PELICAN BOOKS

THE PSYCHOLOGY OF CONSCIOUSNESS

Robert Ornstein teaches at Stanford and the University of
California, San Francisco. He is President of the Institute for
Study of Human Knowledge. His books have won awards
from UNESCO, The American Psychological Association,
and many other sources.

The
Psychology *of*
Consciousness

Robert Ornstein

PENGUIN BOOKS

PENGUIN BOOKS
Viking Penguin Inc., 40 West 23rd Street,
New York, New York 10010, U.S.A.
Penguin Books Ltd, Harmondsworth,
Middlesex, England
Penguin Books Australia Ltd, Ringwood,
Victoria, Australia
Penguin Books Canada Limited, 2801 John Street,
Markham, Ontario, Canada L3R 1B4
Penguin Books (N.Z.) Ltd, 182–190 Wairau Road,
Auckland 10, New Zealand

First published in the United States of America by W. H. Freeman and Company 1972
Published by The Viking Press Inc. 1973
Published in Pelican Books 1975
First revised edition published by Harcourt Brace Jovanovich, Inc., 1977
This second revised edition published by Penguin Books 1986
Published simultaneously in Canada

LIBRARY OF CONGRESS CATALOGING IN PUBLICATION DATA
Ornstein, Robert Evans.
 The psychology of consciousness.
 Bibliography: p.
 Includes index.
 1. Consciousness. I. Title
BF311.O75   1986   153   85-19149
ISBN 0 14 02.2621 4

Printed in the United States of America by
R. R. Donnelley & Sons Company, Harrisonburg, Virginia
Design by Joe Marc Freedman
Set in Primer

For my brother and family

Preface

This is the third edition of a book that has served as a popular introduction to the new understanding about consciousness. I am grateful for the chance to revise it once again, about fifteen years after it was first written.

In that time, a new field has come into being—the study of consciousness. Researchers in the brain and mind areas, as well as cognitive psychologists, have discovered a common language, that of this new field. And more and more workers are beginning to discover something quite humbling: that many of the most advanced questions in psychology and allied sciences have already been met and answered! The answers lie in a different kind of document than the research tradition we are brought up in. They lie in the story and its multiple meanings, meanings that anticipate the divisions of consciousness, the multiple nature of the mind, just being discovered, and divisions of the brain and people.

I am grateful for the chances I have had to introduce some of this exciting understanding to students and readers all over the world. This book is, partly, the result of the response to the original editions: More research work has been published; more students have become interested; more people now understand that consciousness, far from being irrelevant to our society and our future, is at the center of possible human adaptation and survival. Already workers in international political theory are taking work on consciousness as central; workers in ecology are beginning to realize that without a profound change in our understanding of ourselves, no major social goal can be accomplished.

Thanks to the thousands of readers who have taken their time to write about the concerns of the original versions of this book and the students who have used it in more than 12,500 classes throughout the world.

I have also had the advice of many readers of this edition. First is my wife, Sally Mallam, who has gone through the manuscript with care and clarity. Dennis Reed also took his time with early versions of this revision and had major influence on changes that would help the book stay current, as did Evan Nielsen and Brent Danninger.

ROBERT ORNSTEIN
March 1985

Acknowledgments

Excerpts from "Psychology and Scientific Research," Hadley Cantril et al., *Science*, vol. 110, November 4, 1949, November 11, 1949, and November 18, 1949. Copyright 1949 by the American Association for the Advancement of Science. Reprinted with permission.

Excerpts from *The Doors of Perception* by Aldous Huxley. Copyright 1954 by Aldous Huxley. Reprinted by permission of Harper & Row, Publishers, Inc., and Chatto & Windus Ltd.

Excerpts from "They Saw a Game: A Case Study" by A. Hastorf and H. Cantril in *Journal of Abnormal and Social Psychology*, vol. 49, 1954. Copyright 1954 by the American Psychological Association. Reprinted by permission.

"Never Know When it Might Come in Useful," "Moment in Time," "See What I Mean?" "There Is More Light Here," and "The Value of the Past" from *The Exploits of the Incomparable Mulla Nasrudin* by Idries Shah. Copyright © 1966 by Mulla Nasrudin Enterprises. Reprinted by permission of the author.

Excerpt from "The Other Side of the Brain: An Appositional Mind" by Joseph E. Bogen, M.D., from the *Bulletin of the Los Angeles Neurological Societies*, vol. 34, no. 3, July 1969.

Excerpt from "Burnt Norton" in *Four Quartets* by T. S. Eliot. Copyright 1943 by T. S. Eliot, renewed 1971 by Esme Valerie Eliot. Reprinted by permission of Harcourt Brace Jovanovich, Inc., and Faber & Faber.

"The Legend of Nasrudin" from *Thinkers of the East* by Idries Shah. Copyright © 1971 by Idries Shah.

"The Man Who Walked on Water" and "The Blind Men and the Elephant" from *Tales of the Dervishes* by Idries Shah. Reprinted by permission of the author.

Excerpts from *What the Buddha Taught* by Walpola Rahula. Copyright © 1959 by W. Rahula.

Excerpts from *Spiritual Practices of India* by Frederic Spiegelberg. Reprinted by permission of Citadel Press Inc.

Excerpt from "Deautomatization and the Mystic Experience" by Arthur J. Deikman in *Psychiatry*, 1966, vol. 29. Copyright 1966 by The William Alanson White Psychiatric Foundation, Inc.

Excerpt from "The Sufi Tradition" by Elizabeth Hall. Reprinted with permission from *Psychology Today* magazine. Copyright © 1981 American Psychological Association.

"The Teaching-Story" by Idries Shah in *Point,* no. 4., Winter 1968–69. Reprinted with permission.

"The Magic Horse" from *Caravan of Dreams* by Idries Shah (Penguin Books Inc.), © Idries Shah, 1968. Used by permission of the publisher.

"The Story of Tea" and "The Tale of the Sands" from *Tales of the Dervishes* by Idries Shah. Copyright © 1967 by Idries Shah. Published by E. P. Dutton & Co., Inc.

Excerpt from *Current Sufi Activity: Work, Literature, Groups and Techniques* by C. Thurlnas, London, Designist Communications (1980).

Figures on pages 37, 68, 85, 87 from *Psychology: The Study of Human Experience* by Robert Ornstein. Copyright © 1985 by Robert E. Ornstein and the Institute for the Study of Human Knowledge. Reprinted by permission of Harcourt Brace Jovanovich, Inc. Figure on page 68 adapted from Visual Perception by Tom N. Cornsweet, copyright © 1970 by Academic Press, Inc. Figure on page 85 adapted from the graph "The Pepetual Cycle" from *Cognition and Reality: Principles and Implications of Cognitive Psychology* by U. Neisser, published by W. H. Freeman.

Contents

The Psychology of Consciousness

I

Introduction: The Study of Consciousness

Is there any number higher than 100?

A man, having looted a city, tried to sell one of the spoils, an exquisite rug. "Who will give me 100 gold pieces for this rug?" he cried throughout the town.

After the sale was completed, a comrade approached the seller, and asked, "Why did you not ask more for that precious rug?"

"Is there any number higher than 100?" asked the seller.

It is easy, all too easy, to be smug about the rugseller. However, we are like him, since our own conceptions and consciousness limit what is possible for us to understand. The structure of consciousness often acts as a barrier to understanding, as many conceptions may act as barriers to action.

Consider this: It was once thought impossible for a man to run a mile in less than 4 minutes. It was even called the "4-minute-mile" barrier, as if effort of another order were required to run in 3:59:99 instead of 4:00:00. Running times hovered around the magic mark for years; each effort coming so close to the mark, seeming to confirm it as a real entity.

Then one man broke the "barrier" and quite soon many others were able to surmount it, a mark once thought impossible. We seem to set mental limits on the possible boundaries of our world and work within these limits. It is our assumed limitations that this book is about. According to most surveys, we are quite satisfied, satisfied with our lives, and our concept of who we are and what we can do. For most upwardly mobile Westerners prosperity continues, prospects are on the rise. But we are like the rugseller in many ways—our sights are too low. Is there anything beyond what we know of life, liberty, and the pursuit of happiness?

Many people who have a well-determined goal in life have asked me, whether it is whispered quietly after a lecture, or presented more boldly in writing: Why bother? Why is consciousness important? Especially since many successful people feel that they are getting ahead all right as it is, our society is successful . . . I think it is that they are selling themselves short.

It is my view that humans are a much more extraordinary animal than we yet know.

Even in this era when there are psychologists appearing regularly on talk shows, many people, especially successful ones, do not understand that our possibilities are greater in some directions, greater than anything we can currently consider. It is also my view that the *dangers* inherent in human life and even in being human are increasing daily as our control over the physical environment becomes greater and greater.

We Are, Literally, in a Race with Ourselves

We are now biologically obsolete, as we evolved to suit the conditions of a different world, a world that ended at the latest 20,000 years ago. We have not changed much during that period, although it seems a long time to us.

"Prehistory," after all, takes in all this period, from the hunter-gatherers through the beginnings of civilization, to the agricultural, industrial, and other revolutions, and we are quite accustomed to thinking that twentieth-century humans in Western society are very different from those living in "remotest antiquity"—cave dwellers, hunter-gatherers, those who lived just before the agricultural revolution, long before civilization. This smugness is the current version of the shocked thinking of Darwin's time when the citizens of Victorian England simply couldn't accustom themselves to the idea that they were akin to apes. For most of us it is the same—"Surely we have transcended the actions and reactions of those precivilized savages."

But to anyone who is aware of the recent discoveries in human evolution, our own time scale must be reset. Human beings, and our predecessors, evolved over a period lasting hundreds of millions of years. Our predecessors stood up and probably shared food 4 million years ago. Five hundred thousand years ago there were organized settlements in what is now southern France. We certainly have not been able to change significantly in the last 100,000 years, since the Neanderthals.

The last 20,000 years are an insignificant amount of time in evolutionary terms: There has been *no time* to improve the development of our mental capacities, our ability to meet the challenges of the environment, our ability to think, reason, and create. We are the same people who were "designed" to live when our species numbered small groups of thousands, roaming around the savannas of East Africa. We were designed to respond to immediate danger quickly—those who did lived long enough to produce us.

Our dangers, in the current era, are of a different kind: No one is prepared to view 15,000 murders during puberty (the average child, according to recent studies, does, on television and in the cinema); no one is biologically prepared for the destruction that might follow a nuclear war (think of it—billions could die within hours, and this to a race which *numbered only in the millions for most of its history*); no one is prepared biologically for the complexity of the crowds, the noise, and the pollution of the urban surround in many cities. And there is no time for the glacial processes of evolution to produce those changes in us; our own brain took more than 500 million years to "create." We don't have that kind of time!

Will we be able to make the changes necessary to understand our world and alter our course? Our own world has changed radically in our own lifetimes—with computers, air and space travel, the threat of nuclear war. All these are unprecedented. And yet, we have the same mental system that we had ages ago, one that tries, in the face of everything, to keep things stable, simple, and neat.

There are contemporary psychologies described here that allow us, perhaps for the first time, to understand these inflexible tendencies of mind. There are advanced psychologies that agree that the human being is an animal who wishes and attempts desperately to make his life as routine and stable as possible, keeping to fixed assumptions and paradigms, while the world changes continuously.

·   ·   ·

In the next few years we will discover whether human beings will be able to adapt to the enormous changes that have occurred in the past century. Will we be able to feed the world's population? We will know whether it is possible to educate our young to face the contemporary world as it is. Can we avoid a nuclear holocaust? There are countless solutions proposed to the continuous problems of modern life, and I do not wish to in any way reject any of them. However, it is in an understanding of our mental system that may well provide the clues to those who wish to effect changes—for we do have some extraordinary abilities, but also the accumulated limitations of millions of years. At least now we know what some of our mental limitations are!

Our biological evolution is, for all practical purposes, at its end. *There will be no further biological evolution without human "conscious evolution."* And this may not happen without first an understanding of what our consciousness is, what it was originally designed to do, and where the points of possible change may be. That is what *The Psychology of Consciousness* is about.

THE SCOPE OF PSYCHOLOGY

William James

Psychology is the Science of Mental Life, both of its phenomena and [of] their conditions. The phenomena are such things as we call feelings, desires, cognitions, reasonings, decisions, and the like; and, superficially considered, their variety and complexity is such as to leave a chaotic impression on the observer. The most natural and consequently the earliest way of unifying the material was, first, to classify it as well as might be, and, secondly, to affiliate the diverse mental modes thus found, upon a simple entity, the personal Soul, of which they [were] taken to be so many facultative manifestations. Now, for instance, the Soul manifests its faculty of Memory, now of Reasoning, now of Volition, or again its Imagination or its Appetite. This is the orthodox 'spiritualistic' theory of scholasticism and of common-sense. Another and a less obvious way of unifying the chaos is to seek common elements *in* the diverse mental facts rather than a common agent behind them, and to explain them constructively by the various forms of arrangement of these elements, as one explains houses by stones and bricks. The 'associationist' schools of Herbart in Germany, and of Hume, the Mills and Bain in Britain have thus constructed a *psychology without a soul* by taking discrete 'ideas,' faint or vivid, and showing how, by their cohesions, repulsions, and forms of succession, such things as reminiscences, perceptions, emotions, volitions, passions, theories, and all the other furnishings of an individual's mind may be engendered. The very self or *ego* of the individual comes in this way to be viewed no longer as the pre-existing source of the representations, but rather as their last and most complicated fruit.

Now, if we strive rigorously to simplify the phenomena in either of these ways, we soon become aware of inadequacies in our method. Any particular cognition, for example, or recollection, is accounted for on the soul-theory by being referred to the spiritual faculties of Cognition or of Memory. These faculties themselves are thought of as absolute properties of the soul; that is, to take the case of memory, no reason is given why we should remember a fact as it happened, except that so to remember it constitutes the essence of our Recollective Power. We may, as spiritualists, try to explain our memory's failures and blunders by secondary causes. But its *successes* can invoke no factors save the existence of certain objective things to be remembered on the one hand, and of our faculty of memory on the other. When, for instance, I recall my graduation-day, and drag all its incidents and emotions up from death's dateless night, no mechanical cause can explain this process, nor can any analysis reduce it to lower terms or make its nature seem other than an ultimate *datum,* which, whether we rebel or not at its mysteriousness, must simply be taken for granted if we are to psychologize at all. However the associationist may represent the present ideas as thronging and arranging themselves, still, the spiritualist insists, he has in the end to admit that *something,* be it brain, be it 'ideas,' be it 'association,' *knows* past time *as* past, and fills it out with this or that event. And when the spiritualist calls memory an 'irreducible faculty,' he says no more than this admission of the associationist already grants.

And yet the admission is far from being a satisfactory simplification of the concrete facts. For why should this absolute god-given Faculty retain so much better the events of yesterday than those of last year, and, best of all, those of an hour ago? Why, again, in old age should its grasp of childhood's events seem firmest? Why should illness and exhaustion enfeeble it? Why should repeating an experience strengthen our recollection of it? Why should drugs, fevers, asphyxia, and excitement resuscitate things long since forgotten? If we content ourselves with merely affirming that the faculty of memory is so peculiarly constituted by nature as to exhibit just these oddities, we seem little the better for having invoked it, for our explanation becomes as complicated as that of the crude facts with which we started. Moreover there is something grotesque and irrational in the supposition that the soul is equipped with elementary powers of such an ingeniously intricate sort. Why *should* our memory cling more easily to the near than the remote? Why should it lose its grasp of proper [names] sooner than of abstract names? Such peculiarities seem quite fantastic; and might, for aught we can see *a priori*, be the precise opposites of what they are. Evidently, then, *the faculty does not exist absolutely, but works under conditions;* and *the quest of the conditions* becomes the psychologist's most interesting task.

However firmly he may hold to the soul and her remembering faculty, he must acknowledge that she never exerts the latter without a *cue*, and that something must always precede and *remind* us of whatever we are to recollect. "An *idea!*" says the associationist, "an idea associated with the remembered thing; and this explains also why things repeatedly met with are more easily recollected, for their associates on the various occasions furnished so many distinct avenues of recall." But this does not explain the effects of fever, exhaustion, hypnotism, old age, and the like. And in general, the pure associationist's account of our mental life is almost as bewildering as that of the pure spiritualist. This multitude of ideas, existing absolutely, yet clinging together, and weaving an endless carpet of themselves, like dominoes in ceaseless change, or the bits of glass in a kaleidoscope—whence do they get their fantastic laws of clinging, and why do they cling in just the shapes they do?

For this the associationist must introduce the order of experience in the outer world. The dance of the ideas is a copy, somewhat mutilated and altered, of the order of phenomena. But the slightest reflection shows that phenomena have absolutely no power to influence our ideas until they have first impressed our senses and our brain. The bare existence of a past fact is no ground for our remembering it. Unless we have seen it, or somehow *undergone* it, we shall never know of its having been. The experiences of the body are thus one of the conditions of the faculty of memory being what it is. And a very small amount of reflection on facts shows that one part of the body, namely, the brain, is the part whose experiences are directly concerned. If the nervous communication be cut off between the brain and other parts, the experiences of those other parts are non-existent for the mind. The eye is blind, the ear deaf, the hand insensible and motionless. And conversely, if the brain be injured, consciousness is abolished or altered, even although every other organ in the body be ready to play its normal part. A blow on the head, a sudden subtraction of blood, the pressure of an apoplectic hemorrhage, may have the first effect; whilst a very few ounces of alcohol or grains of opium or hasheesh, or a whiff of chloroform or nitrous oxide gas, are sure to have the second. The delirium of fever, the altered self of insanity, are all due to foreign matters circulating through the brain, or to pathological changes in that organ's substance. The fact that the brain is the one immediate bodily condition of the mental operations is indeed so universally admitted nowadays that I need spend no more time in illustrating it, but will simply postulate it and pass on. The whole remainder of [*The Principles of Psychology*] will be more or less of a proof that the postulate was correct.

Bodily experiences, therefore, and more particularly brain-experiences, must take a place amongst those conditions of the mental life of which Psychology need take account. *The spiritualist and the associationist must both be 'cerebralists,'* to the extent at least of admitting that certain peculiarities in the way of working of their own favorite principles are explicable only by the fact that the brain laws are a codeterminant of the result.

Our first conclusion, then, is that a certain amount of brain-physiology must be presupposed or included in Psychology.

In still another way the psychologist is forced to be something of a nerve-physiologist. Mental phenomena are not only conditioned *a parte ante* by bodily processes; but . . . lead to them *a parte post*. That they lead to *acts* is of course the most familiar of truths, but I do not merely mean acts in the sense of voluntary and deliberate muscular performances. Mental states occasion also changes in the calibre of blood-vessels, or alteration in the heart-beats, or [in] processes more subtle still, in glands and viscera. If these are taken into account, as well as acts which follow at some *remote period* because the mental state was once there, it will be safe to lay down the general law that *no mental modification ever occurs which is not accompanied or followed by a bodily change*. The ideas and feelings, e.g., which these present printed characters excite in the reader's mind not only occasion movements of his eyes and nascent movements of articulation in him, but will some day make him speak, or take sides in a discussion, or give advice, or choose a book to read, differently from what would have been the case had they never impressed his retina. Our psychology must therefore take account not only of the conditions antecedent to mental states, but of their resultant consequences as well.

But actions originally prompted by conscious intelligence may grow so automatic by dint of habit as to be apparently unconsciously performed. Standing, walking, buttoning and unbuttoning, piano-playing, talking, even saying one's prayers, may be done when the mind is absorbed in other things. The performances of animal *instinct* seem semi-automatic, and the *reflex acts* of self-preservation certainly are so. Yet they resemble intelligent acts in bringing about the *same ends* at which the animals' consciousness, on other occasions, deliberately aims. Shall the study of such machine-like yet purposive acts as these be included in Psychology?

The boundary-line of the mental is certainly vague. It is much better not to be pedantic, but to let the science be as vague as its subject, and include such phenomena as these if by so doing we can throw any light on the main business in hand. It will ere long be seen, I trust, that we can; and that we gain much more by a broad than by a narrow conception of our subject. At a certain stage in the development of every science a degree of vagueness is what best consists with fertility. On the whole, few recent formulas have done more real service of a rough sort in psychology than the Spencerian one that the essence of mental life and of bodily life are one, namely, 'the adjustment of inner to outer relations.' Such a formula is vagueness incarnate; but because it takes into account the fact that minds inhabit environments which act on them and on which they in turn react; because, in short, it takes mind in the midst of all its concrete relations, it is immensely more fertile than the old-fashioned 'rational psychology,' which treated the soul as a detached existent, sufficient unto itself, and assumed to consider only its nature and properties. I shall therefore feel free to make any sallies into zoology or into pure nerve-physiology which may seem instructive for our purposes, but otherwise shall leave those sciences to the physiologists.

Can we state more distinctly still the manner in which the mental life seems to intervene between impressions made from without upon the body, and reactions of the body upon the outer world again? Let us look at a few facts.

If some iron filings be sprinkled on a table and a magnet brought near them, they will fly through the air for a certain distance and stick to its surface. A savage seeing the phenomenon explains it as the result of an attraction or love between the magnet and the filings. But let a card cover the poles of the magnet, and the filings will press forever against its surface without its ever occurring to them to pass around its sides and thus come into more direct contact with the object of their love. Blow bubbles through a tube into the bottom of a pail of water, they will rise to the surface and mingle with the air. Their action may again be poetically interpreted as due to a longing to recombine with the mother-atmosphere above the surface. But if you invert a jar full of water over the pail, they will rise and remain lodged beneath its bottom, shut in from the outer air, although a slight deflection from their course at the outset, or a re-descent towards the rim of the jar when they found their upward course impeded, would easily have set them free.

If we pass from such actions as these to those of living things, we notice a striking difference. Romeo wants Juliet as the filings want the magnet; and if no obstacles intervene he moves towards her by as straight a line as they. But Romeo and Juliet, if a wall be built between them, do not remain idiotically pressing their faces against its opposite sides like the magnet and the filings with the card. Romeo soon finds a circuitous way, by scaling the wall or otherwise, of touching Juliet's lips directly. With the filings the path is fixed; whether it reaches the end depends on accidents. With the lover it is the end which is fixed, the path may be modified indefinitely.

Suppose a living frog in the position in which we placed our bubbles of air, namely, at the bottom of a jar of water. The want of breath will soon make him also long to rejoin the mother-atmosphere, and he will take the shortest path to his end by swimming straight upwards. But if a jar of water be inverted over him, he will not, like the bubbles, perpetually press his nose against its unyielding roof, but will restlessly explore the neighborhood until by re-descending again he has discovered a path round its brim to the goal of his desires. Again the fixed end, the varying means!

Such contrasts between living and inanimate performances end by leading men to deny that in the physical world final purposes exist at all. Loves and desires are today no longer imputed to particles of iron or of air. No one supposes now that the end of any activity which they may display is an ideal purpose presiding over the activity from its outset and soliciting or drawing it into being by a sort of *vis a fronte*. The end, on the contrary, is deemed a mere passive result, pushed into being *a tergo,* having had, so to speak, no voice in its own production. Alter the pre-existing conditions, and with inorganic materials you bring forth each time a different apparent end. But with intelligent agents, altering the conditions changes the activity displayed, but not the end reached; for here the idea of the yet unrealized end co-operates with the conditions to determine what the activities shall be.

The pursuance of future ends and the choice of means for their attainment are thus the mark and criterion of the presence of mentality in a phenomenon. We all use this test to discriminate between an intelligent and a mechanical performance. We impute no mentality to sticks and stones, because they never sem to move for *the sake of* anything, but always when pushed, and then indifferently and with no sign of choice. So we unhesitatingly call them senseless.

Just so we form our decision upon the deepest of all philosophic problems: Is the Kosmos an expression of intelligence rational in its inward nature, or a brute external fact pure and simple? If we find ourselves, in contemplating it, unable to banish the impression that it is a realm of final purposes, that it exists for the sake of something, we place intelligence at the heart of it and have a religion. If, on the contrary, in surveying its irremediable flux, we can think of the present only as so much mere mechanical sprouting from the past, occurring with no reference to the future, we are atheists and materialists.

PSYCHOLOGY AND SCIENTIFIC RESEARCH

Hadley Cantril, Adelbert Ames, Jr., Albert H. Hastorf, and William H. Illelson

> The traditional code of science—that is, the objectives sought and the methods of investigation—cannot satisfy the requirements of our critical times, and this is why science has failed to measure up to the opportunities and obligations before it. The generally accepted ideas of what natural science is and what it is for are out of date and need radical revision.
>
> —C. J. Herrick (1949)

The Nature of Scientific Inquiry

A feeling of urgency for a more adequate understanding of man and his social relations can be sensed in today's intellectual atmosphere. People are becoming more and more anxious about the ability of psychologists and social scientists to help solve the problems arising from our technological advances and from the swift social transitions they leave in their wake. But, unfortunately, what Herrick has said about the natural sciences applies especially to those sciences which deal with man— psychology and the social sciences in general. Moreover, in these sciences, in contrast to the physical sciences, there seems to be less agreement as to what constitutes significant research.

Obviously, an increase in our understanding of man can come about only as we extend our empirical knowledge and improve our formulations through research of demonstrated significance. Before that is possible we must increase our understanding of the scientific process through which discoveries are made. But sometimes the scientist's interest in building up the content of his discipline sidetracks him from a consideration of the scientific process itself and creates a lag in the understanding and improvement of scientific tools. What follows is an attempt to clarify our thinking about the nature of scientific research in those fields which take upon themselves the primary responsibility of accounting for man's thoughts and behavior. Only then will such research accomplish what we have a right to expect of it.

We shall first consider the nature of scientific inquiry, trying to find out why man pursues scientific inquiry, anyway—what function it serves him and what steps seem to be involved. We shall then distinguish between scientific inquiry and scientific method—a distinction which seems necessary to avoid certain pitfalls and to assure a scientific progress. Then we shall try to point out some of the specific implications to be derived for psychology from a better understanding of the nature of scientific inquiry and the role of scientific method, and we shall indicate to what degree science can be "objective." Finally, some suggestions will be made which might accelerate the kind of scientific research that will increase our understanding of man.

The apparent reason for scientific inquiry is essentially the reason for any inquiry—to solve a problem. Scientific inquiry can never be understood if it is somehow put on a pedestal and viewed as something remote and apart from man's everyday activities. "Science," says Conant (1947,

p. 24), "emerges from the other progressive activities of man to the extent that new concepts arise from experiments and observations."

These activities of life are carried through in an environment which includes people, artifacts, the phenomena of nature. Man's only contact with this environment is through his senses, and the impression man's senses give him are cryptograms in the sense that they have no meaning unless and until they become functionally related to man's purposive activities. The world man creates for himself through what Einstein has called the "rabble of the senses" is one that takes on a degree of order, system, and meaning as man builds up through tested experience a pattern of assumptions and expectancies on which he can base action.

What man brings to any concrete event is an accumulation of assumptions, of awarenesses, and of knowledge concerning the relatively determined aspects of his environment as derived from his past experiences. But since the environment through which man carries out his life transactions is constantly changing, any person is constantly running into hitches and trying to do away with them. The assumptive world a person brings to the "now" of a concrete situation cannot disclose to him the undetermined significances continually emerging and so we run into hitches in everyday life because of our inadequate understanding of the conditions giving rise to a phenomenon, and our ability to act effectively for a purpose becomes inadequate.

When we try to grasp this inadequacy intellectually and get at the "why" of the ineffectiveness of our purposeful action, we are adopting the attitude of scientific inquiry. Man as scientist tries to understand what aspect of his environment is responsible for a hitch and then calls upon what knowledge he has that is relevant to an understanding of the determined, predictable nature of the particular phenomenon in question. Modern man uses the scientific method as a tool because he has found empirically that he can increase his understanding and act more effectively if his pursuits are guided by some knowledge concerning the determined aspects of the phenomenal world. . . .

The processes involved in scientific inquiry would seem to be somewhat as follows: (1) sensing the inadequacy of the conceptual aspects of our assumptive world, thereby being faced with a problem for which we must seek an answer; (2) deciding on all those aspects of a phenomenon that might have a significant bearing on the problem: deciding on those aspects except for which the functional activities in question would not exist; (3) picking out from the various aspects assumed to be involved those that seem most important in terms of the original hitch we faced and that will serve as bases for standards we can think about and manipulate; (4) working out some method of changing those aspects we have chosen as variables or bases for standards and conducting our empirical investigations accordingly; (5) modifying our assumptive world on the basis of the empirical evidence concerning the validity of formulations that have resolved an immediate problem.

The solving of the immediate problem will automatically give rise to new hitches and the above process constantly repeats itself.*

Specifically, it seems that scientific inquiry has two major functions for man. First, it provides man with a bundle of what are called "scientific facts." This bundle is composed of his up-to-the now understandings of the determined, predictable aspects of nature and is used by him for purposes of prediction and control. There are essentially two varieties of these scientific facts: general statements of relationships of determined aspects of nature which we refer to as "scientific laws" and which, in the physical sciences, tend to be expressed in mathematical formulas; second, applications of these general laws to concrete situations for purposes of verification, specific prediction, or control. The characteristic of all these generalized scientific laws is that they disclose predictable aspects of types of phenomena no matter where or when they occur, irrespective of actual concrete situations.

A second function of science is that it provides a conceptual reorgan-

*There seems to be a striking similarity between the processes used in scientific inquiry and the processes man makes use of in building up the assumptive world. Both science and common sense can be regarded as functional activities man uses in carrying out his life transactions. The method of scientific inquiry seems in many ways to be an unconscious imitation of those age-old processes man has employed in his common-sense solutions of problems. In common-sense activity, the assumptions and awarenesses on which man depends for effective action are the hypotheses he has built up from his many experiences; weighted averages he unconsciously uses to give him a high prognosis for effective action.

There are, however, certain important differences between the steps involved in pursuing scientific inquiry and the apparent processes that constitute common sense. A most important difference is the fact that, in using scientific inquiry, man is the operator who decides what he is going to operate on and how. In an everyday life situation, however, man is not only the operator but is also being operated on and must carry out his activities in the midst of the situation itself. When we meet hitches in everyday life and try to overcome them with hunches for effective action, we test these hunches by the action itself in a more or less insightful, more or less conscious way. In scientific inquiry, on the other hand, hunches are tested by controlled experiments and a deliberate attempt is made to intellectualize the process involved (see Dewey, 1948, p. 197).

ization of the knowledge man has already acquired of the determined aspects of nature. Here we are trying to increase our range of understanding, or, as Dewey and Bentley (1945, p. 225; 1946, p. 645) phrase it, to improve our "specifications"; that is, our accuracy in naming. Here, for example, the specifications involved in relativity are more accurate namings of phenomena than are Newton's concepts and, in this sense, Newton's concepts are not to be regarded as "wrong." This function of science includes that of increasing the range of man's conceptual knowledge through the discovery of more and more predictable aspects of nature that up to the present time remain undetermined. . . .

Transactional Observation

Our own philosophical basis for our thinking concerning the nature and function of scientific inquiry and scientific method should be made explicit. We are using as our take-off point what Dewey and Bentley have referred to in a series of articles as a "transactional approach." What they mean by the term *transactional* can best be gathered by their own words. "Observation of this general (transactional) type sees man-in-action not as something radically set over against an environing world, nor yet as merely action 'in' a world, but as action *of* and *by* the world in which the man belongs as an integral constituent" (1945, p. 228). Under this procedure all of man's behavings, "including his most advanced knowings," are treated as "activities not of himself alone, nor even as primarily his, but as processes of the full situation of organism-environment" (1946, p. 506). "From birth to death every human being is a *Party*, so that neither he nor anything done or suffered can possibly be understood when it is separated from the fact of participation in an extensive body of transactions—to which a given human being may contribute and which he modifies, but only in virtue of being a partaker in them" (Dewey, 1948, p. 198). . . .

While it is easy enough to understand this point of view intellectually, it is not nearly so easy to put it into operation in pursuing actual scientific inquiry. It tends to go against the grain of the psychologist's working procedures to regard any formulation merely as a certain "connection of conditions" (Dewey, 1946, p. 217). It is perhaps particularly difficult for psychologists to understand the full implications of the transactional point of view, because, as Dewey and Bentley (1946, p. 546) have pointed out, "The interactional treatment, as everyone is aware, entered psychological inquiry just about the time it was being removed from basic position by the physical sciences from which it was copied." But we must remember that psychology, by comparison, is still in its infancy, that the transactional approach, which Dewey and Bentley trace to the preface of Clerk Maxwell's *Matter and Motion,* dated 1876, antedated the first psychological laboratory.

The Transactional View in Psychological Research

When psychology emancipates itself from dependence on interactionism alone by taking a transactional view of the phenomena which come within its province, we should expect that the division of psychologists into schools would rapidly disappear. Schools (Gestalt, behaviorism, psychoanalysis, etc.) would disappear not because they are "wrong" or "have been overthrown" but because the formulations of each school that meet empirical tests would be encompassed within wider formulations of problems. What are some ways to speed this development?

First of all, the psychologist not only must realize intellectually but must make a part of his assumptive world the idea that man's thought and behavior can be understood only as processes of a "full situation of organism-environment." The point has been made by H. A. Murray and collaborators (1948, p. 466) in their contention that "the main body of psychology started its career by putting the wrong foot forward, and it has been out of step with the march of science much of the time. Instead of beginning with studies of the whole person adjusting to a natural environment, it began with studies of a segment of a person responding to a physical stimulus in an unnatural laboratory environment." Brunswik (1949), in his well-known "ecological analysis," has pointed out the need to understand the complete "representativeness of circumstances" operative in any situation under observation. But while an increasing number of psychologists are calling for a revision in traditional psychological procedure, their voices are still those of men crying in the wilderness of the universe which constitutes so much of psychological inquiry today. The psychological investigator, of all people, cannot separate the observer from what is being observed, the process of knowing from what is known, what is "out there" from whatever goes on in the experiencing organism. Psychology must disavow completely any "field theory" which implies that an environmental field acts *on* a person rather than *through* a person.

Because man inevitably builds up for himself an assumptive world in carrying out his purposive activities, the world he is related to, the world he sees, the world he is operating on, and the world that is operating on him is the result of a transactional process in which man himself plays an active role. Man carries out his activities in the midst of concrete events which themselves delimit the significances he must deal with.

In the process man is himself changed in greater or lesser degree by having his own assumptive world changed through confirmation or denial as a result of action. In his immediate activity man abstracts from the immediate situation certain determined aspects according to his assumptive world. This, as we indicated, includes far more than the immediate occasion; it is a continuum which includes the past and the future, a storehouse of both past experience and ideal. As Bentley (1941, p. 485) has pointed out, "Behaviors are present events converging pasts into futures. They cannot be reduced to successions of instants nor to successions of locations. They themselves span extension and duration. The pasts and the futures are rather phases of behavior than its control." Psychologists must be constantly aware of the effects man's own actions have both on his assumptive world—confirming or denying certain aspects of it—and concurrently on the "environment out there" as it is perceived and experienced. . . .

There is also a tendency in psychology to use catchwords in labeling the fields of social, clinical, educational, or industrial as "applied" fields of psychology, and to separate them from the more traditional "experimental" psychology. Any such division is absurd unless the person who uses it consciously reserves it for rough descriptive purposes. Investigators in these fields must, of course, also rely on experiments. But, beyond that, any such distinction acts as a deterrent in the search for more adequate formulations which will better account for human behavior, whether in the laboratory, the clinic, the factory, or in everyday social life. . . .

We can illustrate the way in which psychological inquiry has been restricted by the use of terms with reference to the field of perception, which has so often been a weather vane in psychology. In working on perception, psychologists early found that certain variations in objective or physiological factors produced marked subjective variations. This naturally led to the idea of correspondence between subjective factors, on the one hand, and objective and physiological factors, on the other hand. Since an alteration of objective and physiological factors could so easily be shown to cause subjective effects, and since the converse could not so easily be demonstrated, the assumption was built up that the subjective aspects of perception had their origin largely in the corresponding objective factors and the accompanying physiological disturbances they caused. Studies of perception have thus concentrated largely on the analysis of objective and physiological factors. Since these objective or physiological factors could be varied quantitatively, scientific methodology in psychology tended to become identified with measurement alone.

This led to a long neglect of those factors not amenable to precise measurement. These neglected factors were, of course, subjective factors described by such symbols as past experience, loyalties, expectancy, and purpose, whether these were operating consciously or unconsciously. This methodological dam has recently been cracked, largely through research in social and clinical psychology, where the effects of subjective factors on perception are especially obvious. More recently, in an attempt to liberate investigators somewhat from correspondence between subjective and objective or physiological factors, demonstrations of perceptual phenomena have been designed which deliberately make use of illusions. By using illusions the investigator gains more freedom to understand the nature of the functional activities involved in the scientific inquiry of perception and thereby gets a better toehold on the function of perception in man's purposive behavior. For example, it can be demonstrated that the perception of *where* a thing is depends upon the perception of *what* a thing is and on *when* it is perceived. Carr (1935, p. 326) has pointed out that "illusions contrasted with correct perceptions are the experimental variants that reveal the common principle involved in both." . . .

Value Judgments and "Objectivity"

It is becoming increasingly clear that the process of mentation involved in scientific inquiry is not a simple one of bringing "impartial analysis" to bear on a set of conditions. The scientist's own value judgments are involved in (1) sensing the inadequacy of his conceptual structure— posing a problem for himself; (2) sensing the functional activities or subphenomena which may be involved in the phenomenon that has caused the original hitch; (3) deciding on which aspects of a phenomenon (variables) can fruitfully be used as bases for standards in experimentation; and (4) designing an experimental procedure to test the validity of these bases for standards. Scientific research thus involves an elaborate process of weighing and integrating which may take place largely on an unconscious level.

In this process, all the unconscious assumptions, all the awarenesses, and all the conceptual abstractions of the individual investigator's assumptive world are operative. Whether any scientist likes to admit it or not, any interpretation he makes must be regarded as a value judgment. To be sure, rational thought and the conscious intellectual manipulation of abstracted variables can, often do, and obviously should play a most important role in the process of scientific inquiry. But to assume that rational thought and conscious manipulation alone are the determinants of the judgments involved in scientific research is to go against the overwhelming evidence already obtained from scientific research itself. The dictionary definition of the word "objective," in the sense that it is used in discussions concerning the objectivity of science, is: "Emphasizing or expressing the nature of reality as it is apart from self-consciousness; treating events or phenomena as external rather than as affected by one's reflections or feelings." For example, our knowledge of perception, showing that "the nature of reality" as we experience it would not exist *except* for the assumptive world we bring to a concrete situation, flatly contradicts the contention that the scientist can be objective in any such sense.

The objectivity of science can therefore only refer to the use of accepted rules of empirical research *after* the problem, the variables, and the experimental design have been decided upon. Here the scientific investigator takes every precaution he can to see that he does not misinterpret what he observes by allowing any subjective bias to enter into the actual conduct of the experiment itself.

Not only is objectivity illusory in the sense of eliminating personal bias, it is also undesirable. We cannot improve on the conclusion reached by Herrick (1949, pp. 180f) after a lifetime of productive research in neurology:

> The bias which arises from unrecognized personal attitudes, interests, and preconceptions is the most treacherous of all the subversive enemies of sound, scientific progress; yet these attitudes and interests are the key factors in all really original scientific investigation. This issue must be faced frankly and courageously. The easy way out is to ignore the troublesome personal ingredients of the problem and say that science has no concern with them.

This is now generally regarded as the standard, or normal, scientific method. But actually this cannot be done, and we cannot afford to try to do it; for the interests and the attitudes of the inquirer shape the whole course of the investigation, without which it is meaningless and fruitless. To neglect these components of scientific work and the satisfactions of a successful outcome is to sterilize not only the process but also the results of the inquiry. The vital germ of untrammeled imaginative thinking is thrown into the discard, and too often we seem quite content with the dead husk which is so easily weighed, measured, classified, and then stowed away in the warehouse.

In the social sciences, Robert Lynd (1939) has made the same point for "outrageous hypotheses."

The myth that "science is objective" may tend to be fostered in most cultures today in an attempt to preserve whatever status quo exists by giving it scientific blessing. But any scientist will resent boundaries placed on his thinking by social, economic, political, religious, or any other ideological barriers and taboos. This danger is especially prevalent in the field of inquiry labeled "social psychology" and in the social sciences, where the data gathered have been largely determined and preconditioned by the purposes and conditions within which the investigator has worked.

Psychologists and social scientists who honestly try to bring their most mature value judgments to bear on concrete social problems are all too frequently labeled as biased, crackpot reformers if they even implicitly criticize existing social relationships. Yet it is because scientific inquiry is shot through with valid judgments that no scientist can avoid some responsibility for the judgments he makes. Because value judgments play so important a role in scientific thinking, ways and means must be discovered of making value judgments themselves the subject matter for scientific inquiry (see Cantril, 1949, p. 363). Value judgments concern the significance of the constant emergents which are not subject to explanation in determined and verifiable terms. Here the scientist has a freedom of choice; here conscience, the "sense of oughtness," must be recognized as the highest standard for effective action. When the subject matter with which the scientist deals consists of human beings trying to act effectively to carry out their purposes, then the social responsibility of anyone who pretends to be an expert obviously becomes very great indeed.

2

The Conscious Human Mind: Selection, Reception, and Creation

Seeing Double

A father said to his double-seeing son, "Son, you see two instead of one."
"How can that be?" the boy replied. "If I were, there would seem to be four moons up there in place of two."

Consider your own consciousness, and reflect for a moment upon its contents. You will probably find a mixture of thoughts, ideas, sensations, fantasies. Images appear and go, ideas emerge fleetingly, only to disappear again, an ache or a pain surfaces, then a desire.

How are we going to get that contract? Will I see him or her or it again? That tastes good. How can I help those people . . . and much more. An object appears—one or more trees, books, chairs. We become aware of other people walking, as they might walk into us, as individual bodies, as voices in the air all around us.

We move in three-dimensional space and actively manipulate perceived objects—we may turn the pages of a book, sit in a chair, speak to someone, listen to a speaker. Normally the content of our consciousness is a representation of outside reality and it can be successful to the extent that we survive. There are successes at all "levels." On a high level it may be: Do we get the job? And on the lower levels it may be: Do we cross the street without getting hit?

In our own personal experience we are sure that "our world" thus has some validity, we usually go a bit further. At almost each moment of each day we make the same mistake as does the double-seeing son— we immediately assume that our own personal consciousness *is* the world, that an outside "objective" reality is somehow *received by us in its completeness*. After all, we've cut the tree and made it into a table, we've drunk the same wine as have all the other people at dinner, we've gotten the job. Most people never really see any issue here; for ordinary purposes the "reality" we experience goes unchallenged.

Remember the early Disney cartoons? In them, a little man at a switchboard, located somewhere like our very own brain, projected physical "pictures" of the world on a sort of consciousness screen, something like a giant projection television. And, though you will, again, laugh, the way you might have at the rugseller, this is the ordinary belief of many, many people. In fact, in years of teaching, and years of discussing these issues, when I inquire about how most people understand how they register or respond to the outside world, they eventually end up at a version of this mental Disneyland in some form.

But even a moment's directed reflection will confirm that the "naïve reality" idea, in which our mind somehow directly mirrors the world, cannot be true. If there were a consciousness screen somewhere in there, who would see it? Does that little man (or woman) inside have another one still farther inside? And, in addition, we sometimes experience things that are not physically present. We hallucinate, daydream, imagine, scheme, wish. And each night we dream and experience events that we produce completely by ourselves.

And consider, too, the enormous variety of physical energies that we contact at each moment of our lives. The air, or more properly, our atmospheric environment, contains and conveys to us energy in the electromagnetic band: visible light, X-rays, radio waves, infrared radiation. In addition the air is mechanically vibrated, by vocal chords, drums, passing cars, the movement of our feet; this conveys energy that transforms into sound information. There is constant energy from the gravitational field; there is varying pressure in our own body; there is the movement of gaseous matter in the air; and there are hundreds more events out there. We generate our own internal stimuli as well—thoughts, internal organ sensations, muscular activity, pains, feelings, and more.

And all this occurs simultaneously, not even as neatly as it can be described, and it continues for as long as we are alive. Imagine being aware of each process at each moment. Immediately you will see that our personal consciousness can never, even at any one instant, represent or reflect all of the external world, but must consist of an extremely small fraction of the entire "reality."

We do not even possess the sensory equipment to perceive many of the energies that strike us, such as ultraviolet or infrared.

And then there are many questions to be considered (which we will try to answer) once it is registered that our consciousness is limited. What is it limited *to*? *Why* is it limited? How do the selections and the exclusions operate? How can we achieve a stable mind if all we can do is to select a little of what is out there? How do we keep from getting overwhelmed?

An individual consciousness is oriented toward action for the most part. It is evolved for the primary purpose of ensuring the individual's biological survival, attention to the outside world, sensitivity (and sometimes oversensitivity) to threatening organisms, and the separation of the individual's welfare from that of others would most often be useful. After all, there must be a "me first" system that takes priority.

Our biological inheritance determines that we *select* the sensory information that is to reach the brain from the mass of information reaching us. This is an exquisite undertaking, and it is done through a vast network of filters, sensors, and censors, all working with microsecond timing. This immediate selection process sorts out survival-related stimuli, from which we are able to, somehow miraculously, construct a stable representation of the world.

There are such a great number of routine miracles in this system that the scientist is dazzled: Somehow a collection of very short waves in the air combine and can become paintings in the mind; other, longer, ones become music; a group of molecules fits right in to receptors in the palate and becomes *cassoulet*. And it is within ourselves that it is all done, and done at every moment of every day.

If we can realize at the outset that our ordinary consciousness is something we must of necessity create in order to survive in the world, we can also credit, at least as a working hypothesis, that there may well be other ways the world may be organized, at least in other organisms if not in ourselves.

Studies of Sensory Selection

The initial processing of the mental operating system of the mind catches a small and specific bit of the outside world and brings it to the brain. So we normally consider that the senses are the "windows" to the world, that we see with our eyes and hear with our ears. But although such a view explains our situation it is not entirely the case, for a primary function of sensory systems (considered as whole systems) is to discard information that is "irrelevant" to the organism, such as X-rays, infrared radiation, or ultrasonic waves. These systems protect us from being overwhelmed and confused by this mass of information. They do this by design. And there is more to their design than this.

The senses routinely perform two miracles. First, each sensory organ acts to transform a particular kind of physical energy—the short waves of light, the molecules of sourness—into a different kind of energy: the electrochemical process of neural firing. This process is called *transduction*. Each sense has specialized receptors responsible for the transduction of external energy into the language of the brain. The eye transduces light, the ear transduces sound waves, the nose transduces gaseous molecules. Second, at some point in the sensory and brain system, there is a second transformation: The billions of electrical explosions and chemical secretions of "neural firing" become trees and cakes, silverfish and laughter—the conscious world of human experience.

These two miracles occur every moment of our lives, and are so continuous and routine that we are naturally unaware of them. We are on our way to understanding how the first miracle works, but everyone in science remains completely mystified by the second.

Consider the most important "avenue" of sensory experience, the eye. It responds to radiant electromagnetic energy in the visible spectrum, and it transmits to us our whole visual world—the richness of the autumn colors, the complexity of the winter sky, the enormous variation in human faces, and much more.

So it is difficult to credit that the entire "visible" spectrum is but one tiny part of the entire bandwidth of energy. The entire spectrum of wavelengths ranges from those less than 1 billionth of a meter long, to those longer than 1,000 meters; yet we can see *only that tiny portion between 400 and 700 billionths of a meter long*. This entire visual spectrum is thus less than a trillionth of the energy that reaches the eye in the electromagnetic band. And in addition to electromagnetic energy, many other forces arrive unbidden at the eye—pressure waves, gaseous matter, mechanical vibrations in the air. The eye is "by design" ignorant of these.

We could not possibly experience the world as it fully exists—we cut out an enormous amount before it even "reaches us," or gets inside the nervous system. If we do not possess receptive systems for a given energy form, if an object is out of range, or too quick, it never gets into our experience. It is almost impossible for us even to imagine an energy-form or object outside our range. What would infrared radiation, or an X-ray "look" like? What would be the "sound" of a one-cycle note? In an amateurish way, this is what perhaps is meant in the Zen saying "the sound of one hand clapping."

The problem may be a bit easier to understand if we descend a bit on the evolutionary scale and examine an animal whose sensory systems limit information even more than does ours.

Perhaps the clearest and most important research has been done on the visual system of the frog. Now it is obvious that the frog occupies a different "evolutionary niche" than do we, and might have different selective procedures in its nervous system. But hardly anyone was prepared for the difference in the two nervous systems!

A group of researchers at MIT, under the direction of Jerry Lettvin, devised an experiment in which visual stimulation could be offered to the eye of an immobilized frog. The frog was so situated that its eye was at the center of a hemisphere seven inches in radius. Small objects could be placed in different positions on the inner surface of this hemisphere by means of magnets, or they could be moved around in the space inside the hemisphere.

The investigators implanted microelectrodes into the frog's optic nerve to measure, as the title of the classic paper expressed it, "What the frog's eye tells the frog's brain." Since the frog's eye itself is somewhat similar to other eyes, these investigators hoped that the electrical recordings from the optic nerve would discriminate the different kinds of "messages" that the eye sends to the brain. It was hoped that an analysis of these messages would reveal the relationship of the evoked patterns of electrical activity to the different objects displayed to the frog on the hemisphere.

There are literally an infinite number of different visual patterns that one could present to a frog—colors, shapes, movements, and various combinations of these—a choice that mirrors the richness of the visual world we experience. However, in presenting these many different objects, colors, and movements to the frog, the investigators uncovered a remarkable phenomenon: *From all the different kinds of stimulation presented, only* four *different kinds of "messages were sent from the retina to the brain.* In other words, no matter what complexity and subtle differences are present in the environment, the frog's eye is "wired up" to send only a few different messages. The frog's eye presumably evolved to *discard* the remainder of the information available.

The structure of its eye limits the frog to an "awareness" of four different kinds of external activities. Lettvin and his co-workers termed the four related systems *sustained contrast detectors, moving-edge detectors, net dimming detectors,* and *net convexity detectors.* The first provides the general outline of the environment; the second responds to any significant movement; the third seems to enhance response to a sudden decrease in light, as when a large enemy is attacking.

The fourth type of message, conveyed by the net convexity detectors, is the one most obviously related to the frog's biological needs, and is the most interesting. These net convexity detectors do not respond to a general change in light or to contrast; they respond only when small dark objects come into the field of vision and move close to the eye. So that is how the frog gets its food, how it can see flying bugs even with its highly refined visual system. The frog has evolved its own perceptual subsystems that are "wired in" to its senses—it almost automatically responds to bugs flying around it!

The same kind of analysis has elucidated the mechanisms of perception and consciousness in other organisms. The results show that sight does not take place *in* the eyes, but with the *assistance* of the eyes. The first part of visual experience is what the eye tells the brain; the second is what the brain tells the eye.

In each human eye there are about 126 million photoreceptor cells whose impulses are channeled into 1 million ganglion cells. Information from the outside world is increasingly simplified and abstracted as the information travels from the outside to the visual cortex of the brain.

Information from the left eye travels via the left optic nerve and information from the right eye goes through the right optic nerve. A change takes place at an intersection called the *optic chiasma:* some of the axons *cross over.* Those from the left sides of both eyes go off to the left side of the brain while those from the right sides of both eyes go off to the right. The arrangement, not the structure, of the axons changes. But the name also changes. After the crossover, the optic nerve is called the *optic tract.*

The million nerve fibers in each of the two optic tracts reach the brain first at the *lateral geniculate nucleus* (LGN) in the thalamus, so the visual cortex is alerted to visual input via the LGN. It appears the LGN is a kind of switching station relaying messages to the visual cortex. While in the LGN, the messages from the two eyes are still separate. The LGN also analyzes color signals. The neural fibers that leave the LGN fan out to inform the visual cortex.

In studies similar to Lettvin's, the rate of firing a single axon can be measured and recorded by a hairlike electrical probe. By flashing a light at an animal's eye and recording the response to individual nerve cells, we can find out which cells respond to the stimulus. The area of stimulation that a cell responds to is called the *receptive field.* The function of the cells in the cortex is different from that of cells in the optic tract. When these cortical cells are recorded from individually, they respond best to specific features in the environment and are thus called *feature analyzers.* (However, the cells may actually serve other functions unknown to us.)

There are over 100 million neurons in the human visual cortex, and we do not yet know the extent of their specialization. Isolating and identifying receptive fields is one way that investigators can determine the features specific cells are designed to notice. *It appears that each species of animal possesses a special set of feature analyzers that pick out the objects and events that are important for it.* In animals such as the frog, such selection is extreme.

The visual system of the cat, which so far is the most thoroughly studied, selects for edges, angles, and objects moving in different directions. In monkeys, some cells seem to respond to specific features of the environment. In one study a group experimented with one rhesus monkey. They probed one cell in the cortex and tried to find out what would make it respond. They placed food in front of the monkey, showed it cards, moving objects, and so on. In fact, they tried everything they could think of and found no response. Finally there was a wild response when they waved their hands good-bye to the cell, in front of the monkey's eye. They then showed lots of new stimuli to the cell. The more similar a stimulus was to a monkey's hand, the greater was the response in that cell. This example shows that, at least in the monkey, we can identify a single cell that responds strongly to an extremely specific feature.

The neuroscientists Hubel and Wiesel of Harvard, in studies which have led to a Nobel Prize, have identified three main categories of cells in the visual cortex of cats, each of which detects specific kinds of patterns.

1. *Simple cells* respond to a bar, line, or edge. Because simple cells respond most strongly to particular angles, they are called *orientation detectors*. They are arranged in columns in the visual cortex; each column contains cells that respond to a particular orientation.
2. *Complex cells* respond to orientation and to movement, such as a diagonal line moving from left to right.
3. *Hypercomplex cells* respond to bars of light in any orientation. The clumsy term "hypercomplex" reflects researchers' surprise at the complexity of the cortical selection system; they never expected that there would be cells beyond the "complex." It may well be that other cells will be found that respond to even more specialized features of the environment (like the hand-responding cell of the monkey).

Each element of the visual system, including the visual cortex, is designed to select special features of the environment, transmit and analyze that information, and ignore the rest. The cells in the visual cortex are probably the building blocks of more complex visual experiences.

Most sensory and perceptual experience follows that of the eye. All human beings are similarly evolved to select common aspects of the physical surround: We possess eyes that receive radiant electromagnetic energy; ears that receive and "pick up" the mechanical vibrations of the air; a nose that contains receptors for gaseous molecules; specialized touch sensors; and a complex foam of cells bursting up from the tongue that are shaped to respond to the molecules in food, giving us taste. So we could go through to the amazing complexity of these and again the hidden assumption would be building that these experiences exhaust the extent of the known world.

After all, there is consensual validation—we all agree that there is a tree out there, a bird singing, dinner beckoning at us on the table. But our agreement on the nature of reality, done among right-thinking people, of course, is of course limited, because all of us share the limitations that have presumably evolved to ensure the biological survival of the race.

Humans agree on certain events only because we are all similarly limited in our receptive structure, training, and culture. Like the double-seeing son, it is very easy for us to confuse our common agreement with external reality. If *everyone* saw double, for instance, we would all operate as if two moons exist, or our numbering system would be doubled—perhaps it is already doubled and we don't know it.

What distinguishes us more complicated organisms, at least compared with the frog, is that the avenues of sensation become more complex and multimodal, and the *flexibility* increases due to the increased complexity of the brain and sensory nervous systems. This "retuning" is more computerlike, the ability to adjust the programs in different environments.

You can personally experience this higher-level selectivity and tuning. At a gathering where several people are talking at the same time, close your eyes and listen to one person speaking, then "tune" him or her out and listen to another person. Perhaps you will be surprised at how easy it is to tune your attention in this way. In fact, we have little reason to be surprised at this ability, since we tune ourselves continuously to suit our needs and expectations, but the mild surprise comes because we are not usually *aware* of such self-tuning.

The selection process is programmable, within the fixed sensory limits. It is often driven by need. When we perspire during the summer, we like the taste of foods that are more salty than usual. We don't consciously reason that we need salt and that we should take more salt in with the diet; we simply *like* foods that at other times we would consider grossly oversalted. And people differ in this as well: Some dishes taste oversalty to many, while others will add salt to them!

Studies of Consciousness, Mind, and Brain

One naïve view of the brain and nervous system has stimulated some useful research in psychology. Remember that the lens of the eye reverses the light from left to right and up to down. One common question reflects this view: If the eye reverses the visual world, then why do we see the world right side up when this image is upside down? But "right side up" and "upside down" have no real biological meaning. The idea that "right side up" is important presupposes that we see *what exists*.

Since we don't "view" an external reality the question is actually meaningless. All that is required in order for us to "see" is for a *consistent* relationship to exist between the external object and the pattern of excitation on the retina. In humans this pattern, as we shall soon see, can be radically transformed and not lead to much difficulty.

If the visual world of the goldfish is inverted by surgical rotation, the goldfish never adapts to the alteration in its sensory input. It may even starve as it swims in circles, looking for food. In contrast if a human being's world is so altered, adaptation is often quick. Since we do not surgically experiment upon people, the studies are done with distorting lenses. After a period of adjustment a man can pedal a bicycle through a crowded town wearing specially designed inverting lenses. The naïve view cannot be correct.

Consciousness operates in a continuous process by which an organism adapts to the immediate environment. The retinal "image" is *never* turned right side up. We do not need such turns or corrections in an image; all we need to adapt to the external world is consistent information. The "image" on the retina is, in fact, inverted, and is consistently obscured by blinks, blind spots, and blood vessels, yet we adapt to all this. The rods and cones, the photoreceptors in the eye, are actually *behind* the blood vessels, and *face away from the incoming light*.

In the late nineteenth century the psychologist George Stratton reasoned that if consciousness is a process of adaptation to the environment, then it ought to be possible to learn to adapt to an entirely different arrangement of visual information *as long as it was consistent*. To test this hypothesis Stratton wore a special prism lens over one eye, so that he saw the world turned 180 degrees on its side. The world was topsy-turvy: up/down and left/right were reversed.

Stratton had great difficulty at first in doing simple things like reaching or grasping. He was dizzy when he walked, and he bumped into things. But within days he began to adapt.

After only three days of wearing the inverted lens he wrote: "Walking through the narrow spaces between pieces of furniture required much less art than hitherto. I could watch my hands as they wrote, without hesitating or becoming embarrassed thereby." By the fifth day he could move around the house easily. On the eighth day he removed the lens and wrote: "The reversal of everything from the order to which I had grown accustomed during the last week gave the scene a surprisingly bewildering air which lasted for several hours." Once Stratton had adapted to the new relationship between information and perception, it took some time to unlearn it.

Stratton wrote in 1896 of his results:

> The different sense-perceptions, whatever may be the ultimate course of their extension, are organized into one harmonious spatial system. *The harmony is found to consist in having outer experiences meet our expectations.* [Italics added]

More than sixty years later, Ivo Kohler conducted further experiments on optical rearrangement. His observers wore distorting lenses for weeks. At first they all had great difficulty in seeing the world, but in a few weeks they had adapted. *One of Kohler's subjects was able to ski while wearing distorting lenses!* People can also learn to adapt to color distortions. In another of Kohler's demonstrations his subjects wore glasses in which one lens was green and one red. In a few hours they sensed no difference in color between the lenses.

The Nature of Immediate Conscious Experience

If you do not think about it, nothing seems simpler than experiencing the environment. At this moment I can see ivy and grass, hear music in the distance, and can easily see the blue sky beyond.

Consider a simple scene: I walk into a room and see my friend Big Dennis. I might speak to him, perhaps ask him about a project he is working on. An ordinary experience not worthy of much analysis—or so it would seem.

But *it takes a lot of work to keep things simple*. It might interest you to know that no computer, no matter how large and sophisticated, could accomplish that simple feat. I know hundreds of people, and it is not extraordinary that I know what to talk about with each one. A computer could not even identify Big Dennis, let alone hold a conversation with him. This simple and ordinary experience is, actually, the result of many difficult and complex operations. We may be aware of *what* we perceive, but we are not normally aware of the mental processes "behind the scenes" that make perception possible. In order to see someone, like my friend Big Dennis, you first "pick up" information from the environment.

Only a few of the millions of stimuli reaching the sense receptors yield any information about Big Dennis and the room. This "raw" sensory information is first picked up and organized.

That expanse of red we see we perceive as the couch, the gray is his shirt, the voice identifies him as Big Dennis, not Fred. Your experience involves much more than what meets the eyes and ears. Once you have "assembled" Big Dennis, you go beyond that immediate information. You immediately assume he is the same person he was before, with the same memories, interests, and experiences. The first component of conscious experiences, perception, involves "picking up" information about the world, organizing it, and making inferences about the environment in a continuous cycle.

To be useful, our perceptions must accurately reflect the world around us. People approaching must be seen if we are to avoid bumping into them. We have to be able to identify food before we can eat it. The senses act as information gatherers and selectors for perception. They select information about color, taste, and sound relevant for survival. What an organism perceives depends on the environment. The characteristics of the environment are described by "ecological psychologists." Two characteristics are:

1. *Affordance*. Each object in the environment offers a rich source of information. A post "affords" information about its right angles; a tomato affords information about its roundness, color, and taste; a tree about its greenness, the color of its fruit, and other attributes.
2. *Invariance*. The external environment contains many different objects. Each offers to the perceiver certain *invariant* features. Even a common object such as a post presents unchanging (or invariant) information about itself as we walk around it. From every angle, we see that the post has right angles, is perpendicular to the earth, is white. There are invariant patterns that are common to all objects: Objects get smaller as their distance from the perceiver increases; lines converge at the horizon; when one object is nearer it blocks out another.

The first tier of consciousness involves an organism "picking up" the information afforded by the environment and using it.

But the sensory information is most often so complex that it must be simplified and organized. The mental operating system is so specialized for organizing sensory information that it attempts to organize things into a pattern even when there is none. We look up at a cloud and see shapes in it—a whale, a dagger.

Op art, popular in the 1960s, played with this predisposition to organize. Op art is at once intriguing and unsettling, because we try continually to organize certain figures that are designed by the artist to have no organization.

The rules of mental organization are the basis of the Gestalt approach to psychology. *Gestalt* is a German word with no direct English equivalent but it roughly means *to create a form*. A gestalt is the immediate organization of the form of an object. You will instantly perceive stimuli as complete forms, not disconnected. You see the lines in the figure as a square. You do not see four individual lines; you notice they are all at right angles to one another, then judge that they are of equal length, and then add them up and say, "That's a square." *The figure is immediately perceived as a whole,* not as the sum of its parts.

Interpretation: Going Beyond the Information Given

In spite of the fact that there is a great richness of sensory information reaching us, the information we receive at any one moment is often incomplete. We may catch but a glimpse of our friend Big Dennis's shirt or hear only a word or two of his voice, yet we recognize him. This mode of mental operation was demanstrated in the Middle Ages by jesters. They constructed garments that were white on one side, red on the other; they walked a straight line between two rows of spectators. The audience was later asked the color of the garments. One group confidently reported that the jesters were dressed all in white; the other group equally confidently said red. They nearly came to blows until the ambiguous garments were shown, so strong is the tendency to "fill in the gaps."

In order to act quickly and flexibly in the world, we assume much of the missing information. For example, you probably did not notice the three typographical errors in the previous paragraph.

We are usually unaware of the actions of our mind. We *experience* neither the individual stimuli nor the "rules of organization" being applied to them. Rather we make what is called in psychology *unconscious inferences*. We almost literally "draw" conclusions about reality on the basis of the suggestions and cues brought in by the senses. The nineteenth-century scientist Hermann Helmholtz thus compared the perceiver to an astronomer, forced to "fill in the gaps" in his information.

> An astronomer, for example, comes to real conscious conclusions of this sort, when he computes the positions of the stars in space, their distances, etc., from the perspective images he has had of them at various times and as they are seen from different parts of the orbit of the earth. His conclusions are based on a conscious knowledge of the laws of optics. In the ordinary acts of vision this knowledge of optics is lacking. Still it may be permissible to speak of the (psychological) acts of ordinary perception as unconscious conclusions, thereby making a distinction of some sort between them and the common so-called conscious conclusions.

The Assumptive World

In order to act quickly we *assume* a lot about the world we perceive. If I tell you that Big Dennis is in a room, you immediately assume the room has four walls, a floor, a ceiling, and probably furniture. On entering a room we do not inspect it to determine whether the walls are at right angles, or that the room is still there when we leave it. If we constantly inspected everything in our environment there would be no time to do anything. If much of our experience is assumed, then it follows that *if our assumptions change, our consciousness will as well.* This was the hypothesis of an important research group headed by Adelbert Ames at Dartmouth, called the "transactionalists." They were called so because they analyzed consciousness as involving a *transaction* between the organism and the environment.

One of their demonstrations emphasized the difficulty of experiencing space as three-dimensional, through visual stimulation in two dimensions. We assume that rooms are rectilinear. But sometimes assumptions are wrong, and the result can be the experience of "impossible" changes in the apparent size of a person who crosses the room, because we do not easily change our learned assumptions about the shape of rooms. It is so hard to change this assumption that it makes us see people of grossly different sizes.

Other determinants of experience are values and needs. One experiment compared the experiences of rich and poor children. When shown a certain coin, children from poor homes experienced it as larger than did the richer children, a finding that has been repeated in other cultures, such as in Hong Kong. In another study students in a class were asked to draw a picture of the teacher. The majority of the honor students drew the teacher slightly smaller than the students in the picture. But the pictures by less-than-average students depict the teacher as much taller than the students.

Albert Hastorf and Hadley Cantril studied the influence of prejudice on perception at a Princeton-Dartmouth football game. During the game, Princeton's star quarterback was injured. Afterward, Hastorf and Cantril interviewed two groups of fans and recorded their opinions of the game on a questionnaire. The Princeton fans said that Dartmouth had been unduly violent and aggressive toward their quarterback. The Dartmouth fans reported that the game was rough but fair. What a football game looks like depends on whether you are from Dartmouth or not.

Is Our Immediate Conscious Experience Innate or Learned?

One question that has long interested philosophers and psychologists is, What would be the visual experience of a person who had been born blind but was suddenly able to see? Richard Gregory had the good fortune to study a man called SB, blind from birth, who had a successful corneal transplant at fifty-two. When the bandages were removed, SB heard the voice of the surgeon, turned to look at him and *saw nothing but a blur*. In a few days he could walk around the hospital corridors without touching the walls and could tell time from a wall clock, but he could not see the world as crisply as we do. He was able almost immediately to recognize objects for which he had developed an "internal picture" through touch. He was surprised by the appearance of the moon. He could see and draw objects that he had known previously by touch, but had difficulty with those objects that he had not had the opportunity to touch while blind. For example, his drawings of a London bus even a year after the operation omitted the front of the bus, which he was, of course, unable to touch. Windows and wheels were drawn in pretty fair detail right from the beginning. When Gregory showed SB a lathe, a tool SB was experienced in using, he had no idea what it was. Then SB was asked to touch the lathe; he closed his eyes, examined it thoroughly with his hand and said, "Now that I have felt it I can see." Although SB had been deprived of *sight,* he had not been deprived of perception.

Cultural Effects

Although we appear to have some innate sensory and perceptual abilities, a completely prewired, built-in mental operating system seems unlikely. Humans live in all types of environments in the world and have lived in many cultures. It is almost certain that much of our perceptual experience is learned. For instance, pygmies of the Congo dwell primarily in dense forest and thus rarely see across large distances. As a result they do not develop as strong a concept of size constancy as we do. Colin Turnbull, an anthropologist who studied pygmies, once took his pygmy guide on a trip out of the forest. As they were crossing a wide plain, they saw a herd of buffalo in the distance.

> Kenge looked over the plain and down to a herd of buffalo some miles away. He asked me what kind of insects they were, and I told him buffalo, twice as big as the forest buffalo known to him. He laughed loudly and told me not to tell him such stupid stories. . . . We got into the car and drove down to where the animals were grazing. He watched them getting larger and larger, and though he was as courageous as any pygmy, he moved over and sat close to me and muttered that it was witchcraft. . . . When he realized they were real buffalo he was no longer afraid, but what puzzled him was why they had been so small, and whether they had really been small and suddenly grown larger or whether it had been some kind of trickery.

People from different cultures may not be "fooled" by the same optical tricks as we because they do not share the same schemata. For example, many of the most famous of the illusions developed by our psychologists depend to a certain extent on living in a world in which right angles and straight lines predominate. Our world is a "carpentered world." By contrast, some African tribes, such as the Zulus, live in round huts with round doors and plough their fields in circles; they do not experience many illusions as strongly as we do.

Our conventions for representing three dimensions on a two-dimensional surface can lead to some interesting confusions. Look at the "impossible" object in the figure below—sometimes called "the Devil's tuning fork," and try to draw it from memory. The figure itself is obviously not "impossible"—after all, it's there on the page. But most Western people cannot reproduce the drawing because we automatically

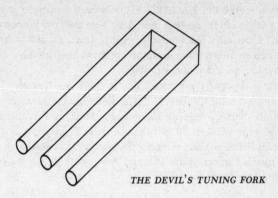

THE DEVIL'S TUNING FORK

interpret the drawing as a fantasy, an object that could not exist in three dimensions. It is our *interpretation* of what is presented to our eyes, not the figure itself, that *is* impossible.

The Initial Processing in Consciousness

A lot goes on "behind the scenes" of our mental stage even before information comes to consciousness. It is not a passive registration of what is out there, but selection and tight organization of a few elements that we allow inside. And if it is so selected and regulated, can we go so far as some wild-eyed yogis who call it an "illusion"? It is illusory in that we make the mistake of the double-seeing son, but if it is an illusion it is a *constrained illusion.* The constraints are that we select the appropriate aspects of the world in order that we survive. Alternative illusions presumably disappeared during the long period of biological evolution.

But most of our experiences of what is outside us are really transpositions of different gradations of stimulation in the outside world. And this characterization of consciousness is often startling to many: There is no color in nature, no sounds, no tastes. It is a cold, quiet, colorless affair outside us. It is *we* who create the sounds from waves in the air, it is *we* who create colors from similar, though shorter, vibrations, and it is *we* who transform molecules that happen to fit into spaces in our tongue into steak and *sauce bérnaise*—these things are *dimensions of the human experience,* not dimensions of the world outside.

To conclude: We don't actually experience the outside world—we grab only a very refined portion of it, *a portion selected for the purpose of survival*. This human selection of reality keeps us out of trouble, it allows us enough information to run the body, to keep healthy, and most importantly, to reproduce and survive.

The mind is designed, not as we like to think, for thought, for creativity, for appreciating the opera, but rather *to allow us to respond to the immediate contingencies of the world outside*. In this it must then be selective, somewhat in the way that a radio is selective, and then it must allow us to receive and consider those items that need action. Then there are much further shifts of mind once we become conscious of these few and precious things.

THE STREAM OF CONSCIOUSNESS

William James

We now begin our study of the mind from within. Most books start with sensations, as the simplest mental facts, and proceed synthetically, constructing each higher stage from those below it. But this is abandoning the empirical method of investigation. No one ever had a simple sensation by itself. Consciousness, from our natal day, is a teeming multiplicity of objects and relations, and what we call simple sensations are results of discriminative attention, pushed often to a very high degree. It is astonishing what havoc is wrought in psychology by admitting at the outset apparently innocent suppositions that nevertheless contain a flaw. The bad consequences develop themselves later on, and are irremediable, being woven through the whole texture of the work. The notion that sensations, being the simplest things, are the first things to take up in psychology is one of these suppositions. The only thing which psychology has a right to postulate at the outset is the fact of thinking itself, and that must first be taken up and analyzed. If sensations then prove to be amongst the elements of the thinking, we shall be no worse off as respects them than if we had taken them for granted at the start.

The first fact for us, then, as psychologists, is that thinking of some sort goes on. I use the word thinking . . . for every form of consciousness indiscriminately. If we could say in English "it thinks," as we say "it rains" or "it blows," we should be stating the fact most simply and with the minimum of assumption. As we cannot, we must simply say that *thought goes on.* . . .

Thought Tends to Personal Form

When I say *every thought is part of a personal consciousness,* "personal consciousness" is one of the terms in question. Its meaning we know so long as no one asks us to define it, but to give an accurate account of it is the most difficult of philosophic tasks. . . .

In this room—this lecture room, say—there are a multitude of thoughts, yours and mine, some of which cohere mutually, and some not. They are as little each-for-itself and reciprocally independent as they are all-belonging-together. They are neither: no one of them is separate, but each belongs with certain others and none beside. My thought belongs with my other thoughts, and your thought with your other thoughts. Whether anywhere in the room there be a mere thought, which is no-body's thought, we have no means of ascertaining, for we have no experience of its like. The only states of consciousness that we naturally deal with are found in personal consciousness, minds, selves, concrete particular I's and you's.

Each of these minds keeps its own thoughts to itself. There is no giving or bartering between them. No thought even comes into direct *sight* of a thought in another personal consciousness than its own. Absolute insulation, irreducible pluralism, is the law. It seems as if the elementary psychic fact were not *thought* or *this thought* or *that thought,* but *my thought,* every thought being *owned.* Neither contemporaneity, nor proximity in space, nor similarity of quality and content are able to fuse thoughts together which are sundered by this barrier of belonging to different personal minds. The breaches between such thoughts are the most absolute breaches in nature. Everyone will recognize this to be true, so long as the existence of *something* corresponding to the term "personal mind" is all that is insisted on, without any particular view of its nature being implied. On these terms the personal self rather than the thought might be treated as the immediate datum in psychology. The universal conscious fact is not "feelings and thoughts exist," but "I think" and "I feel." No psychology, at any rate, can question the *existence* of personal selves. The worst a psychology can do is so to interpret the nature of these selves as to rob them of their worth. . . .

Thought Is in Constant Change

I do not mean necessarily that no one state of mind has any duration—even if true, that would be hard to establish. The change which I have more particularly in view is that which takes place in sensible intervals of time; and the result on which I wish to lay stress is this, that *no state once gone can recur and be identical with what it was before.* . . .

We all recognize as different great classes of our conscious states. Now we are seeing, now hearing; now reasoning, now willing; now recollecting, now expecting; now loving, now hating; and in a hundred other ways we know our minds to be alternately engaged. But all these are complex states. The aim of science is always to reduce complexity to simplicity; and in psychological science we have the celebrated "theory of *ideas*" which, admitting the great difference among each other of what may be called concrete conditions of mind, seeks to show how this is all the resultant effect of variations in the *combination* of certain simple elements of consciousness that always remain the same. These mental atoms or molecules are what Locke called "simple ideas." Some of Locke's successors made out that the only simple ideas were the sensations strictly so called. Which ideas the simple ones may be does not, however, now concern us. It is enough that certain philosophers have thought that they could see under the dissolving-view-appearance of the mind elementary facts of *any* sort that remained unchanged amid the flow.

And the view of these philosophers has been called little into question, for our common experience seems at first sight to corroborate it entirely. Are not the sensations we get from the same object, for example, always the same? Does not the same piano-key, struck with the same force, make us hear in the same way? Does not the same grass give us the same feeling of green, the same sky the same feeling of blue, and do we not get the same olfactory sensation no matter how many times we put our nose to the same flask of cologne? It seems a piece of metaphysical sophistry to suggest that we do not; and yet a close attention to the matter shows that *there is no proof that the same bodily sensation is ever got by us twice.*

What is got twice is the same OBJECT. We hear the same *note* over and over again; we see the same *quality* of green, or smell the same objective perfume, or experience the same *species* of pain. The realities, concrete and abstract, physical and ideal, whose permanent existence we believe in, seem to be constantly coming up again before our thought, and lead us, in our carelessness, to suppose that our "ideas" of them are the same ideas. [Later], we shall see how inveterate is our habit of not attending to sensations as subjective facts, but of simply using them as stepping-stones to pass over to the recognition of the realities whose presence they reveal. The grass out of the window now looks to me of the same green in the sun as in the shade, and yet a painter would have to paint one part of it dark brown, another part bright yellow, to give its real sensational effect. We take no heed, as a rule, of the different way in which the same things look and sound and smell at different distances and under different circumstances. The sameness of the *things* is what we are concerned to ascertain; and any sensations that assure us of that will probably be considered in a rough way to be the same with each other. This is what makes off-hand testimony about the subjective identity of different sensations well-nigh worthless as a proof of the fact. The entire history of Sensation is a commentary on our inability to tell whether two sensations received apart are exactly alike. What appeals to our attention far more than the absolute quality or quantity of a given sensation is its *ratio* to whatever other sensations we may have at the same time. When everything is dark a somewhat less dark sensation makes us see an object white. Helmholz calculates that the white marble painted in a picture representing an architectural view by moonlight is, when seen by daylight, from ten to twenty thousand times brighter than the real moonlit marble would be.

Such a difference as this could never have been *sensibly* learned; it had to be inferred from a series of indirect considerations. There are facts which make us believe that our sensibility is altering all the time, so that the same object cannot easily give us the same sensation over again. The eye's sensibility to light is at its maximum when the eye is first exposed, and blunts itself with surprising rapidity. A long night's sleep will make it see things twice as brightly on wakening, as simple rest by closure will make it see them later in the day. We feel things differently according as we are sleepy or awake, hungry or full, fresh or tired; differently at night and in the morning, differently in summer and in winter, and above all things differently in childhood, manhood, and old age. Yet we never doubt that our feelings reveal the same world, with the same sensible qualities and the same sensible things occupying it. The difference of the sensibility is shown best by the difference of our emotions about the things from one age to another, or when we are in different organic moods. What was bright and exciting becomes weary, flat, and unprofitable. The bird's song is tedious, the breeze is mournful, the sky is sad.

To these indirect presumptions that our sensations, following the mutations of our capacity for feeling, are always undergoing an essential change, must be added another presumption, based on what must happen in the brain. Every sensation corresponds to some cerebral action. For an identical sensation to recur it would have to occur the second time *in an unmodified brain.* But as this, strictly speaking, is a physiological impossibility, so is an unmodified feeling an impossibility; for to every brain-modification, however small, must correspond a change of equal amount in the feeling which the brain subserves.

All this would be true if even sensations came to us pure and single and not combined into "things." Even then we should have to confess that, however we might in ordinary conversation speak of getting the same sensation again, we never in strict theoretic accuracy could do so; and that whatever was true of the river of life, of the river of elementary feeling, it would certainly be true to say, like Heraclitus, that we never descend twice into the same stream.

But if the assumption of "simple ideas of sensation" recurring in immutable shape is so easily shown to be baseless, how much more baseless is the assumption of immutability in the larger masses of our thought!

For there it is obvious and palpable that our state of mind is never precisely the same. Every thought we have of a given fact is strictly speaking, unique, and only bears a resemblance of kind with our other thoughts of the same fact. When the identical fact recurs, we *must* think of it in a fresh manner, see it under a somewhat different angle, apprehend it in different relations from those in which it last appeared. And the thought by which we cognize it is the thought of it-in-those-relations, a thought suffused with the consciousness of all that dim context. Often we are ourselves struck at the strange differences in our successive views of the same thing. We wonder how we ever could have opined as we did last month about a certain matter. We have outgrown the possibility of that state of mind, we know not how. From one year to another we see things in new lights. What was unreal has grown real, and what was exciting is insipid. The friends we used to care the world for are shrunken to shadows; the women, once so divine, the stars, the woods, and the waters, how now so dull and common; the young girls that brought an aura of infinity, at present hardly distinguishable existences;

the pictures so empty; and as for the books, what *was* there to find so mysteriously significant in Goethe, or in John Mill so full of weight. Instead of all this, more zestful than ever is the work, the work; and fuller and deeper the import of common duties and of common goods.

But what here strikes us so forcibly on the flagrant scale exists on every scale, down to the imperceptible transition from one hour's outlook to that of the next. Experience is remoulding us every moment, and our mental reaction on every given thing is really a resultant of our experience of the whole world up to that date. The analogies of brain-physiology must again be appealed to to corroborate our view. . . .

Every brain-state is partly determined by the nature of this entire past succession [of experiences]. Alter the latter in any part, and the brain-state must be somewhat different. Each present brain-state is a record in which the eye of Omniscience might read all the foregone history of its owner. It is out of the question, then, that any total brain-state should identically recur. Something like it may recur; but to suppose *it* to recur would be equivalent to the absurd admission that all the states that had intervened between its two appearances had been pure nonentities, and that the organ after their passage was exactly as it was before. And (to consider shorter periods) just as, in the senses, an impression feels very differently according to what has preceded it; as one color succeeding another is modified by the contrast, silence sounds delicious after noise, and a note, when the scale is sung up, sounds unlike itself when the scale is sung down; as the presence of certain lines in a figure changes the apparent form of the other lines, and as in music the whole aesthetic effect comes from the manner in which one set of sounds alters our feeling of another; so, in thought, we must admit that those portions of the brain that have just been maximally excited retain a kind of soreness which is a condition of our present consciousness, a codeterminant of how and what we now shall feel.*

Ever some tracts are waning in tension, some waxing, whilst others actively discharge. The states of tension have as positive an influence

---

*It need of course not follow, because a total brain-state does not recur, that no *point* of the brain can ever be twice in the same condition. That would be as improbable a consequence as that in the sea a wave-crest should never come twice at the same point of space. What can hardly come twice is an identical *combination* of wave-forms all with their crests and hollows reoccupying identical places. For such a combination as this is the analogue of the brain-state to which our actual consciousness at any moment is due.

as any in determining the total condition, and in deciding what the *psychosis* shall be. All we know of submaximal nerve-irritations, and of the summation of apparently ineffective stimuli, tends to show that *no* changes in the brain are physiologically ineffective, and that presumably none are bare of psychological result. But as the brain-tension shifts from one relative state of equilibrium to another, like the gyrations of a kaleidoscope, now rapid and now slow, is it likely that its faithful psychic concomitant is heavier-footed than itself, and that it cannot match each one of the organ's irradiations by a shifting inward iridescence of its own? But if it can do this, its inward iridescences must be infinite, for the brain-redistributions are in infinite variety. If so coarse a thing as a telephone-plate can be made to thrill for years and never reduplicate its inward condition, how much more must this be the case with the infinitely delicate brain? . . .

What makes it convenient to use . . . mythological formulas is the whole organization of speech, which, as was remarked a while ago, was not made by psychologists, but by men who were as a rule only interested in the facts their mental states revealed. They spoke of their states as *ideas of this or of that thing.* What wonder, then, that the thought is most easily conceived under the law of the thing whose name it bears! If the thing is composed of parts, then we suppose that the thought of the thing must be composed of the thoughts of the parts. If one part of the thing has appeared in the same thing or in other things on former occasions, why then we must be having even now the very same "idea" of that part which was there on those occasions. If the thing is simple, its thought is simple. If it is multitudinous, it must require a multitude of thoughts to think it. If a succession, only a succession of thoughts can know it. If permanent, its thought is permanent. And so on *ad libitum.* What after all is so natural as to assume that one object, called by one name, should be known by one affection of the mind? But, if language must thus influence us, the agglutinative languages, and even Greek and Latin with their declensions, would be the better guides. Names did not appear in them inalterable, but changed their shape to suit the context in which they lay. It must have been easier then than now to conceive of the same object as being thought of at different times in non-identical conscious states.

This, too, will grow clearer as we proceed. Meanwhile a necessary consequence of this belief in permanent self-identical psychic facts that absent themselves and recur periodically is the Human doctrine that our thought is composed of separate independent parts and is not a sensibly continuous stream. That this doctrine entirely misrepresents the natural appearances is what I next shall try to show.

Within Each Personal Consciousness, Thought Is Sensibly Continuous

I can only define "continuous" as that which is without breach, crack, or division. I have already said that the breach from one mind to another is perhaps the greatest breach in nature. The only breaches that can well be conceived to occur within the limits of a single mind would either be *interruptions, time*-gaps during which the consciousness went out altogether to come into existence again at a later moment; or they would be breaks in the *quality*, or content, of the thought, so abrupt that the segment that followed had no connection whatever with the one that went before. The proposition that within each personal consciousness thought feels continuous, means two things:

1. That even where there is a time-gap the consciousness after it feels as if it belonged together with the consciousness before it, as another part of the same self;
2. That the changes from one moment to another in the quality of the consciousness are never absolutely abrupt.

The case of the time-gaps, as the simplest, shall be taken first. And first of all, a word about time-gaps of which the consciousness may not be itself aware. . . . We saw that such time-gaps existed, and that they might be more numerous than is usually supposed. If the consciousness is not aware of them, it cannot feel them as interruptions. In the unconsciousness produced by nitrous oxide and other anaesthetics, in that of epilepsy and fainting, the broken edges of the sentient life may meet and merge over the gap, much as the feelings of space of the opposite margins of the "blind spot" meet and merge over that objective interruption to the sensitiveness of the eye. Such consciousness as this, whatever it be for the onlooking psychologist, is for itself unbroken. It *feels* unbroken; a waking day of it is sensibly a unit as long as that day lasts, in the sense in which the hours themselves are units, as having all their parts next each other, with no intrusive alien substance between. To expect the consciousness to feel the interruptions of its objective continuity as gaps, would be like expecting the eye to feel a gap of silence because it does not hear, or the ear to feel a gap of darkness because it does not see. So much for the gaps that are unfelt.

With the felt gaps the case is different. On waking from sleep, we usually know that we have been unconscious, and we often have an accurate judgment of how long. The judgment here is certainly an inference from sensible signs, and its ease is due to long practice ijn the particular field. The result of it, however, is that the consciousness is, *for itself,* not what it was in the former case, but interrupted and continuous, in the mere time-sense of the words. But in the other sense of continuity, the sense of the parts being inwardly connected and belonging together because they are parts of a common whole, the consciousness remains sensibly continuous and one. What now is the common whole? The natural name of it is *myself, I,* or *me.*

When Paul and Peter wake up in the same bed, and recognize that they have been asleep, each one of them mentally reaches back and makes connection with but *one* of the two streams of thought which were broken by the sleeping hours. As the current of an electrode buried in the ground unerringly finds its way to its own similarly buried mate, across no matter how much intervening earth; so Peter's present instantly finds out Peter's past, and never by mistake knits itself on to that of Paul. Paul's thought in turn is as little liable to go astray. The past thought of Peter is appropriated by the present Peter alone. He may have a *knowledge,* and a correct one too, of what Paul's last drowsy states of mind were as he sank into sleep, but it is an entirely different sort of knowledge from that which he has of his own last states. He *remembers* his own states, whilst he only *conceives* Paul's. Remembrance is like direct feeling; its object is suffused with a warmth and intimacy to which no object of mere conception ever attains. This quality of warmth and intimacy and immediacy is what Peter's *present* thought also possesses for itself. So sure as this present is me, is mine, it says, so sure is anything else that comes with the same warmth and intimacy and immediacy, me and mine. What the qualities called warmth and intimacy may in themselves be will have to be matter for future consideration. But whatever past feelings appear with those qualities must be admitted to receive the greeting of the present mental state, to be owned by it, and accepted as belonging together with it in a common self. This community of self is what the time-gap cannot break in twain, and is why a present thought, although not ignorant of the time-gap, can still regard itself as continuous with certain chosen portions of the past.

Consciousness, then, does not appear to itself chopped up in bits. Such words as "chain" or "train" do not describe it fitly as it presents itself in the first instance. It is nothing jointed; it flows. A "river" or a "stream" are the metaphors by which it is most naturally described. *In talking of it hereafter, let us call it the stream of thought, of consciousness, or of subjective life.*

But now there appears, even within the limits of the same self, and between thoughts all of which alike have this same sense of belonging together, a kind of jointing and separateness among the parts, of which this statement seems to take no account. I refer to the breaks that are produced by sudden *contrasts in the quality* of the successive segments of the stream of thought. If the words "chain" and "train" had no natural fitness in them, how came such words to be used at all? Does not a loud explosion rend the consciousness upon which it abruptly breaks, in twain? Does not every sudden shock, appearance of a new object, or change in a sensation, create a real interruption, sensibly felt as such, which cuts the conscious stream across at the moment at which it appears? Do not such interruptions smite us every hour of our lives, and have we the right, in their presence, still to call our consciousness a continuous stream?

This objection is based partly on a confusion and partly on a superficial introspective view.

The confusion is between the thoughts themselves, taken as subjective facts, and the things of which they are aware. It is natural to make this confusion, but easy to avoid it when once put on one's guard. The things are discrete and discontinuous; they do pass before us in a train or chain, making often explosive appearances and rending each other in twain. But their comings and goings and contrasts no more break the flow of the thought that thinks them than they break the time and the space in which they lie. A silence may be broken by a thunder-clap, and we may be so stunned and confused for a moment by the shock as to give no instant account to ourselves of what has happened. But that very confusion is a mental state, and a state that passes us straight over from the silence to the sound. The transition between the thought of one object and the thought of another is no more a break in the *thought* than a joint in a bamboo is a break in the wood. It is a part of the *consciousness* as much as the joint is a part of the *bamboo*.

On this gradualness in the changes of our mental content the principles of nerve-action can throw some more light. When studying . . . the summation of nervous activities, we saw that no state of the brain can be supposed instantly to die away. If a new state comes, the inertia of the old state will still be there and modify the result accordingly. Of course we cannot tell, in our ignorance, what in each instance the modifications ought to be. The commonest modifications in sense-perception are known as the phenomena of contrast. In aesthetics they are the feelings of delight or displeasure which certain particular orders in a series of impressions give. In thought, strictly and narrowly so called, they are unquestionably that consciousness of the *whence* and the *whither* that always accompanies its flows. If recently the brain-tract a was vividly excited, and then b, and now vividly c, the total present consciousness is not produced simply by c's excitement, but also by the dying vibrations of a and b as well. If we want to represent the brain-process we must write it thus:

$$a\,b^{\,c}$$

—three different processes coexisting, and correlated with them a thought which is no one of the three thoughts that they would have produced had each of them occurred alone. But whatever this fourth thought may exactly be, it seems impossible that it should not be something *like* each of the three other thoughts whose tracts are concerned in its production, though in a fast-waning phase. . . .

Thought Is Always Interested More in One Part of Its Object Than in Another, and Welcomes and Rejects, or Chooses, All the While It Thinks

The phenomena of selective attention and of deliberate will are of course patent examples of this choosing activity. But few of us are aware how incessantly it is at work in operations not ordinarily called by these names. Accentuation and Emphasis are present in every perception we have. We find it quite impossible to disperse our attention impartially over a number of impressions. A monotonous succession of sonorous strokes is broken up into rhythms, now of one sort, now of another, by the different accent which we place on different strokes. The simplest of these rhythms is the double one, tick-tóck, tick-tock, tick-tóck. Dots dispersed on a surface are perceived in rows and groups. Lines separate into diverse figures. The ubiquity of the distinctions, *this* and *that, here* and *there, now* and *then*, in our minds is the result of our laying the same selective emphasis on parts of place and time.

But we do far more than emphasize things, and unite some, and keep others apart. We actually *ignore* most of the things before us. Let me briefly show how this goes on.

To begin at the bottom, what are our very senses themselves but organs of selection? Out of the infinite chaos of movements, of which physics teaches us that the outer world consists, each sense-organ picks out those which fall within certain limits of velocity. To these it responds, but ignores the rest as completely as if they did not exist. It thus accentuates particular movements in a manner for which objectively there seems no valid ground; for, as Lange says, there is no reason whatever to think that the gap in Nature between the highest sound-waves and the lowest heat-waves is an abrupt break like that of our sensations; or that the difference between violet and ultraviolet rays has anything like the objective importance subjectively represented by that between light and darkness. Out of what is in itself an undistinguishable, swarming *continuum*, devoid of distinction or emphasis, our senses make for us, by attending to this motion and ignoring that, a world full of contrasts, of sharp accents, of abrupt changes, of picturesque light and shade.

If the sensations we receive from a given organ have their causes thus picked out for us by the conformation of the organ's termination, Attention, on the other hand, out of all the sensations yielded, picks out certain ones as worthy of its notice and suppresses all the rest. . . . We do not even know without special training on which of our eyes an image falls. So habitually ignorant are men of this that one may be blind for years of a single eye and never know the fact.

Helmholtz says that we notice only those sensations which are signs to us of *things*. But what are things? Nothing, as we shall abundantly see, but special groups of sensible qualities, which happen practically or aesthetically to interest us, to which we therefore give substantive names, and which we exalt to this exclusive status of independence and dignity. But in itself, apart from my own interest, a particular dust-wreath on a windy day is just as much of an individual thing, and just as much or as little deserves an individual name, as my own body does.

And then, among the sensations we get from each separate thing, what happens? The mind selects again. It chooses certain of the sensations to represent the thing most *truly,* and considers the rest as its appearances, modified by the conditions of the moment. Thus my tabletop is named *square,* but after one of an infinite number of retinal sensations which it yields, the rest of them being sensations of two acute and two obtuse angles; but I call the latter *perspective* views, and the four right angles the *true* form of the table, and erect the attribute squareness into the table's essence, for aesthetic reasons of my own. In like manner, the real form of the circle is deemed to be the sensation it gives when the line of vision is perpendicular to its centre—all its other sensations are signs of this sensation. The real sound of the cannon is the sensation it makes when the ear is close by. The real color of the brick is the sensation it gives when the eye looks squarely at it from a near point, out of the sunshine and yet not in the gloom; under other circumstances it gives us other color-sensations which are but signs of this—we then see it looks pinker or blacker than it really is. The reader knows no object which he does not represent to himself by preference as in some typical attitude, of some normal size, at some characteristic distance, of some standard tint, etc., etc. But all these essential characteristics, which together form for us the genuine objectivity of the thing and are contrasted with what we call the subjective sensations it may yield for us at a given moment, are mere sensations like the latter. The mind chooses to suit itself, and decides what particular sensation shall be held more real and valid than all the rest.

Thus perception involves a twofold choice. Out of all present sensations, we notice mainly such as are significant of absent ones; and out of all the absent associates which these suggest, we again pick out a very few to stand for the objective reality *par excellence.* We could have no more exquisite example of selective industry.

That industry goes on to deal with the things thus given in perception. A man's empirical thought depends on the things he has experienced, but what these shall be is to a large extent determined by his habits of attention. A thing may be present to him a thousand times, but if he persistently fails to notice it, it cannot be said to enter into his experience. We are all seeing flies, moths, and beetles by the thousand, but to whom, save an entomologist, do they say anything distinct? On the other hand, a thing met only once in a lifetime may leave an indelible experience in the memory. Let four men take a tour in Europe. One will bring home only picturesque impressions—costumes and colors, parks and views and works of architecture, pictures and statues. To another all this will be non-existent; and distances and prices, populations and drainage-arrangements, door- and window-fastenings, and other useful statistics will take their place. A third will give a rich account of the theatres, restaurants, and public balls, and naught beside; whilst the fourth will perhaps have been so wrapped in his own subjective broodings as to tell little more than a few names of places through which he passed. Each has selected, out of the same mass of presented objects, those which suited his private interest and has made his experience thereby. . . .

If we now pass to its aesthetic department, our law is still more obvious. The artist notoriously selects his items, rejecting all tones, colors, shapes, which do not harmonize with each other and with the main purpose of his work. That unity, harmony, "convergence of characters," as M. Taine calls it, which gives to works of art their superiority over works of nature, is wholly due to *elimination*. Any natural subject will do, if the artist has wit enough to pounce upon some one feature of it as characteristic, and suppress all merely accidental items which do not harmonize with this. . . .

Looking back, then, over this review, we see that the mind is at every stage a theatre of simultaneous possibilities. Consciousness consists in the comparison of these with each other, the selection of some, and the suppression of the rest by the reinforcing and inhibiting agency of attention. The highest and most elaborated mental products are filtered from the data chosen by the faculty next beneath, out of the mass offered by the faculty below that, which mass in turn was sifted from a still larger amount of yet simpler material, and so on. The mind, in short, works on the data it receives very much as a sculptor works on his block of stone. In a sense the statue stood there from eternity. But there were a thousand different ones beside it, and the sculptor alone is to thank for having extricated this one from the rest. Just so the world of each of us, howsoever different our several views of it may be, all lay embedded in the primordial chaos of sensations, which gave the mere *matter* to the thought of all of us indifferently. We may, if we like, by our reasonings unwind things back to that black and jointless continuity of space and moving clouds of swarming atoms which science calls the only real world. But all the while the world *we* feel and live in will be that which our ancestors and we, by slowly cumulative strokes of choice, have extricated out of this, like sculptors, by simply rejecting certain portions of the given stuff. Other sculptors, other statues from the same stone!

Other minds, other worlds from the same monotonous and inexpressive chaos! My world is but one in a million alike embedded, alike real to those who may abstract them. How different must be the worlds in the consciousness of ant, cuttle-fish, or crab!

But in my mind and your mind the rejected portions and the selected portions of the original world-stuff are to a great extent the same. The human race as a whole largely agrees as to what it shall notice and name, and what not. And among the noticed parts we select in much the same way for accentuation and preference or subordination and dislike. There is, however, one entirely extraordinary case in which no two men ever are known to choose alike. One great splitting of the whole universe into two halves is made by each of us; and for each of us almost all of the interest attaches to one of the halves; but we draw the line of division between them in a different place. When I say that we all call the two halves by the same names, and that those names are *"me"* and *"not-me"* respectively, it will at once be seen what I mean. The altogether unique kind of interest which each human mind feels in those parts of creation which it can call *me* or *mine* may be a moral riddle, but it is a fundamental psychological fact. No mind can take the same interest in his neighbor's *me* as in his own. The neighbor's me falls together with all the rest of things in one foreign mass, against which his own *me* stands out in startling relief. Even the trodden worm, as Lotze somewhere says, contrasts his own suffering self with the whole remaining universe, though he have no clear conception either of himself or of what the universe may be. He is for me a mere part of the world; for him it is I who am the mere part. Each of us dichotomizes the Kosmos in a different place.

THE DOORS OF PERCEPTION

Aldous Huxley

> The ancient tradition that the world will be consumed in fire at the
>   end of six thousand years is true, as I have heard from Hell.
> For the cherub with his flaming sword is hereby commanded to
>   leave his guard at the tree of life; and when he does, the whole

creation will be consumed and appear infinite and holy, whereas
it now appears finite & corrupt.
This will come to pass by an improvement of sensual enjoyment. . . .
If the doors of perception were cleansed every thing would appear
to man as it is, infinite.
For man has closed himself up, till he sees all things thro' narrow
chinks of his cavern.

How do you know but ev'ry Bird that cuts the airy way,
Is an immense world of delight, clos'd by your senses five?
    From William Blake, "The Marriage of Heaven and Hell"

Reflecting on my experience, I find myself agreeing with the eminent
Cambridge philosopher, Dr. C. D. Broad, "that we should do well to
consider much more seriously than we have hitherto been inclined to
do the type of theory which Bergson put forward in connection with
memory and sense perception. The suggestion is that the function of
the brain and nervous system and sense organs is in the main *eliminative*
and not productive. Each person is at each moment capable of remembering all that has ever happened to him and of perceiving everything
that is happening everywhere in the universe. The function of the brain
and nervous system is to protect us from being overwhelmed and confused by this mass of largely useless and irrelevant knowledge, by shutting out most of what we should otherwise perceive or remember at any
moment, and leaving only that very small and special selection which
is likely to be practically useful." According to such a theory, each one
of us is potentially Mind at Large. But in so far as we are animals, our
business is at all costs to survive. To make biological survival possible,
Mind at Large has to be funneled through the reducing valve of the
brain and nervous system. What comes out at the other end is a measly
trickle of the kind of consciousness which will help us to stay alive on
the surface of this particular planet. To formulate and express the contents of this reduced awareness, man has invented and endlessly elaborated those symbol-systems and implicit philosophies which we call
languages. Every individual is at once the beneficiary and the victim of
the linguistic tradition into which he has been born—the beneficiary
inasmuch as language gives access to the accumulated record of other
people's experience, the victim in so far as it confirms him in the belief
that reduced awareness is the only awareness and as it bedevils his

sense of reality, so that he is all too apt to take his concepts for data, his words for actual things. That which, in the language of religion, is called "this world" is the universe of reduced awareness, expressed, and, as it were, petrified by language. The various "other worlds," with which human beings erratically make contact, are so many elements in the totality of the awareness belonging to Mind at Large. Most people, most of the time, know only what comes through the reducing valve and is consecrated as genuinely real by the local language. Certain persons, however, seem to be born with a kind of by-pass that circumvents the reducing valve. In others temporary by-passes may be acquired either spontaneously, or as the result of deliberate "spiritual exercises," or through hypnosis, or by means of drugs. Through these permanent or temporary by-passes there flows, not indeed the perception "of everything that is happening everywhere in the universe" (for the by-pass does not abolish the reducing valve, which still excludes the total content of Mind at Large), but something more than, and above all something different from, the carefully selected utilitarian material which our narrowed, individual minds regard as a complete, or at least sufficient, picture of reality.

The brain is provided with a number of enzyme systems which serve to co-ordinate its workings. Some of these enzymes regulate the supply of glucose to the brain cells. Mescalin inhibits the production of these enzymes and thus lowers the amount of glucose available to an organ that is in constant need of sugar. When mescalin reduces the brain's normal ration of sugar what happens? Too few cases have been observed, therefore a comprehensive answer cannot yet be given. But what happens to the majority of the few who have taken mescalin under supervision can be summarized as follows.

1. The ability to remember and to "think straight" is little if at all reduced. (Listening to the recordings of my conversation under the influence of the drug, I cannot discover that I was then any stupider than I am at ordinary times.)
2. Visual impressions are greatly intensified and the eye recovers some of the perceptual innocence of childhood, when the sensum was not immediately and automatically subordinated to the concept. Interest in space is diminished and interest in time falls almost to zero.

3. Though the intellect remains unimpaired and though perception is enormously improved, the will suffers a profound change for the worse. The mescalin taker sees no reason for doing anything in particular and finds most of the causes for which, at ordinary times, he was prepared to act and suffer, profoundly uninteresting. He can't be bothered with them, for the good reason that he has better things to think about.

4. These better things may be experienced (as I experienced them) "out there," or "in here," or in both worlds, the inner and the outer, simultaneously or successively. That they *are* better seems to be self-evident to all mescalin takers who come to the drug with a sound liver and an untroubled mind.

These effects of mescalin are the sort of effects you could expect to follow the administration of a drug having the power to impair the efficiency of the cerebral reducing valve. When the brain runs out of sugar, the undernourished ego grows weak, can't be bothered to undertake the necessary chores, and loses all interest in those spatial and temporal relationships which mean so much to an organism bent on getting on in the world. As Mind at Large seeps past the no longer watertight valve, all kinds of biologically useless things start to happen. In some cases there may be extra-sensory perceptions. Other persons discover a world of visionary beauty. To others again is revealed the glory, the infinite value and meaningfulness of naked existence, of the given, unconceptualized event. In the final stage of egolessness there is an "obscure knowledge" that All is all—that All is actually each. This is as near, I take it, as a finite mind can ever come to "perceiving everything that is happening everywhere in the universe."

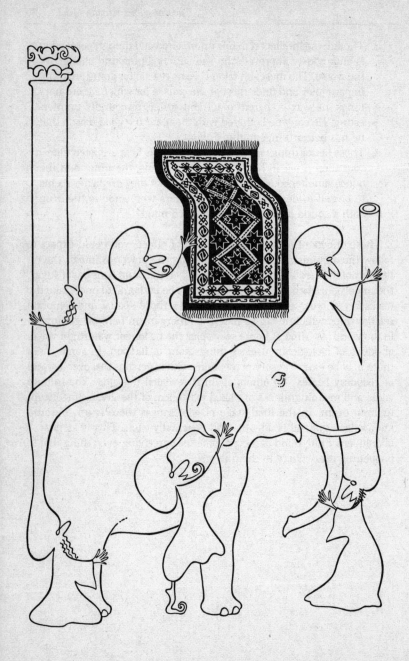

3

The Workings of
the Conscious
Mind

The Blind Men and the Elephant

*Beyond Ghor there was a city. All its inhabitants were blind. A king with his
entourage arrived nearby; he brought his army and camped in the desert. He
had a mighty elephant, which he used in attack and to increase the people's
awe.*

*The populace became anxious to learn about the elephant, and some sight-
less from among this blind community ran like fools to find it. Since they did
not know even the form or shape of the elephant, they groped sightlessly,
gathering information by touching some part of it. Each thought that he knew
something, because he could feel a part.*

*When they returned to their fellow citizens, eager groups clustered around
them, anxious, misguidedly, to learn the truth from those who were themselves
astray. They asked about the form, the shape, of the elephant, and they
listened to all that they were told.*

*The man whose hand had reached an ear said: "It is a large, rough thing,
wide and broad, like a rug."*

*One who had felt the trunk said: "I have the real facts about it. It is like a
straight and hollow pipe, awful and destructive."*

*One who had its feet and legs said: "It is mighty and firm, like a
pillar."*

*Each had felt one part out of many. Each had perceived it wrongly. No
mind knew all: knowledge is not the companion of the blind. All imagined
something, something incorrect. The created is not informed about divinity.
There is no Way in this science by means of the ordinary intellect.*

We do not perceive the outside world as complete. There are many ways fixed in the "hardware" that we reduce the information that reaches us; both as a sculptor whittles away, and as a radio tunes in to a small segment of the ambient spectrum.

But even this drastically reduced flow of information—our sensations, thoughts, emotions, and ideas, is still too much for us, so we have a second and more flexible portion of the mental system. It functions to control the few organized percepts that remain—they are shuttled in and out of consciousness.

Our consciousness is not a reasoned instrument for looking into the future and planning the best action, for we are short-term animals, animals who look for the immediate gain. This gives dismay to our more rational aspects. Politicians seem to get elected or reelected on the basis of the activities of the *previous few months,* not the long term.

The same process occurs in the mind. We screen out much of our surroundings because we do not feel that certain events occur. Once a friend emphasized this to me, unwittingly, by reversing an ordinary saying: "I'll see it when I believe it!" If an object or event does not fit our preconceptions we will misperceive it or ignore it, like mistaking an ear for a rug.

"Ignore" is too simple a description, as it connotes a careful examination, then perhaps deliberation and rejection. We don't examine alternatives, rather we are *determinedly oblivious* to much that happens to us, most of the time, an obliviousness that is for the most part useful: Who wants to continuously pore over the walls in every room to understand that there are usually four of them? Who wants to continuously check the position of his left knee and the feeling in the chest and in the buttocks? Who wants to monitor every movement that leads to crossing the street? No one, no one who wishes to be part of the world, that is.

Our ordinary "obliviousness" to most of the world is useful to us. As we try to achieve a seeming simple stability in consciousness, we make continuous "bets" about the nature of reality. We immediately assume that our rooms are "really" rectangular, that a piece of coal is "really" black (though it may be a shining glare on our eyes), that one person is always "intelligent," that another is usually "aggressive."

It is quite difficult to alter our assumptions even in the face of compelling new evidence. There is a continual trade-off in the mind: We pay the price of a certain conservatism and resistance to new information in order to gain a constant, stable world in which we know how to act in different situations and thus know how to survive.

Like the blind man, any organized community of people holds in common certain fixed assumptions about reality. Some are common to life on earth, such as what will happen to an object if dropped from a table. Some assumptions are common to a whole culture; a language is the encrustation of these assumptions, shared for the convenience of easy communication. Time, its movement and its measure, is another—imagine trying to arrange a meeting otherwise.

The "four-minute mile" was another particularly common assumption in one culture. In addition, each professional and technical community—physicists, mathematicians, philosophers, real estate agents, stockbrokers—share an additional set of implicit and explicit assumptions, sorted into categories into which we can classify the world: "furniture" is a category, "impossible occurrences" is another.

In science the shared assumptions and the categories themselves, explicit and implicit, have been termed a *paradigm* by Thomas Kuhn. The paradigm is the shared conception of what is possible, the boundaries of acceptable inquiry, the limiting cases. It forms the framework for deciding whether ideas are acceptable or whether something is a "fact" or not.

The scientific paradigm operates in the same way as an individual's, a culture's, or an organization's assumptions about reality. Personal categories are by their nature conservative—the conservatism is of effort. Given a simple set of stable categories, and simple innate responses to the world, we need not remeasure everything to see if it fits—our friends remain with the same stable characteristics we encountered when we last met; rooms endure after we leave them; the world becomes a manageable place.

In science a paradigm allows a similar stability of knowledge, again, at the price of an insensitivity to new information. Science isn't special, after all it is done by humans who have the same mental system as all the rest of us, for better or worse!

If several researchers share a paradigm, it enables them to explore jointly one well-delimited area of inquiry and to coordinate (more often, it must be admitted, to dispute) and compare their efforts. A shared paradigm allows them to communicate about an area in a specialized language and set of assumptions, as the residents of a particular town may have their own local phrases and jokes.

A successful paradigm, or successful set of assumptions about the world, enables any group, in this case a scientific one, to agree on problems and priorities; they can select problems amenable to solution. It allows a number of "local road maps" to be drawn up, tested and argued about by many independent workers, many of whom never actually meet. But there is the same kind of danger here: parochialism. Just as the residents of a community may become smug about their town and come to consider it the "only" place in the world, so scientists working under a successful paradigm may begin to lose sight of any possibilities beyond their own particular set of assumptions.

Scientists are trained to be *more oblivious* than the rest of us, the result of the specialization required by their training. Science as a system of information gathering involves a set of deliberate *limitations* on inquiry.

Although the idea that science is controlled obliviousness may sound flip, it is not. The essence of a good experiment is exclusion: One factor (in the jargon called a *variable*) may be allowed to change, or be manipulated, while a very, very few other factors are measured. If, for example, we wished to study the response of brain cells to light, we would be considered slightly loony if we also monitored the blood flow to the feet, the constructions of buildings in Kuala Lumpur, the changes in the orbit of one of Jupiter's moons. And you will see that there are millions of other possibilities, all excluded, almost without thought, so well-learned is the scientists' obliviousness to what is hoped are extraneous details.

In performing scientific research, we are often unaware of the full effect of our tools, be they physical ones or doctrines, like behaviorism or cognitive psychology. The psychologist Abraham Maslow, commenting on the overselective effect that a strict behaviorism once had in psychology, wrote: "If the only tool you have is a hammer, you tend to treat everything as if it were a nail."

I compare science and the scientists' special manner of knowing with the blind men, because there are continuities in all affairs of the mind. The special workings of science are the distillate (sometimes crude, sometimes pure) of the mental processes and mental system that we possess. Scientists have to limit their perceptions more than the normal person, and select a tiny bit of knowledge to consider.

But how does any information ever become "chosen" to enter consciousness? We seem to have evolved an exceedingly complex set of "paths" and gates in the mind, which let some things in easily and keep others waiting, so we keep a very simplified version of events in store.

A good example can be found in answering a simple question: *What day is it?* If our minds were in some way representative of the world there should be no difference, but this is not the case. On a weekday it takes longer to answer this question than it does on a weekend, and Wednesday takes the longest to remember! This probably happens because we judge days by their proximity to the weekend.

Most of the time we cannot even remember things we see everyday: Can you quickly say which letters are on the 7 of the phone dial? And try this: Repeat the months in order and time yourself; count the mistakes. If you are like most people, you did it well! Then try to recite the months of the year in reverse order and time yourself. Probably longer, and most likely few if any mistakes. Then try the months of the year in *alphabetical* order. You wouldn't think so, but it is surprisingly difficult, especially considering that you probably knew what were the months and have just repeated them twice, and you surely know alphabetical order! These are difficult because our mental system is specialized to do only a few things well, and not much else.

Our memory is perhaps the ultimate in selection, and when we select something in memory, it often brings up those other selections that were "laid down" at the same time—a song recalls a whole era, the remembrance of going out on one's first date, which almost "automatically" calls up the kind of car being driven, the clothes, now so out of style.

Our memory is a great mystery. How can a song suddenly bring up memories of an orchard, an automobile, a lost era? How can someone forget an entire era of life or a marriage partner, or suddenly speak a language not spoken in years?

The same kinds of simplifying rules work in recall. Our memory operates like a storehouse, those items on the "fast path" are used and overused. In a sense, it is easy to understand why this system should be the one operating: Things for which we have a lot of use have priority— they influence and organize our experiences.

You can easily see why this system would be functional; like other mental shortcuts it would enable us to have a lot of different kinds of information in our mental register at different times, each set of information associated with different contingencies. When I recently went back to a small hotel that I have previously visited in London, I was surprised to find out that I somehow knew how to turn, on an unfamiliar street, to find the telephone booth. This was something that for years I had been unaware that I remembered.

On the Nature of Consciousness Itself

Consciousness is the "front page" of the mind. In this loose analogy, the mind is like a newspaper—what is most important that day is on the front page. The most important events are immediate crises, such as a breakdown in transportation or a battle, or new and unexpected situations that require actions, such as a flood or a disaster.

Countless ordinary events each day never make the headlines. We would never see 75 MILLION PLEASANT DINNERS LAST NIGHT as a headline, or anything like it. Instead, those who select what goes on the front page ask: Is it unexpected? Is it important? Is it new?

A similar process goes on in the mind. Countless stimuli reach us at any moment. Some are filtered out by the senses, some are organized and simplified by perception, but we must still select the most important ones at any one moment. Therefore, what is in consciousness at any moment are the items of highest priority to us, those items most needing action. These items may be real emergencies such as a threat to safety. Some may be immediate concerns, such as "Watch that car in the left lane; he's weaving all over the road." Some may be chronic concerns, such as solving an intellectual problem. Some may be simply new events, such as a person entering the room.

Since our situation and needs for action change, our consciousness changes continually within a day, from sleep and dreaming to the kind of "borderline" state on awakening, from tiredness to excitement, from daydreaming to directed thinking. These "daily" alterations in consciousness are much more extreme than we normally realize.

It is also possible to deliberately alter consciousness. Techniques for doing so have been developed in almost every culture. Meditation, for instance, turns down the normally active consciousness and allows a more receptive, inward state to emerge. Under hypnosis, the control of our consciousness is given over to another. A person in hypnosis can withstand normally intolerable levels of pain and uncover memories "lost" from consciousness. Mind-altering drugs, such as LSD and cocaine, affect consciousness by altering the neurotransmitters of the brain.

William James, in a now classic passage, described the potential varieties of consciousness:

Our normal waking consciousness, rational consciousness as we call it, is but one special type of consciousness, whilst all about it, parted from it by the filmiest of screens, there lie potential forms of consciousness entirely different. We may go through life without suspecting their existence; but apply the requisite stimulus, and at a touch they are there in all their completeness, definite types of mentality which probably somewhere have their field of application and adaptation. No account of the universe in its totality can be final which leaves these other forms of consciousness quite disregarded. How to regard them is the question,—for they may determine attitudes though they cannot furnish formulas, and open a region though they fail to give a map. At any rate, they forbid a premature closing of our accounts with reality. (James, 1890)

The Automatization of the Mind

The reason that only new and important information gets into consciousness is that well-learned actions and patterns of events become automatized. Automization takes place in the mind when a series of movements or actions are repeated, as in writing or walking. The repetition in some ways solidifies the action, and it becomes in essence a set routine. Familiar actions are accomplished "without thinking," without much involvement of consciousness, leaving us free to notice new events.

Watch a baby learning to walk. Notice how he concentrates very hard on the specific movements; eventually, the complex coordination of movements becomes automatized. Do you remember how it was when you first learned to drive a car? At first, the individual actions required to operate the car were painfully uncoordinated. All of your attention was focused on the car. "Let's see. Press the left foot down. Move the gear lever into first. Let the left foot off the clutch. Press on the gas." While learning to operate a car, it is very hard to think about anything else—like where you are supposed to be driving!

However, once the movements become automatized you can carry on a conversation, sing, or admire the scenery without necessarily being conscious of operating the car. The action of shifting gears, even the total activity of driving, becomes automatized.

Other schemata also become automatized, in addition to those concerned with actions. The automatization of perceptual schemata serves to simplify the world. Mental operations, like physical skills, also become automatized: When someone says George Washington, chopping down a cherry tree "automatically" comes to mind.

The Functions of Consciousness

The functions of an organism's consciousness differ between animals. The frog, for instance, sees only a few selected features of the physical world and responds, for the most part, "automatically" to them. A cat may respond to many more of the features of the world, but lacks much of the range of human flexibility.

The range of options and of capacities is what most distinguishes the consciousness of human beings. We can survive in widely different environments, from life on the dry plains of Africa to the frigid mountains of Alaska; no other animal can do that.

There are four main functions of human consciousness:

1. *Simplification and selection of information.* There is much "editing" that goes on in the mind—from the first cuts at the senses to those of perception, memory, and thinking—but still there is far too much information available at once, so there needs to be a choice in what the organism does at any moment. It is in consciousness that the choice is made.

2. *Guiding and overseeing actions.* Consciousness connects brain and body states with external occurrences. In order to function in a complex environment, actions must be planned, guided, and organized: We must know when and where to walk; when to speak and what to say; when to eat, drink, eliminate, and sleep. These actions must be coordinated with events in the outside world. At any moment the *content* of consciousness is what we are prepared to act on next.

3. *Setting priorities for action.* It is not enough for our actions to be coordinated with events in the outside world; they must reflect our internal needs. Pain can flood consciousness in the same way that an emergency fills the front page of a newspaper. The priority system gives certain events, those affecting survival, fast access or a controlling influence on consciousness. Survival and safety come first; while hunger will not intrude as dramatically as does pain, the need will be felt if left unattended.

4. *Detecting and resolving discrepancies.* Since the information selected to enter consciousness is usually about *changes* in the

external and internal worlds, when there is a discrepancy between our stored knowledge about the world and an event, it is more likely to come to consciousness. For instance, a woman in a bikini would probably not attract too much attention on the beach, but if she wore the same outfit to a formal dinner it would certainly be noticed. Discrepancies may arise internally, as well. For instance, you are usually not conscious of your breathing. However, when you have a cold your breathing may enter your consciousness, and this may tell you to slow down or to see a doctor. Consciousness involves actions to reduce the discrepancy, as when you straighten out a crooked painting on the wall because it does not fit with the other paintings.

The Structure of Consciousness

Continuing the newspaper analogy, the contents of consciousness are those few important events demanding immediate action. But consciousness is only the "front page" of the mind; behind it are many different levels of awareness, containing our plans and expectations, our assumptions, or our basic knowledge of how to operate in the world.

So the mind is divided in the two ways a newspaper is divided: The first is the division between the front page and the rest of the paper; between consciousness and other forms of awareness. The second is the division of the front page (consciousness) itself.

Consciousness and Subconscious Levels of Awareness

Only the most important events that need our attention enter consciousness. But "behind" consciousness, as the later pages of a newspaper follow the front page, are different *levels of awareness* of the outside world.

There is a quite important difference between awareness and consciousness, although in most discussions they are confused. When something is in awareness *it means that we are keeping track of it.* We are aware of a great deal, much more than we know. For instance, to walk we must be aware of our own movements, the touch of feet on the pavement, whether there is a crack, a curb, or a stone. But we are not *conscious* of these things as we walk, nor are we *conscious* of our breathing, our arm movements, the background noises, or traffic.

Sleep provides a striking example of the difference between awareness and consciousness. During sleep, when our consciousness is shut down, we are nevertheless aware of sounds. If the sounds have a particular significance, our consciousness can be aroused. Sleepers will awaken to their own names or to a word like *fire*, although they will not awaken to random words spoken. A mother sleeps through the noise of sirens in the streets, but awakens at the far softer sound of her baby crying. For that to occur, we must have been *aware* of many of the words and sounds of the environment and have selected only the important ones to enter consciousness. Therefore, *when we know we are aware of something, we are conscious of it.*

Awareness. The content of awareness includes our plans, the automatized functions, our expectations and assumptions, all those "things" and more that make up our world, and of which we keep track.

Sometimes we do not notice events in our awareness until they are gone, as when you notice that the clock has stopped ticking. Sometimes we say, "I just heard the clock stop." In order to hear the clock stop, you must have been aware of the ticking at some level of perception. A dramatic illustration of this level of awareness occurred when a train line was torn down some time ago in New York. An elevated railroad once ran along Third Avenue in New York City. At a certain time late each night, a noisy train ran. The train line was torn down some time ago, with some interesting aftereffects. Shortly after the demolition, many people in the neighborhood began to call the police quite late to report "something strange" occurring—unusual noises, suspected thieves or burglars were reported.

The police determined that these calls took place at about the same time the late-night train would have passed these peoples' houses had the line not been demolished. What they were "hearing," of course, was the *absence* of the familiar noise of the train.

There are many other levels of our consciousness; important ones are:

Preconscious memories. Those memories that enable us to operate in the world, be it specific *episodes* in our life, such as our experiences the day we were married, or our generalized *representation* of how the world operates, where Osaka or Scotland are, for instance.

Non-conscious processes. The concerns of this level are primarily the automatic functioning of the body, the pumping of the heart, regulation of hormones, blood pressure.

The unconscious. A very controversial "level" of consciousness proposed by Sigmund Freud and defended for generations by the adherents of psychoanalysis. It is supposed to be a repository of "forbidden" thoughts and desires, an area to which we move, or "repress," things we don't want to have anything to do with, like lusts for people we should not, desires to kill. Most contemporary psychologists are not too taken with this idea, and it has not held up well in fair-minded studies, although there may be some very weak effects, some of which are called up by subliminal stimulation, of which more later. We are not so seething with unexpulsed lust as Freud may have thought, but we are hardly rational either. We both have far more capability to override the "unconscious" than Freud thought (and followers still think!) but we are also prey to many more "unconscious" influences than he ever dreamed—food, the charge in the air, leftover moods, mistaken applications of mental routines, and many more. But there probably is a small unconscious in all these subconscious determinants of consciousness itself.

The Cycle of Conscious Experiences

This analysis presented so far would be adequate if we were only to analyze experiences and events we have seen before. However, the world is constantly changing and to get along we must be able to discover the meaning of new events.

The idea of a *cycle of conscious experiences* (after Neisser's "Perceptual Cycle") is based on the idea that our own personal "world" is discovered in a continuous process, directed by our schemata. When one person says a glass is half empty and another says it is half full, we have an example of how people search their environment differently. One person is looking at what is gone, the empty space; the other is looking at what is left, the liquid.

Three factors figure in the cycle. First is our schemata. The basic unit of the mental operating system is called a *schema*—plural, *schemata*. A schema is the framework that ties events together in the mind. Schemata allow us to perceive things as connected and thus act in an organized way. Schemata not only link our past experience with present events, they also direct our discovery of the world.

The second factor is our movements and manipulations of the world; the third is sensory information about physical changes in the external world. The figure on page 68 is a diagram of the cycle. The schemata direct exploration: Sensory information provided by these exploratory movements modifies the view of the world produced by the brain, which in turn changes the schema. New movements are directed, and exploration begins anew. This continuous cycle produces continually changing experiences, and thus different people may "carve out" different conscious experiences, in the way that James's sculptor did. Half empty . . .

Do We Receive or Invent the External World?

Consciousness involves extracting only those stimuli that convey important information, but how do we accomplish this? There are two major conscious processes described, as usual in the academic world, by two opposing camps of theorists.

One system seems to operate like a radio set; they both "tune into" the environment and pick up information they are built to receive. In part, then our perception is a direct function of stimulation. For instance,

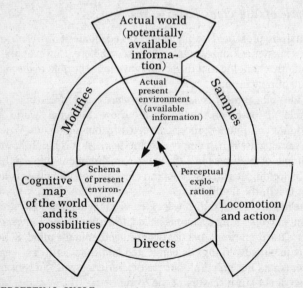

THE PERCEPTUAL CYCLE
This diagram represents the theory that perception is a continuous process of changing experience directed by schemata, themselves modified by sensory information provided by the selective exploration of the environment. (After Neisser, 1976)

the information for color vision is *directly* present at the receptors; it stimulates the receptors, and we experience color. The proponents of this view say that information about distance, relative size, shape, and perspective are all similarly available to the human perceiver.

This aspect of the process of human consciousness is similar to that of other organisms. The worm, the fish, the eagle, the tiger, and the human being, to take a few examples, all live in quite different environments. Different organisms have evolved differently in different environments, and each organism has evolved specialized perceptual systems to "pick up" information that is relevant to the organism. It deserves emphasis. The *environment is different for each organism,* so that the information that is appropriate for each organism is different to a greater or lesser extent. Insofar as perception is successful, it responds directly, as does a radio, to the specific features of the world it is designed to pick up.

If this theory is right, then there should be, waiting to be discovered, cells or networks of cells in the brain that respond to the relative size of two objects, to the convergence at the horizon, and to other features of our natural world, as do the cells in the visual system that respond to color and to corners. If such networks are discovered, we would have a more precise understanding of what is built in and what is built up in the perceptual process.

But because the information reaching the brain is often chaotic and quite often incomplete, consciousness must also include the process of constructing a "representation" or model of the world (as an ordinary globe is fashioned to represent the earth). Hence, the transmitted information from the senses "sparks off" the creation of a mental image of what could have caused this sensation. Many of the classic demonstrations such as the distorted room show that the mental operating system includes acts of creation as well as the reception of information. We process, infer, and analyze information until we arrive at a reliable solution, the percept. Of course, our percepts must also be correct when checked out in the real world. That is, the percepts we do construct should keep us from bumping into walls, drinking boiling hot fluids, or not recognizing our friends when we see them.

Consciousness involves some of both processes. Perhaps some of the basic or "primary" qualities of the environment are "picked up" directly by the perceiver. But even these must be interpreted. What is the *meaning* of the man approaching, of an object disappearing into the distance? We are probably a little like a radio and a little like a computer.

. . .

It is quite fragile, this mental system of ours—and it is often a wonder that it does work as well as it does. It should not come as too much of a surprise that it is difficult to "personally develop" consciousness, since almost all of our mind is geared to the acquisition and maintenance of schemata designed to serve us for survival. In the next chapter we turn our focus further into the specific machinery of consciousness, into brain systems that underly our responses to body needs, and one system at the highest levels of the brain that seems to contain some of the escape routes.

THEY SAW A GAME: A CASE STUDY

Albert H. Hastorf and Hadley Cantril

On a brisk Saturday afternoon, November 23, 1951, the Dartmouth football team played Princeton in Princeton's Palmer Stadium. It was the last game of the season for both teams and of rather special significance because the Princeton team had won all its games so far and one of its players, Kazmaier, was receiving the All-American mention and had just appeared as the cover man on *Time* magazine, and was playing his last game.

A few minutes after the opening kick-off, it became apparent that the game was going to be a rough one. The referees were kept busy blowing their whistles and penalizing both sides. In the second quarter, Princeton's star left the game with a broken nose. In the third quarter, a Dartmouth player was taken off the field with a broken leg. Tempers flared both during and after the game. The official statistics of the game, which Princeton won, showed that Dartmouth was penalized 70 yards, Princeton 25, not counting more than a few plays in which both sides were penalized.

Needless to say, accusations soon began to fly. The game immediately became a matter of concern to players, students, coaches, and the administrative officials of the two institutions, as well as to alumni and the general public who had not seen the game but had become sensitive to the problem of big-time football through the recent exposures of subsidized players, commercialism, etc. Discussion of the game continued for several weeks.

One of the contributing factors to the extended discussion of the game was the extensive space given to it by both campus and metropolitan newspapers. An indication of the fervor with which the discussions were carried on is shown by a few excerpts from the campus dailies.

For example, on November 27 (four days after the game), the *Daily Princetonian* (Princeton's student newspaper) said:

> This observer has never seen quite such a disgusting exhibition of so-called "sport." Both teams were guilty but the blame must be laid primarily on Dartmouth's doorstep. Princeton, obviously the better team, had no reason to rough up Dartmouth. Looking at the situation rationally, we don't see why the Indians should make a deliberate attempt to cripple Dick Kazmaier or any other Princeton player. The Dartmouth psychology, however, is not rational itself.

The November 30th edition of the *Princeton Alumni Weekly* said:

> But certain memories of what occurred will not be easily erased. Into the record books will go in indelible fashion the fact that the last game of Dick Kazmaier's career was cut short by more than half when he was forced out with a broken nose and a mild concussion, sustained from a tackle that came well after he had thrown a pass.
>
> This second-period development was followed by a third quarter outbreak of roughness that was climaxed when a Dartmouth player deliberately kicked Brad Glass in the ribs while the latter was on his back. Throughout the often unpleasant afternoon, there was undeniable evidence that the losers' tactics were the result of an actual style of play, and reports on other games they have played this season substantiate this.

Dartmouth students were "seeing" an entirely different version of the game through the editorial eyes of the *Dartmouth* (Dartmouth's undergraduate paper). For example, on November 27 the *Dartmouth* said:

> However, the Dartmouth-Princeton game set the stage for the other type of dirty football. A type which may be termed as an unjustifiable accusation.
>
> Dick Kazmaier was injured early in the game. Kazmaier was the

star, an All-American. Other stars have been injured before, but Kazmaier had been built to represent a Princeton idol. When an idol is hurt there is only one recourse—the tag of dirty football. So what did the Tiger Coach Charley Caldwell do? He announced to the world that the Big Green had been out to extinguish the Princeton star. His purpose was achieved.

After this incident, Caldwell instilled the old see-what-they-did-go-get-them attitude into his players. His talk got results. Gene Howard and Jim Miller were both injured. Both had dropped back to pass, had passed, and were standing unprotected in the backfield. Result: one bad leg and one leg broken.

The game was rough and did get a bit out of hand in the third quarter. Yet most of the roughing penalties were called against Princeton while Dartmouth received more of the illegal-use-of-the-hands variety.

On November 28 the *Dartmouth* said:

Dick Kazmaier of Princeton admittedly is an unusually able football player. Many Dartmouth men traveled to Princeton, not expecting to win—only hoping to see an All-American in action. Dick Kazmaier was hurt in the second period, and played only a token part in the remainder of the game. For this, spectators were sorry.

But there were no such feelings for Dick Kazmaier's health. Medical authorities have confirmed that as a relatively unprotected passing and running star in a contact sport, he is quite liable to injury. Also, his particular injuries—a broken nose and a slight concussion—were no more serious than is experienced almost any day in any football practice, where there is no more serious stake than playing the following Saturday. Up to the Princeton game, Dartmouth players suffered about 10 known nose fractures and face injuries, not to mention several slight concussions.

Did Princeton players feel so badly about losing their star? They shouldn't have. During the past undefeated campaign they stopped several individual stars by a concentrated effort, including such mainstays as Frank Hauff of Navy, Glenn Adams of Pennsylvania and Rocco Calvo of Cornell.

In other words, the same brand of football condemned by the *Prince*—that of stopping the big man—is practiced quite successfully by the Tigers.

Basically, then, there was disagreement as to what had happened during the "game." Hence we took the opportunity presented by the occasion to make a "real life" study of a perceptual problem.*

Procedure

Two steps were involved in gathering data. The first consisted of answers to a questionnaire designed to get reactions to the game and to learn something of the climate of opinion in each institution. This questionnaire was administered a week after the game to both Dartmouth and Princeton undergraduates who were taking introductory and intermediate psychology courses.

The second step consisted of showing the same motion picture of the game to a sample of undergraduates in each school and having them check on another questionnaire, as they watched the film, any infraction of the rules they saw and whether these infractions were "mild" or "flagrant."† At Dartmouth, members of two fraternities were asked to view the film on December 7; at Princeton, members of two undergraduate clubs saw the film early in January.

The answers to both questionnaires were carefully coded and transferred to punch cards.

Results

Table 1 shows the questions which received different replies from the two student populations on the first questionnaire.

Questions asking if the students had friends on the team, if they had ever played football themselves, if they felt they knew the rules of the game well, etc., showed no differences in either school and no relation to answers given to other questions. This is not surprising since the students in both schools came from essentially the same type of educational, economic, and ethnic background.

Summarizing the data of Tables 1 and 2, we find a marked contrast between the two student groups.

*We are not concerned here with the problem of guilt or responsibility for infractions, and nothing here implies any judgment as to who was to blame.

†The film shown was kindly loaned for the purpose of the experiment by the Dartmouth College Athletic Council. It should be pointed out that a movie of a football game follows the ball, is thus selective, and omits a good deal of the total action on the field. Also, of course, in viewing only a film of a game, the possibilities of participation as spectator are greatly limited.

TABLE 1
DATA FROM FIRST QUESTIONNAIRE

Question	Dartmouth students (N = 163) %	Princeton students (N = 161) %
1. Did you happen to see the actual game between Dartmouth and Princeton in Palmer Stadium this year?		
Yes	33	71
No	67	29
2. Have you seen a movie of the game or seen it on television?		
Yes, movie	33	2
Yes, television	0	1
No, neither	67	97
3. (Asked of those who answered "yes" to either or both of above questions.) From your observations of what went on at the game, do you believe the game was clean and fairly played, or that it was unnecessarily rough and dirty?		
Clean and fair	6	0
Rough and dirty	24	69
Rough and fair*	25	2
No answer	45	29
4. (Asked of those who answered "no" to both of the first questions.) From what you have heard and read about the game, do you feel it was clean and fairly played, or that it was unnecessarily rough and dirty?		
Clean and fair	7	0
Rough and dirty	18	24
Rough and fair*	14	1
Don't know	6	4
No answer	55	71
(Combined answers to questions 3 and 4 above)		
Clean and fair	13	0
Rough and dirty	42	93
Rough and fair*	39	3
Don't know	6	4
5. From what you saw in the game or the movies, or from what you have read, which team do you feel started the rough play?		
Dartmouth started it	36	86
Princeton started it	2	0
Both started it	53	11
Neither	6	1
No answer	3	2
6. What is your understanding of the charges being made?†		
Dartmouth tried to get Kazmaier	71	47
Dartmouth intentionally dirty	52	44
Dartmouth unnecessarily rough	8	35
7. Do you feel there is any truth to these charges?		
Yes	10	55
No	57	4
Partly	29	35
Don't know	4	6
8. Why do you think the charges were made?		
Injury to Princeton star	70	23
To prevent repetition	2	46
No answer	28	31

*This answer was not included on the checklist but was written in by the percentage of students indicated.
†Replies do not add to 100% since more than one charge could be given.

TABLE 2
DATA FROM SECOND QUESTIONNAIRE CHECKED WHILE SEEING FILM

| Group | N | Total number of infractions checked against | | | |
| | | Dartmouth team | | Princeton team | |
		Mean	SD	Mean	SD
Dartmouth students	48	4.3*	2.7	4.4	2.8
Princeton students	49	9.8*	5.7	4.2	3.5

*Significant at the .01 level.

Nearly all *Princeton* students judged the game as "rough and dirty"—not one of them thought it "clean and fair." And almost nine-tenths of them thought the other side started the rough play. By and large they felt that the charges they understood were being made were true; most of them felt the charges were made in order to avoid similar situations in the future.

When Princeton students looked at the movie of the game, they saw the Dartmouth team make over twice as many infractions as their own team made. And they saw the Dartmouth team make over twice as many infractions as were seen by Dartmouth students. When Princeton students judged these infractions as "flagrant" or "mild," the ratio was about two "flagrant" to one "mild" on the Dartmouth team, and about one "flagrant" to three "mild" on the Princeton team.

As for the *Dartmouth* students, while the plurality of answers fell in the "rough and dirty" category, over one-tenth thought the game was "clean and fair" and over a third introduced their own category of "rough and fair" to describe the action. Although a third of the Dartmouth students felt that Dartmouth was to blame for starting the rough play, the majority of Dartmouth students thought both sides were to blame. By and large, Dartmouth men felt that the charges they understood were being made were not true, and most of them thought the reason for the charges was Princeton's concern for its football star.

When Dartmouth students looked at the movie of the game, they saw both teams make about the same number of infractions. And they saw their own team make only half the number of infractions the Princeton students saw them make. The ratio of "flagrant" to "mild" infractions was about one to one when Dartmouth students judged the Dartmouth team, and about one "flagrant" to two "mild" when Dartmouth students judged infractions made by the Princeton team.

It should be noted that Dartmouth and Princeton students were thinking of different charges in judging their validity and in assigning reasons as to why the charges were made. It should also be noted that whether or not students were spectators of the game in the stadium made little difference in their responses.

Interpretation: The Nature of a Social Event*

It seems clear that the "game" actually was many different games and that each version of the events that transpired was just as "real" to a particular person as other versions were to other people. A consideration of the experiential phenomena that constitute a "football game" for the spectator may help us both to account for the results obtained and to illustrate something of the nature of any social event.

Like any other complex social occurrence, a "football game" consists of a whole host of happenings. Many different events are occurring simultaneously. Furthermore, each happening is a link in a chain of happenings, so that one follows another in sequence. The "football game," as well as other complex social situations, consists of a whole matrix of events. In the game situation, this matrix of events consists of the actions of all the players, together with the behavior of the referees and linesmen, the action on the sidelines, in the grandstands, over the loud-speaker, etc.

Of crucial importance is the fact that an "occurrence" on the football field or in any other social situation does not become an experiential "event" unless and until some significance is given to it: an "occurrence" becomes an *"event"* only when the happening has significance. And a happening generally has significance only if it reactivates learned significances already registered in what we have called a person's assumptive form-world (Cantril, 1950).

Hence the particular occurrences that different people experienced in the football game were a limited series of events from the total matrix

---

*The interpretation of the nature of a social event sketched here is in part based on discussions with Adelbert Ames, Jr., and is being elaborated in more detail elsewhere.

of events *potentially* available to them. People experienced those occurrences that reactivated significances they brought to the occasion; they failed to experience those occurrences which did not reactivate past significances. We do not need to introduce "attention" as an "intervening third" (to paraphrase James on memory) to account for the selectivity of the experiential process.

In this particular study, one of the most interesting examples of this phenomenon was a telegram sent to an officer of Dartmouth College by a member of a Dartmouth alumni group in the Midwest. He had viewed the film which had been shipped to his alumni group from Princeton after its use with Princeton students, who saw, as we noted, an average of over nine infractions by Dartmouth players during the game. The alumnus, who couldn't see the infractions he had heard publicized, wired:

> Preview of Princeton movies indicates considerable cutting of important part please wire explanation and possible air mail missing part before showing scheduled for January 25 we have splicing equipment.

The "same" sensory impingements emanating from the football field, transmitted through the visual mechanism to the brain, also obviously gave rise to different experiences in different people. The significances assumed by different happenings for different people depend in large part on the purposes people bring to the occasion and the assumptions they have of the purposes and probable behavior of other people involved. This was amusingly pointed out by the New York *Herald Tribune*'s sports columnist, Red Smith, in describing a prize fight between Chico Vejar and Carmine Fiore in his column of December 21, 1951. Among other things, he wrote:

> You see, Steve Ellis is the proprietor of Chico Vejar, who is a highly desirable tract of Stamford Conn., welterweight. Steve is also a radio announcer. Ordinarily there is no conflict between Ellis the Brain and Ellis the Voice because Steve is an uncommonly substantial lump of meat who can support both halves of a split personality and give away weight on each end without missing it.
>
> This time, though, the two Ellises met head-on, with a sickening, rending crash. Steve the Manager sat at ringside in the guise of

Steve the Announcer broadcasting a dispassionate, unbiased, objective report of Chico's adventures in the ring. . . .

Clear as mountain water, his words came through, winning big for Chico. Winning? Hell, Steve was slaughtering poor Fiore.

Watching and listening, you could see what a valiant effort the reporter was making to remain cool and detached. At the same time you had an illustration of the old, established truth that when anybody with a preference watches a fight, he sees only what he prefers to see.

That is always so. That is why, after any fight that doesn't end in a clean knockout, there always are at least a few hoots when the decision is announced. A guy from, say, Bill Graham's neighborhood goes to see Billy fight and he watches Graham all the time. He sees all the punches Billy throws, and hardly any of the punches Billy catches. So it was with Steve.

"Fiore feints with a left," he would say, honestly believing that Fiore hadn't caught Chico full on the chops. "Fiore's knees buckle," he said, "and Chico backs away." Steve didn't see the hook that had driven Chico back.

In brief, the data here indicate that there is no such "thing" as a "game" existing "out there" in its own right which people merely "observe." The "game" "exists" for a person and is experienced by him only in so far as certain happenings have significances in terms of his purpose. Out of all the occurrences going on in the environment, a person selects those that have some significance for him from his own egocentric position in the total matrix.

Obviously in the case of a football game, the value of the experience of watching the game is enhanced if the purpose of "your" team is accomplished, that is, if the happening of the desired consequence is experienced—i.e., if your team wins. But the value attribute of the experience can, of course, be spoiled if the desire to win crowds out behavior we value and have come to call sportsmanlike.

The sharing of significances provides the links except for which a "social" event would not be experienced and would not exist for anyone.

A "football game" would be impossible except for the rules of the game which we bring to the situation and which enable us to share with others the significances of various happenings. These rules make possible a certain repeatability of events such as first downs, touchdowns, etc. If a person is unfamiliar with the rules of the game, the behavior he sees lacks repeatability and consistent significance and hence "doesn't make sense."

And only because there is the possibility of repetition is there the possibility that a happening has a significance. For example, the balls used in games are designed to give a high degree of repeatability. While a football is about the only ball used in games which is not a sphere, the shape of the modern football has apparently evolved in order to achieve a higher degree of accuracy and speed in forward passing than would be obtained with a spherical ball, thus increasing the repeatability of an important phase of the game.

The rules of a football game, like laws, rituals, customs, and mores, are registered and preserved forms of sequential significances enabling people to share the significances of occurrences. The sharing of sequential significances which have value for us provides the links that operationally make social events possible. They are analogous to the forces of attraction that hold parts of an atom together, keeping each part from following its individual, independent course.

From this point of view it is inaccurate and misleading to say that different people have different "attitudes" concerning the same "thing." For the "thing" simply is *not* the same for different people whether the "thing" is a football game, a presidential candidate, Communism, or spinach. We do not simply "react to" a happening or to some impingement from the environment in a determined way (except in behavior that has become reflexive or habitual). We behave according to what we bring to the occasion, and what each of us brings to the occasion is more or less unique. And except for these significances which we bring to the occasion, the happenings around us would be meaningless occurrences, would become "inconsequential."

From the transactional view, an attitude is not a predisposition to react in a certain way to an occurrence or stimulus "out there" that exists in its own right with certain fixed characteristics which we "color" according to our predisposition (Kilpatrick, 1952). That is, a subject does not simply "react to" an "object." An attitude would rather seem to be a complex of registered significances reactivated by some stimulus which assumes its own particular significance for us in terms of our purposes. That is, the object as experienced would not exist for us except for the reactivated aspects of the form-world which provide particular significance to the hieroglyphics of sensory impingements.

4

The Machinery of Consciousness

Never Know When It Might Come in Useful

Nasrudin sometimes took people for trips in his boat. One day a fussy pedagogue hired him to ferry him across a very wide river. As soon as they were afloat, the scholar asked whether it was going to be rough.

"Don't ask me nothing about it," said Nasrudin.

"Have you never studied grammar?"

"No," said the Mulla.

"In that case, half your life has been wasted."

The Mulla said nothing.

Soon a terrible storm blew up. The Mulla's crazy cockleshell was filling with water. He leaned over toward his companion. "Have you ever learned to swim?"

"No," said the pedant.

"In that case, schoolmaster, all your life is lost, for we are sinking."

The two characters in this story represent two major kinds of consciousness. The rational one is portrayed by the pedagogue, involved in and insisting on neat and tidy perfection; the second form of consciousness is represented by the boatman and the skill of swimming, which involves movement of the body in space—a way of operating in reality often devalued by the neat, rational mind of the pedagogue.

These two characters can also represent different types of people. The verbal-logical grammarian is similar to the scientist, the logician, the mathematician, who are committed to reason and "correct" proof. The boatman, ungraceful and untutored in formal terms, represents the artist, the craftsman, the dancer, the dreamer, whose output is often unsatisfactory to the purely rational mind.

But stories such as these have an extraordinary tendency to anticipate the discoveries of modern science. These characters in the story represent different types of specialization of the top levels of the human brain—the profound divisions in the cortex. And analyzing this particular story should also allow us to go further in many of the stories in this book drawn from Idries Shah's collections—*they allow us to dissect the components of our mind and lay bare a blueprint of the human mental structure, in a way beyond any other form*. We could discuss this story in many other functions: For instance it makes our current precarious situation quite clear, as well as our reliance on only one kind of person to help guide society. But here we use the story to shed light on the structure of the brain.

In the past several decades, neuroscientists have discovered the nature of the evolutionary progression that took place in the building of the brain. This has led in human beings to the "crown of the system"—the elaborate and separated dual cortex. It has taken hundreds of millions of years for this machinery of consciousness to develop.

The Cortex and the Lower Brain Structures

The cortex was the *last* part of the brain to evolve, and the area whose functioning results in the most characteristically human activities: language, reasoning abilities, and the ability to create art.

The cortex is only about one-eighth of an inch thick; it is folded upon itself inside the human skull. Spread out, it would be about the size of a newspaper page. Humans have the most enfolded cortex, perhaps because such a large cortex had to fit into a small head to survive birth. But below the cortex and its important divisions lies the repository of millions of years of evolution—brain structures designed to underly the operation of the body, and which provide the underpinning for consciousness.

The brain regulates the action of the other organs of the body and coordinates actions on the external world. Ultimately, everything the brain does is manifested in action, or movements. Roger Sperry, a neuroscientist who has contributed much to our understanding of the brain, writes:

> The brain's primary function is essentially the transforming of sensory patterns into patterns of motor coordination. . . . In man, as in the salamander, the primary business of the brain continues to be the governing, directly or indirectly, of overt behavior.

The brain has *only one way of communicating*: All messages to and from the brain come in the language of neurons, and that language is firing. The kind of stimulus that gets the brain's attention is one that signals a *change* from the existing state. This action of the neuron, the sensitivity to a change in state, is a major simplifying operation of brain activity and is how we are alert to the "news" in the outside environment.

The changes may be as subtle as a change in air pressure or the weather, or they may be as jarring as a novel or unexpected statement. For example, if we record the electrical activity of the brain as we read the sentence: "He spread the warm bread with jam," there is little indication of disruption in the ongoing electrical activity. However, if we read the sentence, "He spread the warm bread with *socks*," the brain electrical activity changes significantly, spikes and all sorts of disruptions appear, an indication of a surprised response to the unexpected.

The brain seems to contain our expectations or "models" in neural form. Apparently the brain's model of possible endings to the sentence "He spread the warm bread with . . ." does not include "socks." The brain constantly interprets and classifies the information it receives, "matching" it against a "model" it develops of the world.

A major difference between organisms' brains is their ability to control the flexibility of action. Consider what happens when a frog is confronted by a fallen tree. The frog has such a specialized sensory system and brain that it probably would not notice the tree unless it hits it. A human can cut it, play seesaw on it, make tables out of it, even make paper for this book. This greater flexibility of action that characterizes the human adaptation is due to a larger brain, and to many, many more cortical cells.

How the Senses Feed the Brain

The senses are the brain's outposts, and they *relate* the external physical world and internal psychological experience.

The measurement of this relationship, called *psychophysics,* was the first idea of investigation of scientific psychology in the late nineteenth century. Using the methodology and techniques of physics as their model, the first psychologists tried to determine precisely how changes in the outside world affected the internal world of human experience.

They pursued their investigations in what seemed a radical way at the time, but what was a rather straightforward way: They clanged bells, sounded tones of different timbres, and shined lights of varying degrees of brightness at people and then measured how much a stimulus had to change in order for a person to report a change in experience.

There are some absolute limits to what we can sense, limits set by the range of physical energy to which the senses respond. A light must attain a certain intensity before we notice it; a sound must be loud enough for us to hear it. The least amount of physical energy necessary for us to notice a stimulus is called the *absolute threshold*. The absolute threshold is defined as the minimum strength for a stimulus to be *noticed* by an observer 50 percent of the time.

The absolute threshold is not the amount of energy required to *activate* the sensory system, but the amount of energy required for us to *experience* the stimulus. Although the senses have absolute limits, they can be activated with little energy. The eye responds to the smallest quantity of light, the ear to movements in the air only slightly greater than those of the air molecules themselves; although we rarely, if ever, notice these phenomena.

But, of course, most sensory experiences are not absolute. Real experience is composed of things that are brighter, darker, heavier, lighter, or sweeter than other things. An important factor in sensory experience is the *discrimination of differences in stimuli*.

This minimum increase in a physical stimulus necessary to notice a difference is called the *difference threshold* or, more commonly, the *just noticeable difference (JND)*. Unlike the absolute threshold, the JND is not constant. The experience of a stimulus is always relative to its surrounding context. So, for example, if it takes 1 additional candle to notice a difference in illumination in a room with 10 candles, then in a room with 100 candles you would need 10 additional candles to notice a difference. There would be no *noticeable* difference if 101 rather than 100 candles were lit.

So equal changes in physical intensity of a stimulus do not produce equal changes in experience. A single candle flame emits a fixed amount of physical energy, but it is experienced differently depending on the surrounding circumstances. In a darkened room, it provides enormous illumination; in a bright room, it is hardly noticed.

Although the psychological world does not have a one-to-one relationship with the physical world, there is a consistent relationship between them. The amount of added energy in a stimulus required to produce a JND is always the same proportion of the stimulus. For example, if a 64-watt light is required to notice a change in illumination from 60 watts, then 128 watts would be needed to detect a change from 120 watts. This consistent proportional relationship is stated mathematically as follows:

$$\frac{\text{CHANGE IN STIMULUS}}{\text{STIMULUS}} = \text{CONSTANT}$$

But it is not the absolute *differences* between lights, sounds, and such that our senses are designed to notice, but the relative intensity of things. Thus, when danger is approaching, the important thing to know is *how fast* it is approaching, not merely how much louder one threatening sound is than another.

A third principle, recently discovered by the Harvard psychophysicist S. S. Stevens, is that the *different senses actually transform the information they select differently*. This principle, called the Power Law, states that *within each sensory system* equal ratios of stimulus intensity produce equal ratios of change in experience. When these relationships are charted on a graph, they produce characteristic curves. Note in the following figure that the response curves for the experience of length, brightness, and pain are very different.

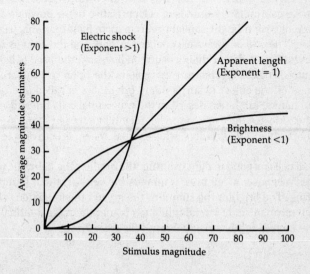

Scaling sensory experience on a graph reveals a lot about how *we are built and the function of the underlying machinery of consciousness*. The flat line that represents the experience of length indicates that the relationship between our experience of length and actual physical length is direct. This makes sense because we do not often have to estimate very long distances visually.

On the other hand, we encounter an extremely large range of brightness. We can see a single candle flame on a dark night thirty miles away, and we are able to glance at the sun, which is about 1,000 trillion times brighter. Since there is such an enormous range of brightness to judge daily, our sensory system has to attenuate, or turn down, that range because a lot of brightness information has to be assessed in a very small "space."

The flattened curve of brightness on the graph indicates that *brightness information is indeed compressed*. The pain curve is also a good representation of the experience of pain. Because it is important to be aware of potential injury as fast as possible, the experience of pain is *amplified,* not attenuated. So, *a small amount of pain gets our undivided attention very quickly*. The upward curve on the pain graph shows that we react very strongly to pain. *Our amplified response to pain makes it an extremely effective early warning system for possible bodily harm— part of the priority system in consciousness*.

Every sensory experience depends on the previous sensory experience, so we can judge thousands of colors relative to the previous ones.

A lump of coal in bright sunlight reflects more light than this page in the shade. The coal is always experienced as dark and the page as light, because the coal is darker than its surroundings and the page is lighter.

The physiological mechanism that allows the brain to compare the brightness of one object to surrounding brightness is called *lateral inhibition*. Lateral inhibition describes the way retinal cells fire and affect each other. Most of the evidence on lateral inhibition comes from studies on the horseshoe crab, *Limulus,* whose visual system is both simple and large.

Retinal cells respond to light by firing: the brighter the light, the more they fire. Whenever a cell fires, it inhibits the cells next to it (laterally) from firing. The brighter the stimulus, the greater the inhibition. Thus, the basic mechanism of lateral inhibition is that the more a retinal cell fires, the more it inhibits neighboring cells from firing.

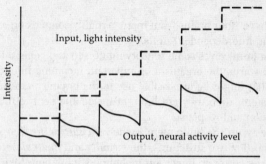

Position

LATER INHIBITION ACCENTUATES CHANGE
There is a uniform progression of changes between successive steps in this photograph. But you do not perceive the changes as uniform. Lateral inhibition makes nerve cells in the retina respond so that changes are accentuated—the relationship between the input (light intensity) and the output (neural activity level) is not uniform. (After Cornsweet, 1970)

Lateral inhibition helps us see sharp changes, like corners, in the environment. It may enhance discrimination between two slightly different figures. Because it exaggerates changes in the environment, we can be fooled (see the figure above).

As we have seen, there are built-in systems in the sensory apparatus that help determine the nature of our experiences. Of course the same is true in analyzing how the brain evolved.

.   .   .

There is a kind of archaeology to the brain. The brain was built by the processes of evolution, over a period of millions of years. There are four different "layers" of functions that developed.

> *Keeping Alive:*
> 1. Arousal and wakefulness; the brain stem
> 2. Emotions and the inner state of the body; the limbic system
> *Creating Anew:*
> 3. Making new associations (learning, memory, perception); the cortex
> 4. Creating symbols (language, art); the divided hemispheres.

We do not have "four brains," but more: a highly complex organ with specialized and interdependent units.

The brain stem receives some sensory input, sets the general level of alertness, and warns the organism of important incoming information. Only events that might be of possible use to the organism are *selected* by the brain stem; then they are brought inside and sent to the brain for interpretation and response.

About midway up the brain stem is the *reticular activating system (RAS)*, comprised of two structures, the *medulla* and the *thalamus*. The RAS arouses the cortex to important incoming stimulation. Like a telephone bell, the RAS alerts the cortex in a general way about arriving information (such as "visual stimulus on its way"). When a sleeping dog is stimulated by electrodes in the RAS, it awakens immediately and searches the environment. The RAS also controls the general level of arousal (wakefulness, sleep, attention, excitement, et cetera). Therefore, it controls both the *existence* and the *intensity* of consciousness.

Information is first received in the medulla and lower brain stem, then the thalamus relays the information to the *appropriate* part of the cortex.

Just below the cortex is the limbic system, which consists of a border of cellular structures between the brain stem and the cortex; it is often called the "mammalian brain" because the same structure is found in all mammals. The limbic system is the area of the brain that helps to maintain *homeostasis* or a constant environment in the body.

The limbic system contains specific structures that control emotions as well as the most primitive of reactions. Emotions have a far greater role in our mental operations than we would like to think, as their existence precedes that of the human brain. As we have seen, emotions "color" memories. Emotional needs, as well as the more basic physiological and safety needs, tend to "preempt" consciousness. Recall the last time you tried to think clearly when you were enraged.

This evanescence of consciousness is why we are so easily mentally disturbed; it doesn't take a lot to "flood" consciousness with terror or despair. Disorders of thought can arise due to deficiencies in the body— an unexplained fever can lead the person to thoughts of despair, until he or she realizes that it is an illness. Many formal studies have shown how easily we are misled by the internal signals of our body.

One of the studies was more sexual than usual. In it, young men looked at photos of nudes from *Playboy* and other magazines and listened to their heartbeat on a loudspeaker. Of course, since this was a psychology experiment there was deception: For some, the beats they heard were falsely "fed back" to them, in this case they were speeded up. When the young men were asked to rate the attractiveness of the girls, they rated those associated with the "fast" heartbeats as *more attractive* than those associated with normal heartbeats.

So it is easy to misread the internal system that is minding the body— many mental disorders have been found to result from brain tumors; a person going deaf may begin to think in a paranoid manner, as she begins to interpret the soft signals as others whispering around her. And on top of this careening roller coaster of moods, needs, urgencies sits consciousness, altering constantly to keep us on course, clearing up a mess here, straightening out a picture there.

The controlling area of most of the "keeping alive" functions, the limbic system, also coordinates many of the brain's operations. It *assigns priorities to the messages transmitted to the cortex,* sending some on directly and deferring others. It not only integrates a wide variety of incoming messages, but also cooordinates and elaborates the complex outgoing messages (or responses) from the brain. Thus, the activity of the limbic system lays the groundwork that makes complex consciousness possible.

One of the important limbic structures is the hypothalamus, the most amazing part of the brain. It is about the size of a pea. Its major job is to regulate many activities relating to survival: eating, drinking, sleeping, waking, body temperature, balance, heart rate, hormones, sex, emotions. Information coming to the brain is processed through another limbic structure, the *hippocampus,* to determine if it is *new,* or if it *matches stored information.*

The third level of the brain, the cerebral cortex, appeared in our ancestors quite recently, about 50 million years ago. The cortex performs the functions that have greatly increased our adaptability. It directs the other parts of the brain and is what makes each one of us unique. In the cortex decisions are made; the world is organized; our individual experiences are stored in memory; speech is produced and understood; paintings are seen; music is heard.

One feature of the brain in all primates is its division into hemispheres. But only in humans are these hemispheres specialized for different functions. This "lateral specialization" is the fourth system of the brain. It is the most recent development in human evolution, less than 4 million years old.

It is uniquely human. The left hemisphere, which controls the right side of the body, also controls language and logical activities. The right hemisphere, which controls the left side of the body, controls spatial, simultaneous, and artistic activities. Each hemisphere is also divided into four different lobes: frontal, temporal, parietal, and occipital.

The cerebral cortex of the brain is divided into two hemispheres, joined by a large bundle of interconnecting fibers called the *corpus callosum*. The left side of the body is controlled mainly by the right side of the cortex, and the right side of the body by the left side of the cortex. When we speak of *left* in ordinary speech, we are referring to that side of the body and to the *right* hemisphere of the brain.

Both the structure and the function of these two "half-brains" underlie in some part the two modes of consciousness that coexist within each one of us. Although each hemisphere shares the potential for many functions and both sides participate in most activities, in the normal person the two hemispheres tend to specialize.

The left hemisphere (connected to the right side of the body) is predominantly involved with analytic, logical thinking, especially in verbal and mathematical functions. Its mode of operation is primarily linear. This hemisphere seems to process information sequentially. Since logic depends on sequence and order, this mode of operation must of necessity underlie logical thought. Language and mathematics, both left-hemisphere activities, also depend predominantly on sequence.

If the left hemisphere is specialized for analysis, the right hemisphere (again, recall, controlling the left side of the body) seems specialized for synthesis. Its language ability is quite limited. This hemisphere is primarily responsible for orientation in space, artistic endeavor, crafts, body image, recognition of faces. It processes information more diffusely than does the left hemisphere, and its responsibilities demand a ready integration of many inputs at once. If the left hemisphere can be termed predominantly analytic and sequential in its operation, then the right hemisphere is more holistic and relational, and more simultaneous in its mode of operation.

This right-left specialization is most prevalent in right-handed men, it is slightly different in women and left-handers. Left-handers, who are about 9 percent of the population, are less consistent; some have reversed specialization of the hemispheres, but some have mixed specialization, for example, language in both sides. Some are specialized in the same way as right-handers.

Women have less differences between their hemispheres than do men—damage to one side, as described below, will affect a woman's brain, on the average, less than a male brain, and there are differences in development as well. And even in right-handers these differences are not absolute, but are relative specializations of each "half-brain."

At least in very young people, each side does possess the potential for both modes; for example, brain damage to the left hemisphere in young children often results in the development of language in the right side. And in adults the right hemisphere does possess some language, the left some spatial abilities; it's just that each side is better than the other at its best talent.

For over a century, neurological evidence of the differential specialization of the human cerebral hemispheres has been slowly accumulating. A very valuable part of this evidence has come from the study of people whose brains have been damaged by accident or illness. It is, then, in the work of clinical neurology that the primary indications of our hemispheric specialization are to be found.

In 1864, the great neurologist Hughlings Jackson considered the left hemisphere to be the seat of the "faculty of expression" and noted of a patient with a tumor in the right hemisphere, "She did not know objects, persons, and places." Since Hughlings Jackson, many other neurologists, neurosurgeons, and psychiatrists have confirmed that two modes of consciousness seem to be lateralized in the two cerebral hemispheres of human beings. In hundreds of clinical cases, it has been found that damage to the left hemisphere very often interferes with, and can in some cases completely destroy, language ability. Often patients cannot speak after such left-hemisphere lesions, a conditions known as *aphasia*. An injury to the right hemisphere may not interfere with language performance at all, but may cause severe disturbance in spatial awareness, in musical ability, in recognition of other people, or in awareness of one's own body. Some patients with right-hemisphere damage cannot dress themselves adequately, although their speech and reason remain unimpaired.

There is a tendency in clinical and neurological reports to term the left and right hemispheres the *major* and the *minor,* respectively. This seems more a social than a neurological distinction. The dominant or major mode of our culture is verbal and intellectual, and this cultural emphasis can bias observations. If an injury to the right hemisphere does not affect speech or reason, the damage has often been considered minor. Injury to the left hemisphere affects verbal functions, thus was once termed the "major" hemisphere. However, the conception of the function of the two hemispheres is changing, largely because of the superb work of Roger Sperry and Joseph Bogen and the increasing evidence, from thousands of new articles, of the brain's lateral specialization.

Each hemisphere is a major one, depending on the mode of thought under consideration. If one is a wordsmith, a scientist, or a mathematician, damage to the left hemisphere may prove disastrous. If one is a musician, a craftsman, or an artist, damage to the left hemisphere often does not interfere with one's capacity to create music, crafts, or arts, yet damage to the right hemisphere may well obliterate a career. The position of the fussy pedagogue who devalues the nonverbal boatman becomes less and less tenable.

In more precise neuropsychological studies, Brenda Milner and her associates at McGill University in Montreal have attempted to correlate disorders in specific kinds of tasks with lesions in specific areas of the brain. For example, right temporal lobectomy severely impairs learning, whereas left-temporal-lobe lesions of equal extent produce little deficit. Lesions in specific areas of the left hemisphere are associated with specific kinds of language disorders: An impairment of verbal memory is associated with lesions in the anterior (front) left temporal lobe; speech impairment seems to result from lesions in the posterior (rear) left temporal lobe.

On less empirical grounds, the Russian physiologist A. R. Luria has reported that mathematical function is also disturbed by lesions of the left side. Milner and her associates also report that the recognition of musical pitch seems to be in the province of the right hemisphere.

The "Split Brain"

The two cerebral hemispheres communicate through the corpus callosum, which joins the two sides anatomically. Roger Sperry and his colleagues, notably Joseph Bogen, initiated radical treatment for severe epilepsy in humans in which the callosum was cut.

After the surgery, if a patient held an object, such as a pencil, hidden from sight in his right hand, he could describe it verbally, as would be normal. But if the object was in his left hand he could not describe it at all. Recall that the left hand informs the right hemisphere, which possesses only a limited capability for speech. With the corpus callosum severed, the verbal (left) hemisphere is no longer connected to the right hemisphere, which communicates largely with the left hand; so the *verbal apparatus literally does not know what is in the left hand.* If, however, the patient was offered a set of objects out of sight, such as a key, a book, a pencil, and so on—and was asked to select the previously given object with his left hand—he could choose correctly, although he still could not state verbally just what object he was taking. It was as if you were privately asked to perform an action and I were then expected to discuss it.

Another experiment tested the lateral specialization of the two hemispheres using split visual input. The right half of each eye sends its messages to the left hemisphere, the left half to the right hemisphere. In this experiment the word *heart* was flashed before the patient, with the *he* to the left of the eye's fixation point, and the *art* to the right. Normally, if any person were asked to report this experience, he or she would report having seen *heart.* But the split-brain patients responded differently, depending on which hemisphere was responding.

When asked to point with the left hand to the word he had seen, the patient pointed to *he.* When asked to point with his right hand, he pointed to *art.* The simultaneous experience of each hemisphere was unique and independent of each other in these patients. The verbal hemisphere gave one answer, the nonverbal hemisphere another.

Most right-handed people write and draw with the right hand only, but many can also write and draw to some extent with their left. After surgery, Dr. Bogen tested the ability of the split-brain patients to write and draw with either hand. The right hand retained the ability to write, but it could no longer draw very well. In copying the geometrical figures in the figure below, the left hand certainly conveys the relationship of the parts, even though the line quality may be poor. Note the right hand's performance: The cross contains the correct elements, yet the ability to link the disconnected elements is lacking. No one could consider a cube a set of disconnected corners!

More recent tests of hemisphere functioning confirm that the right hemisphere is superior at part-whole relations, which might indicate that it is responsible for maintaining our internal representation of the world. Robert Nebes asked split-brain patients to match arcs of circles to completed circles. The right hemisphere was superior in accomplishing this task, which requires the ability to generalize from a segment to the whole.

As startling as the split-brain studies are, an important question remains: How do the hemispheres operate in *normal* people doing *normal* things? One way we have of finding out what an intact brain is doing is measuring electrical activity in the brain through an electroencephalograph (EEG). Brain activity is measured in waves. Alpha wave activity indicates an awake brain on "idle"; beta waves indicate an awake brain actively processing information. In one study the right hemisphere showed more alpha activity than the left while the subject was writing a letter; the left hemisphere showed more beta. While arranging blocks in space,

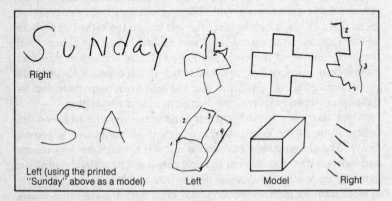

The response of a split-brain patient to the request to write Sunday *and to copy the two figures.*

the left hemisphere showed more alpha than the right and the right hemisphere showed beta waves. When people write, they turn off the right side of the brain; while arranging blocks in space they turn off the left hemisphere. This finding has been proved consistent and reliable.

More recent studies show that the primary factor in hemisphere specialization is *not* the type of information (words and pictures versus sounds and shapes) considered, but how the brain processes the information.

A recent study compared subjects' brain activity while reading two types of written material: technical passages and two folk tales. There was no change in the level of activity in the left hemisphere, but the right hemisphere was more activated while the subject was reading the stories than while reading the technical material. This finding might be explained by examining the nature of the material. Technical material is almost exclusively logical. Stories, on the other hand, are simultaneous; many things happen at once; the sense of a story emerges through a combination of style, plot, and evoked images and feelings. Thus, it appears that language *in the form of stories* can stimulate activity of the right hemisphere.

In another experiment brain activity was recorded while subjects mentally rotated objects in space. This operation normally involved the right hemisphere. When asked to do the task analytically, by counting the boxes, subjects by and large "switched over" to their left hemisphere. Thus, people can use their hemispheres differently in problem solving at will.

Education, Society, and the Hemispheres

Some critics have seized on the results of research on hemispheric specialization to justify their rejection of conventional science and educational systems. Like many new discoveries, the nature of the brain's specialization has often been misrepresented.

Many concerned people in psychology, education, medicine, and environmental sciences realize that those of us in industrialized societies have not developed our abilities to think in terms of whole systems. When they read about current research in hemispheric specialization, some respond as if all the world's problems would be solved if we simply suppressed our left hemispheres and ran ourselves and society with only the "intuitive" thought of the right hemisphere. Although such conclu-

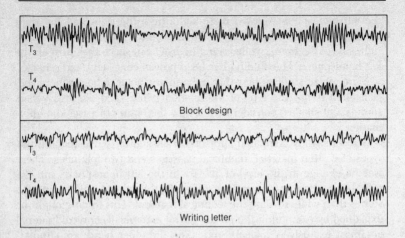

T_3

T_4

Block design

T_3

T_4

Writing letter

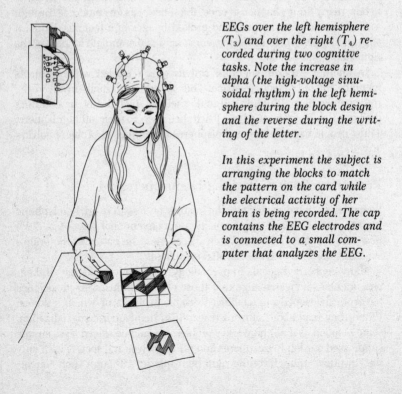

EEGs over the left hemisphere (T_3) and over the right (T_4) recorded during two cognitive tasks. Note the increase in alpha (the high-voltage sinusoidal rhythm) in the left hemisphere during the block design and the reverse during the writing of the letter.

In this experiment the subject is arranging the blocks to match the pattern on the card while the electrical activity of her brain is being recorded. The cap contains the EEG electrodes and is connected to a small computer that analyzes the EEG.

sions are simplistic, some people have at least realized that our intellectual training emphasizes analytical skills.

As a result of our preoccupation with isolated facts, it is not surprising that we face so many problems whose solutions depend upon our ability to grasp the relationship of parts to wholes. The problem is not that our technology is "leading us to destruction," but that our technical innovations have outstripped our perspective and judgment. We live in a world that is often difficult for us to understand.

Split- and whole-brain studies have led to a new conception of human knowledge, consciousness, and intelligence. All knowledge cannot be expressed in words, yet our education is based almost exclusively on the written or spoken word. One reason it is difficult to expand our ideas of education and intelligence is that as yet we have no standard way of assessing the nonverbal portion of intelligence.

The two ways of knowing are not competitive but are complementary. Without a holistic perspective our ability to analyze may be as useless to us as it was to the right hand of the split-brain patient. Similarly, an intuitive insight is lost unless we have a way to express it. Many people whom we consider "unintelligent" or "retarded" may in fact possess a different kind of intelligence and may be quite valuable to society. The neurologist Norman Geschwind has put the dilemma this way:

> One must remember that practically all of us have a significant number of special learning disabilities. For example, I am grossly unmusical and cannot carry a tune. We happen to live in a society in which the child who has trouble learning to read is in difficulty. Yet we have all seen some dyslexic children who draw much better than controls, i.e., who have either superior visual-perceptual or visual-motor skills. My suspicion would be that in an illiterate society such a child would be in little difficulty and might, in fact, do better because of his superior visual-perceptual talents, while many of us who function well here might do poorly in a society in which a quite different array of talents was needed to be successful. As demands of society change, will we acquire a new group of the minimally brain-damaged?

In addition to the differences in hemispheric maturation, the hemispheres in males are more specialized than those in females. The representation of analytic and sequential thinking is more clearly present in the left hemisphere of males than in females, and spatial abilities are more lateralized in the right hemisphere of males than females. Thus, damage to the left hemisphere interferes with verbal abilities more in males than in females and damage to the right hemisphere interferes with spatial abilities more in males than in females.

Only recently has an important bit of evidence on the male and female brains been discovered. While examining the corpus callosums of several brains, Christine De Lacoste and her colleagues, in work beginning at Berkeley, found that they could begin to identify them as male and female by sight. The corpus callosums of the men were as different ("dimorphic" in the jargon) from the women as are men's and women's arms; an observer can easily group them into the different sexes by sight alone. The women's corpus callosums are larger than the men's, and they are larger toward the back of the brain. This is the area of the brain involved in the transmission of information about movements in space and about visual space. It is just the area of the corpus callosum that one might expect to be different, given that spatial abilities like throwing seem to be less lateralized in females, involving both sides of the brain rather than just one. This difference appears as early as twenty-six weeks *in utero*; that is, it is an inborn difference in the major system of brain communication.

So there are two systems, at the "top" of the human brain, which govern our abilities to create, in language and in art, and discover new connections in the world. These two hemispheres appeared in our ancestors as *specialized systems* sometime during the long period of human evolution. There is evidence for them at least 100,000 years ago and probably earlier. They are the most distinctively human part of the brain, that portion that makes us most different from other animals.

There are many other systems of the brain that help to determine consciousness. Although the two hemispheres have received the most publicity and Roger Sperry the Nobel Prize, these latecomer functions of the brain are not typical of the brain's job in life. Although language, poetry, philosophy, and the building of computers seem to us to be the most important functions we have, what the brain, and hence consciousness, is doing most of the time is quite different.

It is the primary job of the brain to run the body, to govern our actions, to keep our limbs in the right place, our heart beating the right way, and to monitor, thousands and thousands of times per second, with its billions of neurons, our internal operations.

The priority system in consciousness is the mental "read out" of this process—consciousness is involved when something needs deliberate rather than automatic control or intervention. The main operations of the brain do not really include thinking and reason, they are largely concerned with blood flow, blood chemistry, and the maintenance of the *milieu intérieur*.

This is why pain interrupts philosophical dialogue; why the longing for food eventually disrupts our concentration; why disruptions, say, in the weather, which disrupt brain functions, also disrupt thought.

That the brain, and hence our consciousness, serves to govern the body is a different approach to those currently interested in simulating the brain and mental processes on machines. They exhibit the same kind of "idealism" as do many who seek to "transcend" their current consciousness in one whoosh.

We may not like our limited brain/mind system. Certainly many would like to think, with the top part of our brain, that we are different than we are, and many academics and idealistic philosophers have often convinced themselves and the rest of us that we are somewhat "rational."

But we are animals with a brain and mental system limited to a few things: keeping out of trouble, minding the store, and organizing our actions around the short-term contingencies of our environment. It is the system that "got us here." Whether it can get us anywhere else is certainly a difficult question to pursue.

THE OTHER SIDE OF THE BRAIN: AN APPOSITIONAL MIND

Joseph E. Bogen

It is here proposed that one way of interpreting the considerable evidence now available is to postulate the existence of two different ways of thinking; and a variety of neurologic findings will be discussed from this point of view. . . .

This article concludes with a few philosophic considerations and has appended an informal discussion of some related opinions of others.

Imperception

Hughlings Jackson wrote in 1864: "If, then, it should be proved by wider evidence that the faculty of expression resides in one hemisphere, there is no absurdity in raising the question as to whether perception—its corresponding opposite—may not be seated in the other" (Taylor, 1958, p. 220).

Jackson's proposal was not only reasonable, but was subsequently supported by his observation of a patient with a right hemisphere tumor (Taylor, 1958, p. 148):

> She did not know objects, persons and places . . . there was what I would call "imperception," a defect as special as aphasia.*
>
> I think, as Bastian does, that the posterior lobes are the seat of the most intellectual processes. This is in effect saying that they are the seat of visual ideation, for most of our mental operations are carried on in visual ideas. I think too that the right posterior lobe is the "leading" side, the left the more automatic. This is analogous to the difference I make as regards use of words, the right is the automatic side for words, and the left side for that use of words which is speech.

But the tide was running against Jackson, for most neurologists of the late nineteenth century were increasingly preoccupied with the localization of various functions (or the lack of it) within the left hemisphere. . . .

For at least three decades after 1900, little consideration was given to the special capacities, if any, of the right hemisphere. This was true of the entire spectrum, from the extreme localizers such as Henschen to prominent proponents of the holistic school such as Henry Head. When Henschen specifically considered the right hemisphere in his 1926 review, he allowed it only a compensatory role following left hemisphere lesions. Even then, "In every case the right hemisphere shows a manifest inferiority as compared with the left, and plays an automatic role only." In Henschen's view, the right hemisphere was probably a "regressing organ" although "it is possible that the right hemisphere is a reserve organ." . . .

---

*Aphasia: defect or loss of the power of expression by speech, writing, or signs, or of comprehending spoken or written language.

The most prominent neurologists emphasized the prevailing view. Lord Brain (1962, p. 81) averred: "The posterior half of the left cerebral hemisphere is thus the site of those neuronic linkages which underlie the elaboration of meanings in response to auditory and verbal stimuli." In their popular textbook, Grinker, Bucy, and Sahs (1959, p. 621) said: "The hemisphere which controls handedness, expression, and comprehension is known as the dominant hemisphere."

And W. Ritchie Russell (1963) wrote: "The processing of past and present information arriving in the dominant hemisphere seems to provide a scaffolding on which thought activity depends." The preoccupation of clinical neurologists with the left hemisphere diffused into medical knowledge as a whole; and the overall impression was expressed by Strong and Elwyn (1943, p. 374), "In man the higher control functions are vested principally in one cerebral hemisphere, the left one in right-handed individuals . . . the dominant hemisphere . . . lesions of the other hemisphere producing as a rule no recognizable disturbances." . . .

Disorders of Spatial Thought

A disorder of spatial thought is often associated with bilateral or diffuse brain disease; but it can also occur when the injury is restricted to one hemisphere. This was the import of Nielsen's best-known article on the subject (1937), although his argument was somewhat alloyed by his tendency to lump object agnosia* and spacial agnosia together. In spite of this, he was able to conclude in a subsequent review (1940), "The right occipital lobe is far more often dominant than would be anticipated on the basis of left-handedness." . . .

In 1963, Hécaen and Angelergues summarized findings in 415 patients with various lesions in the posterior of the brain. In general, disorders of spatial thought were associated with right hemisphere lesions. "The right hemisphere appears to play a special role in the appreciation of space and the recognition of faces." . . .

Neuropsychological studies on patients with tumors are often contaminated by secondary symptoms and patients with vascular lesions are frequently symptomatic in both hemispheres. . . . Because removals for epilepsy leave relatively clean lesions of known extent, the study of Milner (1958) was of special importance: Patients with left temporal

---

*Agnosia: loss of the power to recognize the import of sensory stimuli.

lobectomy had certain verbal disabilities in contrast to right temporal lobectomy patients who had impairment in the comprehension of pictures. Changes in brain function consequent to longstanding epilepsy (as well as the not infrequent head injuries) complicate the interpretation of these results. However, Milner (1971) and her colleagues have continued on with a variety of studies contributing to an imposing body of evidence for right hemisphere specialization. Most of these tests concern "spatial thought," but not all, so that Milner and some others have come to use the term "nonverbal" rather than "spatial" or "perceptual." . . .

Music and the Right Hemisphere

Suzerainty of the right hemisphere is not restricted to "visuospatial" functions. Over thirty years ago, Dide (1938) espoused a right hemisphere superiority for "kinesthetic" function. There is other evidence for nonspatial abilities special to the right hemisphere. For example, Luria (1966, p. 90) considered "the right hemisphere dominant with respect to certain mental processes [including] music . . . and the awareness of a personal disability"; and he has published a striking case of a composer whose best work was done after he was rendered aphasic by a massive stroke in the left hemisphere (1965).

Survival of musical ability in spite of severe aphasia has long been known. Perhaps the earliest recorded example was the description by Dalin in 1745, quoted by Benton and Joynt (1960):

> He had an attack of a violent illness which resulted in a paralysis of the entire right side of the body and complete loss of speech. . . . He can sing certain hymns, which he had learned before he became ill, as clearly and distinctly as any healthy person. However, it should be noted that at the beginning of the hymn he has to be helped a little by some other person singing with him. Similarly, with the same type of help, he can recite certain prayers without singing, but with a certain rhythm and in a highpitched, shouting tone. Yet this man is dumb, cannot say a single word except "yes" and has to communicate by making signs with his hand.

Henschen (1926), who considered the right hemisphere "primitive" in almost every other respect, was led by his extensive literature review to admit: "In cases of motor aphasia the faculty of singing words is conserved, in spite of the inability to speak a single word. In such cases the patient probably sings by means of the right hemisphere."

More recently, Critchley (1953, p. 375) mentioned a patient with severe aphasia who conducted his own orchestra. Head (1926, p. 500) wrote: "We know very little of the behavior of auditory images in aphasia; but the direct reproduction of melody and the recognition of time and tune are not affected, apart from the difficulty of forming the words of a song, or reading the notes of the music." . . .

The musical capacity of the right hemisphere is most clearly shown after left hemispherectomy* in the normally developed adult. In the one such patient who survived over a year, the paucity of speech was in marked contrast to his ability to sing a variety of songs learned in early life (Smith, 1966).

Recognition of the lateralization of language to the left hemisphere is based on two observations: language deficit following left hemisphere lesions, and retention of speech following right hemisphere injury. Similarly, the preservation of musical ability (aside from written music) with left hemisphere lesions is complemented by a loss of musical ability with right hemisphere lesions leaving speech intact. . . . Schlesinger (1962) extensively reviewed the question of amusia,† noting the numerous reported examples of both amusia without aphasia and of aphasia without amusia; and he concluded, "In contrast to propositional language, the psychoneural component of musical ability, more especially the expression of musical aptitude, seems to be mediated by both hemispheres."

When Wertheim (1963) reviewed the literature on amusia, he concluded that a lesion of the left anterior temporal area could cause receptive deficits. We may note that such deficits are usually demonstrated by tests requiring speech or writing by the patient, so there is often a question of contamination by a deficit in language function. On the other hand, musical expression can be tested more readily without recourse to language; and Wertheim found expressive amusia to be associated with lesions of the right frontal lobe. Wertheim concluded: "Actually there is a tendency to consider that the musical functions have

*Hemispherectomy: surgical removal of cerebral cortex.
†Amusia: inability to produce (expressive) or to comprehend (receptive) musical sounds.

a bilateral hemispheric representation and it is to be assumed that musical dysfunctions have a lesional substratum far wider than is generally admitted."

Hécaen (1962) discussed the localization of lesions causing amusia. He considered the problem not yet settled, referred to the opinion of Kleist that hemispheric dominance varies between individuals, and concluded by suggesting that right-sided lesions cause defects in the "recognition of musical sounds" whereas left hemispheric lesions cause a "disorganization of musical understanding."

Hécaen's clinically derived insight has further meaning in the light of the experimental observations of Milner (1962). She gave the Seashore music tests to patients with left and right temporal lobectomy. Those with left lobectomy showed little deficit, whereas those with right lobectomy were impaired particularly as regards timbre and tonal memory. Milner's findings were confirmed by Chase (1966) in a different series of patients. Subsequently Kimura (1964) reported evidence for better recognition of melodies by the right hemisphere; and Shankweiler (1966) found greater impairment of melody recognition following temporal lobectomy on the right.

Assuming that the right hemisphere is well supplied with auditory images or "engrams," including words, but not organized as they are on the left side, we can better interpret a variety of clinical observations. For example, as Alajouanine and Lhermitte (1964) say, "There are numerous cases of aphasia with disorders of understanding spoken language without agnosia; on the other hand, cases of pure auditory agnosia without aphasia are quite rare; such a situation results from bilateral temporal lobe lesions."

Indeed, Nielsen and Sult (1939) reported that auditory agnosia without aphasia can sometimes result from a unilateral right hemisphere lesion, subsequently confirmed by Brain (1941). More recently Spreen et al. (1965) reported a carefully documented case of auditory agnosia without aphasia, caused by a circumscribed right hemisphere softening.

If the right hemisphere capacity for spatial function, and for the tonal (as opposed to the notational) aspect of music is recognized, we can see in a new light the intriguing observations of Alajouanine (1948) on three patients with artistic creativity who suffered aphasia. One was a famous writer whose memory, judgment, and esthetic sense were unimpaired by a severe expressive aphasia; his loss of creativity was attributed by

Alajouanine to a "disturbance of literary technique due to disease which converted that delicate artist and subtle grammarian into an agrammatist." He says of a famous musician (Ravel) who was struck down at the peak of his career that his "analytic recognition" of musical notation and piano playing at sight were grossly disabled; on the other hand, melodic, rhythmic and stylistic sense were unimpaired, and playing or singing from memory was largely retained: "Although all artistic realization is forbidden . . . his artistic sensibility does not seem to be in the least altered." He says of a prominent painter who suffered a sudden and severe aphasia: "His artistic activity remains undisturbed; indeed, he has even accentuated the intensity and sharpness of his artistic realization and it seems that in him the aphasic and the artist have lived together on two distinct planes."

Cases of left hemisphere lesions interfering with language, but leaving other functions intact, do not as strongly support a belief in special right hemisphere capacity as would similar findings after total left hemispherectomy; but explanation of such cases springs so simply and surely from that belief as to urge its adoption.

The Hypothesis of an Appositional Mode of Thought

If the right hemisphere is dominant for certain higher functions, we may naturally suppose that there might be others. This direction of thought could eventually lead us to the view that every higher function is distributed unequally between the hemispheres, and that we might hope to determine the ratio or gradient of distribution for each function. . . . The distribution of functions between the hemispheres involves many difficulties, not the least of which is the variation among individuals. But there is a more serious objection to this approach. As soon as we try to distribute or to localize in any way a particular function, we are soon faced with the heart of the problem—what is *a* function? Is recognition of animate objects a faculty separable from recognition of the inanimate, as suggested by Nielsen (1946, pp. 234, 246)? Is love of children a function to be localized in some particular part of the brain as Gall once maintained? It is on such questions as these that all localization of higher function has foundered. Furthermore, if we could solve this fundamental difficulty (rather than ignore it as is so often done), we would have another; our understanding of brain function would consist of a myriad of items without cohesion.*

For the above reasons it may be helpful to take as simple a view as possible by returning to the original and hardly arguable fact: the left hemisphere is better than the right for language and for what has sometimes been called "verbal activity" or "linguistic thought"; in contrast we could say that the right hemisphere excels in "non-language" or "non-verbal" function. The principal difficulty here is not that "non-language" (or "non-verbal") is so non-specific, but moreover it is misleading, because there is a significant right hemisphere capacity (Bogen, 1969, p. 150; Kinsbourne, 1971; Zangwill, 1967).

First of all, the aphasic often utters words or sentences. In fact, as Head pointed out: "When an aphasic cannot employ more abstract terms, he often uses descriptive phrases, similes, and metaphorical expressions in an appropriate manner."

Second, injuries to the right hemisphere produce certain defects in language or verbal activity. It is interesting that, according to Weinstein, the language defects after right hemisphere lesions often are different from those in dysphasia,† the errors being "existential" rather than phonetic or semantic.

Third, a gross defect in understanding speech usually requires, in addition to a left hemisphere lesion, an associated deconnection of the right temporal lobe.

Fourth, ictal‡ utterance more often occurs with an epileptogenic focus in the right temporal lobe than in the left.

Fifth, certain kinds of verbal activity (poetry) may first appear subsequent to an aphasiogenic left hemisphere lesion.

Sixth, vocalization as well as alteration of ongoing speech have been produced by stimulation of the right hemisphere.

Seventh, the right hemisphere of the split-brain patient can read many words as well as understand spoken sentences.

Lastly, two adults having left hemispherectomy could each speak at least a few words; and a third had good comprehension of speech and could articulate long sentences while singing.

---

*See Luria (1966, pp. 1–16) for a particularly clear and concise consideration of these issues.
†Dysphasia: impairment of speech, consisting of lack of coordination and failure to arrange words in their proper order.
‡Ictal: pertaining to a stroke.

Although we now possess many more facts that Hughlings Jackson did, he was fully aware of the need to characterize the hemispheric difference. He repeatedly recognized the presence in the right hemisphere of a verbal capacity. He wrote (Taylor, 1958, pp. 130, 186):

> I think the facts of cases of loss of speech from damage to but one—the left—half, show conclusively that as regards the use of words the brain is double in function. But the very same cases show that the two hemispheres are not merely duplicated in this function. Both halves are alike in so far as each contains processes for words. They are unlike in that the left alone is for the use of words in speech and the right for other processes in which words serve. . . . the speechless patient has lost the memory of the words serving in speech; . . . he has not lost the memory of words serving in other ways. In healthy people every word is in duplicate. The "experiment" which disease brutally makes on man seems to me to demonstrate this; it takes one set of words away and leaves the other set.

Jackson also pointed out (p. 130*m*) that the distinguishing feature of the major hemisphere is not its *possession* of words but rather its *use* of them in propositions: "A proposition is not a mere sequence . . . it consists of words referring to one another in a particular manner [so that each] modifies the meaning of the other."

Henry Head (1926, I, 42) summarized Jackson's view neatly: "The words removed are those employed in the formation of propositions; those which remain to the speechless patient are the same words used non-propositionally." . . . As Denny-Brown (1962) put it:

> Nor am I happy about the use of "symbolic" to describe the lost activity (though we ourselves have used it in the past). . . . The type of defect that is peculiar to the phenomenon of dominance is propositional, its most vulnerable aspect being the proposition "as if" in relation to some highly particularized situation.

Although we might be satisfied by a characterization of the left brain as "propositional," we can no longer follow Jackson and call the right brain's use of words "automatic." In the first place, such a distinction between voluntary and automatic inevitably implies a certain view of causation or free will. This is an important subject, but for our purposes here it can be divisive and diversionary. We would be better served by a verbal distinction which does not force this issue upon us prematurely.

There is a second objection: Jackson said both sides had a capacity for "automatic" use of words, and that only the left side had a capacity for their propositional use. But we are looking for a way to characterize the right hemisphere so as to emphasize its possession of capacities *not* present on the left. . . .

There is a third and most important objection to Jackson's proposal to call the right hemisphere "automatic"; this was in the main based on the "automatic utterance of aphasics"—it accounts for them well enough but not for the other abilities retained in aphasia.

The preservation of intellect in spite of severe aphasia has been argued for many years, both pro and con (Goldstein, 1960; Zangwill, 1964; Bay, 1964). For the present, without entering into this question at length, we can recall the conclusion of Weisenberg and McBride (1935) mentioned earlier that, "Purposeful and effective thinking can be carried through when language is extremely inadequate." Such abilities might perhaps be argued away as dependent upon residual capacity of the left hemisphere. However, this argument cannot apply to the wealth of non-automatic functions elicited in testing of the right hemisphere of the split-brain human or the patient with left hemispherectomy. It is also doubtful that "automatic" adequately describes the capacity of the right hemisphere to respond appropriately at a time when the left hemisphere has been paralyzed by intracarotid amytal (Rosadini and Rossi, 1967).

The right hemisphere recognizes stimuli (including words), apposes or collates this data, compares this with previous data, and, while receiving the very same stimuli as the other hemisphere, is often arriving at different results. As Teuber (1965) wrote, it is a question of "different modes of organization [in the two hemispheres]." This statement reflects the results of Teuber's study together with Semmes, Weinstein, and Ghent in 1960, from which they concluded that organization of somato-sensory function in the left hemisphere is relatively discrete as compared to a more diffuse representation in the right hemisphere. In a recent article, Semmes (1968) has extended this conclusion to encompass other functions.

Hécaen, Ajuriaguerra, and Angelergues (1963) had a different approach when they wrote:

It is indeed remarkable that the apraxias* expressing an impairment of relations between the subject and his body or between the body and the surrounding space are found in connection with lesions of the minor hemisphere. This fact might lead us to the assumption that the paramount importance of language in the organization of the major hemisphere leaves to the minor hemisphere the task of organizing the functions arising from, and marked by, the pre-verbal mode of communication.

This statement clearly resembles the hypothesis being proposed here, except for their use of the word "pre-verbal."

Humphrey and Zangwill described in 1951 three patients who spontaneously reported cessation of dreaming after a posterior brain injury. They tentatively suggested:

> It may be argued that just as the aphasic is unable to express his thought in propositional form, so the agnosic patient may fail to express his ideation at the lower level of phantasy and dream. While not denying that the trend and content of any given dream, or indeed of any given proposition, cannot be interpreted without reference to psychological factors, we would like at the same time to suggest that visual thinking, dreaming, and imagination are liable to organic dissolution in a manner directly comparable to the dissolution of symbolic thought in aphasia.

There is here a clear suggestion of two modes of thought: "symbolic" or "propositional" predominantly associated with the left hemisphere, and "visual thinking and imagination" whose lateralization was doubted by these authors.†

It was Zangwill's superb review of 1961 which first enabled us to relate our dysgraphia-dyscopia‡ data to the emerging evidence of others. In that review he tentatively characterized left and right hemisphere dominance as "symbolic" and "visuo-spatial" respectively. When we first ventured (Bogen and Gazzaniga, 1965) to suggest that two different

---

*Apraxia: inability to carry out purposeful movements in the absence of paralysis or other motor or sensory impairment.

†On casual inquiry it seems that cerebral commissurotomy is typically followed by alteration in dreaming. Several patients (but not all) have specifically denied any dreams after operation in contrast with frequent, vivid dreams before.

‡Dysgraphia: inability to write properly. Dyscopia: inability to copy.

thought processes are lateralized, one in each hemisphere, we attempted to combine the terminology of Milner and Zangwill, using the terms "verbal" and "visuo-spatial." Recognition of a non-automatic verbal capacity in the right hemisphere has rendered this usage obsolete.

Even when good ipsilateral* control obscures the lateralized dissociation of dysgraphia and dyscopia following cerebral commissurotomy,† special tests can show a right hemisphere superiority for matching spatial forms. This finding by Levy-Agresti led her with Sperry (1968) to suggest:

> The data indicate that the mute, minor hemisphere is specialized for Gestalt perception, being primarily a synthesist in dealing with information input. The speaking, major hemisphere, in contrast, seems to operate in a more logical, analytic, computerlike fashion [and] the findings suggest that a possible reason for cerebral lateralization in man is basic incompatibility of language functions on the one hand and synthetic perceptual functions on the other.

The difficulty in characterizing the ability of the right hemisphere (see Table 3) arises largely from our ignorance—we have barely scratched the surface of a vast unknown. We would do well therefore to choose arbitrarily a word, homologous in structure with the word "propositional" but sufficiently ambiguous to permit provisional use. For example, we can say that the right hemisphere has a highly developed "appositional" capacity. This term implies a capacity for apposing or comparing of perceptions, schemas, engrams, etc., but has in addition the virtue that it implies very little else. If it is correct that the right hemisphere excels in capacities as yet unknown to us, the full meaning of "appositional" will emerge as these capacities are further studied and understood. The word "appositional" has the essential virtue of suggesting a capacity as important as "propositional," reflecting a belief in the importance of right hemisphere function.

Ontogenetic Lateralization of the Two Modes of Thought

We recognize that the lateralization of higher function is not invariable. For example, there are cases of right-handers whose right cerebral le-

---

*Ipsilateral: situated on or pertaining to the same side.
†Commissurotomy: surgical incision of the connecting fibers between the two cerebral hemispheres.

TABLE 3
DICHOTOMIES WITH LATERALIZATION SUGGESTED

Suggested by	Right Hemisphere	Left Hemisphere
Jackson (1864)	Expression	Perception
Jackson (1874)	Audito-articular	Retino-ocular
Jackson (1876)	Propositionizing	Visual imagery
Weisenberg & McBride (1935)	Linguistic	Visual or kinesthetic
Anderson (1951)	Storage	Executive
Humphrey & Zangwill (1951)	Symbolic or propositional	Visual or imaginative
McFie & Piercy (1952)	Education of relations	Education of correlates
Milner (1958)	Verbal	Perceptual or non-verbal
Semmes, Weinstein, Ghent, Teuber (1960)	Discrete	Diffuse
Zangwill (1961)	Symbolic	Visuospatial
Hécaen, Ajuriaguerra, Angelergues (1963)	Linguistic	Pre-verbal
Bogen & Gazzaniga (1965)	Verbal	Visuospatial
Levy-Agresti & Sperry (1968)	Logical or analytic	Synthetic perceptual
Bogen (1969)	Propositional	Appositional

sions caused aphasia as well as left hemiplegia;* and in left-handers the situation is much less determinate. More important, there have been reports in which a unilateral lesion disturbs both propositional and appositional functions. But we must not permit the rich diversity of natural phenomena to obscure our recognition of the common and representative types (Bogen, 1969, p. 150).

Zangwill (1964) recently wrote that in earliest infancy, "the two hemispheres are equipotential, or nearly so with regard to the acquisition of speech. . . . Lateralization of speech begins early, almost certainly in the second year, and would appear to proceed *pari passu* with the acquisition of speech." The hypothesis of an appositional mode of thought implies that in this regard, too, the hemispheres are equipotential; and as the ability to propositionize tends to dominate the activity of the left hemisphere, the appositional mode is more free to exploit the intellectual capacities of the other side. The extent to which appositional ability develops must depend on the nature and extent of environment expo-

*Hemiplegia: paralysis of one side of the body.

sure, just as the development of propositional capacity is highly culture-dependent.*

In the adult, left hemispherectomy may be followed by the partial reappearance of propositional function in the remaining brain (Smith, 1966); and after massive right-sided ablations, we can expect that appositional capacity of the left hemisphere will re-emerge to a degree dependent on the patient's age, intelligence, and completeness of lateralization before the ablation. Even in the young patient, however, there may not be a complete return of the ability proper to the other side. For example, there is some evidence that, even after a long recovery period, patients with left hemispherectomy tend to remain deficient in verbal comprehension while patients with right hemispherectomy remain relatively deficient in block designs.

In the event of congenital cerebral hemiatrophy,† one hemisphere must do the work of both. The possibility of two different, parallel modes of thought going on simultaneously in one hemisphere naturally raises the question as to their structural allocation. That is, do they use the same neural elements simultaneously, or different combinations of them, or are the neural elements of each mode spatially distinct? Even a cursory discussion of these questions must be put off to the future. For the moment we need only to recognize the existence of two types of thinking, and that in the common circumstance they come to dominate the activities of their respective hemispheres.

The Duality of the Brain

According to Hippocrates (Chadwick and Mann, 1950, p. 183), "The human brain, as in the case of all other animals, is double." This duality is so apparent to the most casual inspection that it has intrigued neurologists for centuries, especially since it occasionally happens that one hemisphere is destroyed with preservation of the personality. It is straightforward to conclude that if possession of a "mind" requires only one hemisphere, having two hemispheres makes possible the possession of two minds. This view was forcibly argued at least as early as 1844 by Dr. A. L. Wigan. He wrote:

*Nature-nurture interaction in language development was discussed by Lenneberg (1969).

†Cerebral hemiatrophy: wasting away of a cerebral hemisphere on one side of the brain.

The mind is essentially dual, like the organs by which it is exercised. (p. 4)

This idea has presented itself to me, and I have dwelt on it for more than a quarter of a century, without being able to find a single valid or even plausible objection. (p. 9)

I believe myself then able to prove—1. That each cerebrum is a distinct and perfect whole as an organ of thought. 2. That a separate and distinct process of thinking or ratiocination may be carried on in each cerebrum simultaneously. (p. 26)

Wigan defended this position with a variety of reasons, including the many instances of two simultaneous, opposing, concurrent trains of thought; of these he said, "On any other hypothesis they are utterly inexplicable." But the original impetus was his knowledge of some surprising autopsies, beginning with one he observed himself:

One hemisphere was entirely gone—that was evident to my senses; the patient, a man about 50 years of age, had conversed rationally and even written verses within a few days of his death. (p. 40)

Dr. Conolly mentions the case of a gentleman who had so serious a disease that it spread through the orbit into the cerebrum, and by very slow degrees destroyed his life. He was a man of family and independence . . . on examining the skull, one brain was entirely destroyed—gone, annihilated—and in its place (in the narrator's emphatic language) "a yawning chasm." All of his mental faculties were apparently quite perfect and his mind was clear and undisturbed to within a few hours of his death. (p. 41)

Dr. James Johnson mentions to me another example of a gentleman under his care, who retained the entire possession of his faculties until the last day of his existence, yet on opening the skull, one cerebrum was reduced by absorption to a thin membrane— the whole solid contents of the one half of the cranium, above the tentorium, absolutely gone. . . . (p. 42)

If, for example, as I have so often stated, and now again repeat, one brain be a perfect instrument of thought—if it be capable of all the emotion, sentiments, and faculties, which we call in the aggregate, mind—then it necessarily follows that Man must have two minds with two brains; and however intimate and perfect their unison in their natural state, they must occasionally be discrepant when influenced by disease, either direct, sympathetic, or reflex. (p. 271)

We will leave to the future an expanded discussion of the implications for psychiatric illness of this conception. For the present, we should stop to inquire: Why was Wigan forgotten? Was he simply overlooked? No— for he was quoted by Brown-Séquard, when the latter wrote in 1877: "I have come to the conclusion that we have two brains, perfectly distinct the one from the other." Brown-Séquard was not alone, for Ferrier wrote in 1886 (p. 426), "The brain as an organ of motion and sensation, or presentative consciousness, is a single organ composed of two halves; the brain as an organ of ideation, or representative consciousness, is a dual organ, each hemisphere complete in itself." Several years later, Sir Victor Horsley asserted (Paget, 1919): "We are not single animals: We are really two individuals joined together in the middle line."

The likely explanation of the eclipse of the two-brain view was the emergence of the concept of cerebral dominance. The social disabilities of the dysphasic (especially in a society which emphasized "rational" thought) were so much more obvious than the defects of the right-brain-injured person that when dysphasia was accepted as a left hemisphere symptom, the right hemisphere was soon forgotten. And the increasing preoccupation of neurologists with the pecularities of the left hemisphere diverted them from a more comprehensive view. Hughlings Jackson (a student of Brown-Séquard) summarized in 1874 (Taylor, 1958, p. 129) what was soon to be generally accepted:

> Not long ago, few doubted the brain to be double in function as well as physically bilateral; but now that it is certain from the researches of Dax, Broca, and others, that damage to one lateral half can make a man entirely speechless, the former view is disputed. Thus, Broca and Moxon supposed that but one half of the brain—the left in the vast majority of people—is educated in words.

Whatever the eminence of its advocates (Brown-Séquard, Ferrier, Horsley, etc.), an idea may be abandoned because of an accumulation of adverse evidence. In this case, it appears that it was the theoretical suppositions accompanying the concept of "cerebral dominance" that resulted in the loss of the two-brain view; it was not the appearance of any adverse evidence. We should not suppose that the flowering of experimental neuro-physiology, at the same time as the emergence of the concept of dominance, supplied similar information, for animal experiments have repeatedly supported Wigan's view.

The first experimental hemispherectomies were done by Goltz (von Bonin, 1960). He wrote in 1888:

> I will begin by relating an experiment which I hope will be acclaimed by all true friends of science. I succeeded in observing for 15 months an animal in which I had taken away the whole left hemisphere. (p. 118)
>
> We have seen that a dog without a left hemisphere can still move voluntarily all parts of his body and that from all parts of his body, action can be induced which can only be the consequence of conscious sensation. This is incompatible with that construction of centers which assumes that each side of the body can serve only those conscious movements and sensations which concern the opposite half of the body. (p. 130)
>
> Finally, as far as Man is concerned, the fact that a dog after an extirpation of a whole hemisphere shows essentially the same personality with only slightly weakened intelligence might make it possible to take out even very large tumors if they are confined to one half of the brain. (p. 158)

Subsequent experimental hemispherectomy has provided no contradiction of Goltz. . . . But what of the Human for whom the concept of cerebral dominance was invented?

Following Krynauw (1950) the removal of an entire hemisphere from the human as a treatment for certain kinds of epilepsy became relatively common. And it has been noted over and over again, as Glees (1961, p. 486) wrote: "Even the removal of a complete hemisphere (about 400 grams of brain substance) may be said to have little effect on intellectual capacity or social behavior, producing at most a lessened capacity for adaptability and a more rapid mental exhaustion." Furthermore, it is particularly interesting that of the 150 cases reviewed by H. H. White (1961) and the 35 cases reviewed by Basser (1962) approximately half involved the left hemisphere and half the right hemisphere. And following the removal of one hemisphere (or brain, Wigan would say), there remained a "person," no matter which hemisphere was removed.

It can be argued that hemispherectomy for epilepsy is done in a setting of abnormal maturation, and that the crucial test comes with hemispherectomy in a normally developed adult. We recall that Goltz suggested hemispherectomy for tumors; Dandy (1928) carried out such operations, as have a number of subsequent surgeons. Because of the relative rarity of such operations, as well as the progressive nature of the disease, there have been only a few long-term psychometric studies (Smith, 1966, 1969; Rowe, 1957; Bell and Karnosh, 1949; Mensh et al., 1952; Bruell and Albee, 1962). Although the patients have more severe neurological deficit than after hemispherectomy for infantile hemiplegia, they have confirmed the original observation that only one hemisphere is needed to sustain, in Wigan's words, "the emotions, sentiments, and faculties which we call in the aggregate, mind."

The Split Brain

The most reasonable argument may prove incorrect when experimentally tested. Wigan argued that if one hemisphere can sustain a mind, "it necessarily follows" that a man with two hemispheres must have two minds. This conclusion has been tested in part by sections of the neocortical commissures, sometimes called "splitting the brain."

When the optic chiasm of a cat or a monkey is divided sagittally, the input into the right eye goes only into the right hemisphere and similarly the left eye informs only the left hemisphere. If an animal with this operation is trained to choose between two symbols while using only one eye, later tests show that it can make the proper choice with the other eye. But if the commissures, especially the corpus callosum, have been severed before training, the initially covered eye and its ipsilateral hemisphere must be trained from the beginning. That is, the training does not transfer from one hemisphere to the other if the commissures have been cut. This is the fundamental split-brain experiment of Myers and Sperry (1953; Sperry, 1961; Myers, 1965; Sperry, 1967).

The second eye can be trained to choose the opposite member of the pair. Then, the symbol which is considered correct depends on which eye is covered. In other words, one hemisphere is solving the problem one way and one hemisphere solving it the other.

Subsequent experiments by Trevarthen (1962) showed that the two hemispheres can work not only independently but also simultaneously. More recently Gazzaniga and Young (1967) showed that monkeys whose hemispheres are disconnected can solve independent problems with each hand simultaneously, in contrast to unoperated monkeys whose ability to do these two tests simultaneously is quite limited. The same phenomenon, of independent problem solving by the two hands simultaneously, has also been shown in the human. Indeed, the many studies (Bogen, Sperry, and Vogel, 1969; Sperry, Gazzaniga, and Bogen, 1969; Sperry 1964c; Gazzaniga, 1970; Sperry, Vogel, and Bogen, 1970) of our patients with cerebral commissurotomy have abundantly supported Dr. Wigan's conclusion. The data are consistent with the interpretation that disconnection of the hemispheres splits not only the brain but also the psychic properties of the brain. As Sperry wrote (1964c), "Everything we have seen so far indicates that the surgery has left each of these people with two separate minds, that is, with two separate spheres of consciousness."

The Illusion of Mental Unity

Using special tests following a special operation, cerebral commissurotomy, we can regularly elicit a behavioral dissociation from which are inferred two separate, parallel streams of thought. The crucial question is whether these two minds exist with the commissures intact. It may be that an essential function of the corpus callosum is to keep the two hemispheres in exact synchrony, so that only one Mind can exist, that is, until the commissures are cut. This may be stated differently as a question: Does cerebral commissurotomy produce a splitting or doubling of the Mind, or is it more correctly considered a maneuver making possible the demonstration of a duality previously present?

Every experiment involves the introduction of artifice or alteration, so that every experimental result can be explained as attributable more to the technique than to the process under investigation. Ultimately, this question is settled by production of the same result with a different technique. In this particular case, we can choose with certainty between the alternatives only if some other approach illustrates the same duality of mind.

Pending further evidence, I believe (with Wigan) that each of us has two minds in one person. There is a host of detail to be marshalled in this case. But we must eventually confront directly the principal resistance to the Wigan view: that is, the subjective feeling possessed by each of us that we are One. This inner conviction of Oneness is a most cherished opinion of Western Man. It is not only the common sense of the layman but also the usual assumption of the most prominent neurobiologists. Ramon y Cajal (1960) wrote: "It is impossible to understand the architectural plan of the brain if one does not admit as [one of the] guiding principles of this plan the unity of perception." The issue was drawn with surpassing clarity by Sir Charles Sherrington (1947, p. xvii):

> This self is a unity . . . it regards itself as one, others treat it as one. It is addressed as one, by a name to which it answers. The Law and the State schedule it as one. It and they identify it with a body which is considered by it and them to belong to it integrally. In short, unchallenged and unargued conviction assumes it to be one. The logic of grammar endorses this by a pronoun in the singular. All its diversity is merged in oneness.

The strength of this conviction is no assurance of its truth. An unarguable certainty in men's minds was no guarantee of the flatness of the World, the geocentricity of the Universe, spontaneous generation, the inheritance of acquired characteristics, the Vital nature of organic compounds, the conservation of mass, etc. Commonsensical (at one time) were all of these, self-evident—and all eventually recognized as wrong.

In the last resort, Common Sense has often been defended by the misuse of theological arguments. In this case, for example, some might appeal to St. Augustine's dictum, that whatever its multiplicity of manifestations, there is but one Soul—"Quoniam omnia ista una anima est, proprietates quidem diversae." The Soul is indeed the proper concern and the authority of the theologian.*

But we are concerned here with the Mind, an entity created in their own subjective image by certain pre-Christian philosophers of the ancient world (Plato, Cicero) and concretized by a mathematician (Des-

---

*Although the hypothesis presented here does not concern the Soul, the reader may feel entitled to some indication of my personal position. Such convictions are not easily capsulized; but I do believe that while it is not necessary to cerebrate in order to be aware, it is necessary to be aware in order to think. Everyday clinical experience has led me to believe, that in so far as an escape of the Soul from the body can be correlated with anatomico-physiological events, that most likely such event is irreversible damage to the reticular core of the central cephalid brain stem (as is commonly seen in advanced tentorial herniation). At this crucial inner level, there is no duplication of either function or structure (Magoun, 1958).

cartes) long before the availability of physiological or even any precise anatomical knowledge of the brain. Bartemeier* wrote:

> The Platonic-Augustinian idea was that man was essentially a soul, dwelling temporarily in the body. This was also the heart of Descartes' theory, and is often confused with Christian doctrine (it is called the "official dogma" by Gilbert Ryle, 1950). St. Thomas Aquinas would have none of this: "Passio proprie decta non potest competere animae nisi per accidens, inquantum scilicet compositum patitur." (S. T. 1a 2 ae, QXXII al). (Trans.: Emotion in the strict sense cannot apply to the soul, except incidentally, in so far, in other words, as it affects the psychophysical composite.) This implies a clear distinction between soul and psyche.

Modern psychologists have occasionally taken exception to the unitary concept of mind; one such as Lashley (1958) who wrote: "Psychologists, however, at least in recent times, have seen no reason to keep mind unitary." Lashley was in truth an exceptional psychologist; most of his contemporaries and successors have continued to discuss Mind in the singular. So it was with Hebb (1954), when he suggested that we abandon the idea altogether. In the same paper, Hebb emphasized the unrecognized influence of out-dated psychology on the subsequent thinking of physiologists. Surely one of the most outstanding examples must be the practically universal acceptance in Western scientific thought of this venerable belief in the singularity of the Mind.

Summary of the Hypothesis

The hypothesis which is the main burden of this paper may be summarized as follows:

One of the most obvious and fundamental features of the cerebrum is that it is double. Various kinds of evidence, especially from hemispherectomy, have made it clear that one hemisphere is sufficient to sustain a personality or mind. We may then conclude that the individual with two intact hemispheres has the capacity for two distinct minds. This conclusion finds its experimental proof in the split-brain animal

*There is an especially clear and concise discussion by Rather (1965) of the views of Plato, Cicero, St. Augustine, and Descartes. See particularly pages 7, 8, 45, and 125.

whose two hemispheres can be trained to perceive, consider, and act independently. In the human, where *propositional* thought is typically lateralized to one hemisphere, the other hemisphere evidently specializes in a different mode of thought, which may be called *appositional*.

The rules or methods by which propositional thought is elaborated on "this" side of the brain (the side which speaks, reads, and writes) have been subjected to analyses of syntax, semantics, mathematical logic, etc., for many years. The rules by which appositional thought is elaborated on the other side of the brain will need study for many years to come.

A Potpourri of Dichotomies

Having believed for several years in the duality of the mind, I have collected a variety of related opinions from various sources (see Table 4). They are included here in the hope that they may be of interest, and perhaps a little enlightening, in an appositional sort of way.

The belief that man is possessed of two ways of thought, occasionally conflicting, is common in everyday speech, where it often takes the form of supposing a struggle between "reason" and "emotion," or between "the mind" and "the heart." This is, of course, a mere figure of speech, as pointed out by the Reverend McCleave (1959):

> The matter of heart transplant raises no moral question. Society and our culture have used the heart as a symbol for so long that in the minds of many the symbol has become a reality. I do not believe that the heart is life, that it contains love, compassion, or mercy, nor do I believe that it is the dwelling place of the soul. The heart is simply another organ of the body.

Even in olden times it was recognized that "the heart" was a figure of speech and that both of the contending forces exist within the mind. In 1763, Jerome Gaub wrote (Rather, 1965),

> If you yourselves have neither been taught by a certain interior sense to agree with my previous assertion that the mind contains two very different principles of action. . . . I hope that you will believe Pythagoras and Plato, the wisest of the ancient philosophers,

TABLE 4
DICHOTOMIES WITHOUT REFERENCE TO
CEREBRAL LATERALIZATION

Suggested by	Dichotomies	
C.S. Smith	Atomistic	Gross
Price	Analtyic or reductionist	Synthetic or concrete
Wilder	Numerical	Geometric
Head	Symbolic or systematic	Perceptual or non-verbal
Goldstein	Abstract	Concrete
Reusch	Digital or discursive	Analogic or eidetic
Bateson & Jackson	Digital	Analogic
J. Z. Young	Abstract	Maplike
Pribram	Digital	Analogic
W. James	Differential	Existential
Spearman	Education of relations	Education of correlates
Hobbes	Directed	Free or unordered
Freud	Secondary process	Primary process
Pavlov	Second signaling	First signaling
Sechenov (Luria)	Successive	Simultaneous
Levi-Strauss	Positive	Mythic
Bruner	Rational	Metaphoric
Akhilinanda	Buddhi	Manas
Radhakrishanan	Rational	Integral

who, according to Cicero, divided the mind into two parts, one partaking of reason and the other devoid of it.

Great literature has characteristically concerned itself with this issue. For example, it has been said of Dostoievski that "The anguish arising from the dual nature of man rings forth in great chords throughout his work."

Not all mental duality is anguished: Dr. Samuel Johnson is said to have been much annoyed by dreams in which he found himself in repartée with an antagonist of superior wit. "Had I been awake," said he, "I should have known that I furnished the wit on both sides."

André Gide averred: "There is always a struggle between what is reasonable and what is not." It is perhaps because we live in a society in which rational thought is held in particularly high esteem that the "other" is often considered to be base or undesirable even when it is unnamed. More likely this evaluation is not cultural in origin, but arises from the fact that the hemisphere which does the propositioning is also the one having a near monopoly on the capacity for naming. C. S. Smith (1968) recently remarked on "the curious human tendency to laud the more abstract." He went on to suggest that scientists are becoming increasingly aware of the need for a simultaneous and synchronous use of two points of view, "one, intellectual, atomistic, simple and certain, the other based on an enjoyment of grosser forms and qualities." In a presidential address to the American Association for the Advancement of Science, D. K. Price (1969) goes so far as to suggest that today's "cosmopolitan rebellion" reflects not so much a generation gap or a racial problem, but rather a confrontation between two "processes of thought" one of which he terms "analytic, reductionist, simple, or provable," and the other he describes variously as "synthetic, concrete, complex, and disorderly."

When Ruesch and Kees (1956) proposed that Man thinks simultaneously in two different ways, they used the popular terminology of this computer age and called them *digital codification* (discursive, verbal, or logical) and *analogic codification* (non-discursive, non-verbal, or eidetic). The same terminology (digital and analogic) was urged by Bateson and Jackson (1964).

In a recent discussion of the duality of the brain, J. Z. Young (1962) supposed the cerebrum to represent reality in two ways, "abstract" and "maplike." In the same conference, Pribram (1962) referred to the distinction made by William James (1890, I, 49) between two types of discrimination: differential and existential. Pribram went on to the usual distinction of "digital" and "analogue." He also suggested that the maintenance of stability in space utilizes a different mechanism than that which provides stability in time.

Although terminology has varied with the times, the notion of two modes of thought has frequently been proposed by psychologists. For example, Hobbes (Murphy, 1951, p. 27) supposed that "mental discourse is of two sorts," free or "unordered" thinking on the one hand and "directed" or purposeful thinking on the other. Similar views have since been advanced by both experimental (for example, reflexologic) and introspective (for example, psychoanalytic) schools. Pre-eminent among experimental psychologists was I. P. Pavlov. He considered human thought to be particularly distinguished by the presence of a second signaling system, differentiated out of the first signaling system of the cerebrum.

The first signaling system concerns phenomena immediately connected with real reactions of the external world. The second signaling system depends on language and has a capacity of abstraction. This distinction between two modes of thought was used by Pavlov to explain human neuroses, and he is quoted by Frolov (1937, p. 233) as saying: "Thanks to the two signaling systems . . . the mass of human beings can be divided into thinking, artistic, and intermediate types. The last named combines the work of both systems in the requisite degree." Pavlov's view may well have stemmed in part from a knowledge of Sechenov's suggestion, quoted and supported by Luria (1966, p. 74) that the cerebrum has two basic forms of integrative activity: organization into "simultaneous and primarily spatial groups"; and into "temporally organized successive series."*

Probably the most influential proponent of introspective psychology in this century was Sigmund Freud. So well known was the antagonism between Pavlov and Freud that it is quite revealing to find them here in agreement! Freud (1946, IV, 119ff) supposed the brain to have two modes of thought, apparently arriving at this quite independently of Pavlov and on altogether different grounds. He considered "secondary process" thinking to develop with the growth of language. "Primary process" thinking he considered concrete rather than verbal, as well as having a more mobile cathexis. Fenichel (1945), a well-known disciple of Freud, described primary process thinking as: "carried out more through pictorial, concrete images, whereas the secondary process is based more on words . . . it is remote from any (sic) logic. But it is thinking nevertheless because it consists of imaginations according to which later actions are performed." Fenichel emphasized that such "pictorial thinking" is "less fitted for objective judgment" because it is: "relatively unorganized, primitive, magical, undifferentiated, based on common motor reactions, ruled by emotions, full of wishful or fearful misconceptions, archaic, vague, regressive, primal." He considered it to lack "lofty intellectual interest" and to be typified by "emotional fantasy" and in general "not in accord with reality." Perhaps Fenichel protests too much! One is reminded of a song from *My Fair Lady*, "Why Can't a Woman Be Like a Man?" Perhaps Fenichel's condemnatory tone reflects his own

*Although this distinction (Sechenov-Luria) suggests no lateralization, it implies what may well be the most important distinction between the left and right hemisphere modes; that is, the extent to which a linear concept of time participates in the ordering of thought.

unconscious denial of the value of "non-logical" or pictorial thought.*

Spearman's experience with a variety of "intelligence" tests led him to accept a verbal factor and a spatial factor as well as [his factor "g"] called the "general intelligence." (Supposing verbal and spatial abilities tend to lateralize to left and right hemispheres, one can easily suppose that the factor "g" is distributed, not necessarily equally, between the hemispheres.) Spearman asserted furthermore that intelligence can be considered to consist of two components, a capacity for abstract reasoning which he called the "education of relations" and a capacity for analogical reasoning which he called "education of correlates." In referring to this view, McFie and Piercy (1952) wrote, "Intellectual functions most sensitive to dominant hemisphere lesions appear to be cases of 'education of relations,' while functions sensitive to minor hemisphere lesions may be classified as cases of 'education of correlates.'"

The notable studies of Goldstein (1948, 1960) were characterized by a psychological approach in which anatomic correlations were avoided and the emphasis was given to the nature rather than the origin of symptoms. Throughout Goldstein's work there recurs a division of mental function into two modes of thought: an "abstract attitude" involving discursive reasoning, and a "concrete attitude" which is "un-reflective" and "more realistic." His belief that one of these is a "higher" function than the other and his disaffection for anatomical localization are not necessarily bound up with the essential point, that there are two types of thinking generated in the same cerebrum.

It is not only in the Western world that the dual nature of man is recognized. For example, Benedict (1953) studied the Bagobo people of Malaysia:

> Inhabiting every individual two souls called *Gimokud* are recognized—shadowy, ethereal personalities that dominate the body more or less completely. The right-hand soul, known in Bagobo terminology as the *Gimokud Takawanan,* is the so-called "good soul" that manifests its self as the shadow on the right hand of one's path. The left-hand soul called *Gimokud Tebang* is said to be a 'bad soul' and shows itself as the shadow on the left hand of the path.

*Some reinterpretation may be afforded by the hypothesis of an appositional mind not only for the primary process, but also for what Fromm (1968) has called the fundamental observations of psychoanalysis: the Unconscious; repression; resistance; and the therapeutic value of conscientiation. [Also see Maslow, 1957.]

There are many examples of various peoples believing that man is dual. In addition to those discussed by Herz (1960) and Domhoff (1969), Griaule (1950, p. 54) has emphasized the West African belief in the coexistence of two spiritual entities which he translated "soul" and "vital principle." The cultural anthropologist Levi-Strauss (1965) concluded:

> Primitive man is clearly capable of positive thought . . . but it is his myth-creating capacity which plays the vital part in his life . . . I believe that these two ways of thinking have always existed in man, and they go on existing, but the importance they are given is the same here and there.

In the East are much more highly developed systems of thought comparable to those of the Western world. I must admit to a vast ignorance of Oriental philosophy; but it seems to me as reasonable to suppose that the pre-Confucian concept of Yang and Yin reflects a projection onto the surroundings, as to suppose that it is forced on thoughtful man by the external world. With respect to Vedanta, or Hindu thought, we are on slightly firmer ground. Akhilananda (1946) distinguished intellect *(buddhi)* from mind *(manas);* and Professor Huston Smith has informed me (personal communication) that this distinction between buddhi and manas is common among Hindu psychologists. He pointed out further that this was once rendered into English by Radhakrishnan as "rational thought" and "integral thought."

It seems that certain contemporary Western psychologists are converging toward the Vedantic view. Bruner (1962, p. 74) recently wrote: "The elegant rationality of science and the metaphoric nonrationality of art operate with deeply different grammars; perhaps they even represent a profound complementarity."

Certain other psychologists are not so converging. K. J. Hayes (1962) argued what may be called a mosaicist view, that intellect is an "accumulation" of a large number of individual skills or faculties. In recent conversation, he has pointed out that the occurrence of so many terminological dichotomies is not obviously related to the bilateral symmetry of the brain, but that it can be ascribed to a nearly universal predilection for the logical simplicity of a binary system. On the other hand, perhaps this predilection is itself one expression of the duality of the mind [see also Bogen and Bogen, 1969].

5

The Temporal Dimension of Consciousness

Moment in Time

"What is Fate?" Nasrudin was asked by a scholar.

"An endless succession of intertwined events, each influencing the other."

"That is hardly a satisfactory answer. I believe in cause and effect."

"Very well," said the Mulla, "look at that." He pointed to a procession passing in the street.

"That man is being taken to be hanged. Is that because someone gave him a silver piece and enabled him to buy the knife with which he committed the murder; or because someone saw him do it; or because nobody stopped him?"

Like the scholar in the story, we live our daily lives in a realm of causality—a past and a future, in the province of the clock. The clock is an embodiment of linearity and sequence. Inside a clock rotations of a wheel, vibrations of a tuning fork or crystal, or other similarly precise repetitive processes are mechanically translated into movements of an external indicator. These yield seconds, then minutes, then hours, as the movements' sum. For any ordinary purpose, the more constant the internal mechanism of the clock the better, for on hour must be defined as the equal of any other in a linear time system, otherwise a consistent sequencing of events could not be maintained.

According to the clock, one event follows another, one hour follows another, in a strict unchanging sequence; eight o'clock always follows seven and preceeds nine. Spring is followed in time by summer. The consistent linear sequence of time is so much a given part of our ordinary consciousness that it seems a bit strange to examine it; we might wonder whether time could operate in any other manner.

But consider this normal "sense" of time. Our normal consciousness consists of objects and people, who can only exist in time. Our experiences seem to follow each other linearly, as do the hours of the clock. We notice our friends growing up and growing old "in time." To paraphrase Benjamin Lee Whorf, our experience consists of a stream of duration, which carries us out of the past and into the future. The normal modality is linear; it includes a past, present, and future and consists of a sequence of enduring events, one following another.

This kind of temporal experience forms a basis of our personal and cultural life. The clock of hours, minutes, and seconds allows us to "time" meetings and races, to arrive at the moment when an event such as a lecture is to begin. It allows us to plan for a future, to arrange actions well in advance, to coordinate our individual and social lives with those of others. All in all, it forms an integral part of the sustaining, invisible fabric of normal life and normal consciousness. This mode of time is as much a necessary dimension of ordinary consciousness as is vision. Words must follow a recognizable sequence to make sense; causes must precede effects for science to exist; if 5,000 people are to appear on schedule, the concept *three o'clock next Thursday* must have some real meaning.

Although this kind of temporal experience is necessary for the functioning of our daily lives, this mode does not exhaust the possibilities. In chapters 2 and 3 we noted that the contents of normal consciousness are a personal construction. We now consider the possibility that the normal mode of experiencing time is only one particular personal construction of reality. There is nothing sacred about our clock. Many civilizations have existed without the clock as we know it.

The question here is not whether the clock, and the sequential, enduring time that go with it, are "successful" in terms of survival. They are. Indeed, they have become *necessary* for the functioning of a complex technological society. Nevertheless, other modes of experiencing time are available to us.

Each person each day may move in and out of linear and nonlinear modes of experience. Let us resume the metaphor of two modes of consciousness, identified with the day and the night: It is the *daytime* that is governed by the clock and by linearity. The clock is quite important in our jobs, in our studies, in coordination of action. Clock time is an important element in the active mode of consciousness. To perform successful manipulative action, precise and sequential concept of time is very helpful. In work or at school, it is quite important whether we arrive at 9:00 A.M. or 9:17. In the former case we are "on time"; in the latter we are "late."

The precise timing of events underlies scientific inquiry. It necessarily governs any inference we make about causality. The more linear and objective the endeavor, the smaller the basic unit in which sequential time is measured. In scientific inquiry, the second is defined as "1,192,631,700 cycles of the frequency associated with the transition between the two energy levels of the isotope cesium 133." The smallest sequential unit of our ordinary day is a second, unless we are "timing" a race, where we may use a stopwatch to measure hundredths of a second or perhaps employ an even more sophisticated electronic counter. But many other cultures less technically advanced and linearly organized than ours do not break time into such small units. One Indian culture uses the "time to boil rice" as the smallest basic unit. The Trobrianders and the Hopi Indians of the Southwest do not even seem to employ the linear construction. Theirs is a world of the present.

The story that begins this chapter contrasts the two major dimensions of temporal experience. One is typified by the scholar, similar to the pedagogue of the last chapter, who seeks a linear explanation for events (such as, "he did this because . . ."). The other is represented in this story by Mulla Nasrudin: a comprehensive, complete perception of events as intertwined entities, each reciprocally influencing the other.

The chaos of the events in the external world can be selected and analyzed into a linear sequence, and valid inferences can well be made from this particular selection and construction—this is the way in which we usually operate, especially in science. But the events can also be viewed simultaneously as a "patterned whole," as the drawing at the beginning of this chapter indicates, with all action seen at once, and here drawn in one single, connected stroke. It does not postulate duration, a future or a past, a cause or an effect, but a patterned "timeless" whole.

In reviewing the differences between the modes of operation of the two cerebral hemispheres of the brain, Joseph Bogen observed that one of the most important differences between them is "the extent to which a linear concept of time participates in the ordering of thought." As he

and other neuropsychologists have pointed out, our two cerebral hemispheres seem neurologically specialized to process information in two
different and complementary modes, the left hemisphere working more
linearly than the right. The left hemisphere of the cortex, which subtends
language and mathematics, seems to process information primarily in
a sequential manner, appropriate to its specialties. The right side of the
cortex processes its input more as a "patterned whole," that is, in a more
simultaneous manner than does the left.

This simultaneous processing is advantageous for "spatial literacy,"
the integration of diffuse inputs—such as orientation in space and movement such as dance—when motor kinesthetic and visual input must be
quickly integrated. This mode of information processing, too, would seem
to underlie an immediate "intuitive," rather than a mediated "intellectual," integration of complex entities.

Time in Psychology

In considering time, most psychologists have unfortunately taken for
granted that a "real" time, external to our personal and social construction, does exist and that this time is linear. If this were the case, we
would possess a physical "sense" of time just as we have a visual "sense."
The implicit idea of many of these researchers has been that we therefore
perceive an external and real time (identified with the clock) with a
special organ of perception.

Even a little reflection will reveal, however, that the clock is not a
time "receiver" but a special time *definer*. Nevertheless, linear clock
time is so ingrained in our own personal constructions of reality that it
has even influenced scientific research paradigms and has thus led to
much confusion in psychology. In 1891, Henry Nichols wrote modern
psychology's first review of the research performed on time experience,
sounding a theme that was to become the *leitmotif* of many later reviews
of such work.

Casting an eye backward we can but be struck by the wide variety
of explanations offered for the time-mystery. Time has been called
an act of mind, or reason, of perception, of intuition, of sense, or
memory, of will, of all possible compounds and compositions to be
made up of them. It has been deemed a General Sense accompanying all mental content in a manner similar to that conceived of

pain and pleasure. It has been assigned a separate, special, disparate sense, to nigh a dozen kinds of "feeling," some familiar, some strangely invented for the difficulty. It has been explained by "relations," by "earmarks," by "signs," by "remnants," by "struggles," and by "strifes," by "luminous trains," by "blocks of specious-present," by "apperception." It has been declared *a priori,* innate, intuitive, empirical, mechanical. It has been deduced from within and without, from heaven and from earth, and from several things difficult to imagine as of either.

With a tributary of research ideas so broad yet so shallow it was hardly surprising that the mainstream of psychological thought drew less and less from time as a dimension of consciousness. With John Watson's purging of "mentalism" from psychology in the early 1900s, time's tributary almost dried up. The flow of research on consciousness as a whole began to slacken, the work on time even more so.

The reasons why time research has been and remains so scattered and so offensive to an "objectively" minded psychology can be clearly seen. To perform an analysis of the experience of time, one can point neither to an *organ* of consciousness, such as the eye, nor to a physical continuum, such as the wavelength of light, for study by objective methods. There is no immediate physical or physiological point of departure for a scientific analysis of time experience. There is no process in the external world that directly gives rise to time experience, nor is there anything immediately discernible outside ourselves that can apprehend any special "time stimuli." It is, therefore, not too surprising that psychological research on time as a dimension of consciousness has been so diverse, so incoherent, and so easily forgotten.

Yet some researchers continue to overlook the lack of a time organ, and attempt to approach temporal experience as if it really were a sensory process, as if we had a special time "sense." In ordinary speech we often use the phrase "a good sense of time" to refer to someone who is consistent with respect to the clock, to someone who is "on time." This may be a useful everyday idea, but as a scientific concept it has seriously impeded an understanding of temporal experience.

Even within ordinary experience, time has too many referents to be considered a unitary sense. The novelist Lawrence Durrell cites a few of the many times of experience: "One lies here with time passing and wonders about it. Every sort of time trickling through the hourglass, time immemorial, and for the time being, and time out of mind. The time of the poet, the philosopher, the pregnant woman, the calendar."

The simple confusion of one construction of time with another has caused great difficulties for professional researchers in many disciplines, among them philosophy, biology, psychology, and physics. This confusion stems from the underlying, implicit belief that a "real" linear time exists somewhere outside of man. To take one example, in *The Problem of Time,* Gunn points out that one stumbling block in physics has been the confusion of different time concepts, of physical time with either mathematical or clock time. This mirrors the case within the psychology of consciousness, where the confusion has been between the time of experience and either biological time or the linear time of the clock.

Many psychological experiments have been performed to find out how "accurately" such "real" time is perceived. "Real time" is, of course, identified with the clock. To call the clock "real time" is somewhat like calling American money "real money"; it is parochial at best. A useful psychological analysis should be concerned with time as a dimension of consciousness, as it exists in itself, not with how it relates to hours, days, burning rope, a sundial, or some other mode of defining time. It should answer the question, How is linear time constructed?

In considering time as a dimension of consciousness, we must distinguish between the different modes of temporal experience to ensure that we not confuse one mode with another. First, we will briefly consider the general dimensions of linear time: the present, duration, simultaneity, the concept of causality. Then we will undertake a closer analysis of duration, the mode we usually experience, and consider one approach to understanding how this continuing experience is constructed. Finally, after a brief recounting of drug experiences, we will consider other aspects of time experience, especially the nonlinear mode, in which all action is experienced as a "patterned whole."

The Dimensions of Linear Time Experience

The Present

We continually experience the immediate present passing by, the time that is always *now.* This is the time of our immediate contact with the world, very short, continuously changing, fading away, forever being replaced by a new *now.* William James quotes an anonymous poet: "The moment of which I speak is already far away." In the linear mode, time is directional, a duration carrying us from the past into the future; the present is always fleeting away behind us, as the poet laments. In the nonlinear mode, however, the present exists and is all that exists.

In modern psychological research the idea of a fleeting, immediate present seems to have held up under some rigorous experimental analyses. There is an immediate memory process, fleeting and decaying quickly, that is distinct from the more permanent memory. George Miller and others have shown that the information-processing capacity of this immediate memory is fixed at a very low amount and is difficult to modify by training.

Duration

The other continuous mode in which we experience linear time is that of duration. This constitutes our normal experience of time passage, of hours lengthening and shortening, of a recent event seeming "a long time ago," of one interval passing more quickly for one person than another or more quickly for the same person at one time than at another. Duration is the continuing, persevering, normal time of our lives. The short, decaying present is continuing but always fading from consciousness. The experience of duration is malleable. One "hour" seems quite long, another brief. Our experience of duration seem to be constructed on the remembrances of things past—retrospection.

Our linear experiences of time are divided along the lines of memory: the present (within these terms) constructed from short-term storage, the past or duration from the contents of long-term memory. There will obviously be a high correlation between these experiences, but since not all experience enters our permanent store, the correlation will not be perfect.

Simultaneity

A less immediate dimension of our consciousness of time is its cultural definition. Our culture is largely linear, scientific, clock oriented. We "break" time into small units, and "time" events precisely. But other cultures do not share this orientation. Some "break" the flow of events into larger chunks of simultaneity, and some dispense with the linear, sequential mode entirely.

When do we experience events as occurring "at the same time"? What *is* "at the same time"? Henri Bergson pointed out that this experience depends on one's frame of reference, on how finely the "grain" of time experience is divided. The experience depends on the mode of consciousness employed as well. If we take one second as the basic unit, we must construct an experience of what occurred "at the same time" that is quite different from what we would construct if we considered all events within the time needed to boil rice as being "at the same time."

Causality can be inferred only within a linear mode of temporal consciousness. The information processing of this mode divides the flow of events into serial lists that can be sequentially analyzed, studied, and manipulated. Succession and duration are the underpinnings of causality, for without a concept of past and future, of discrete events that follow temporally, it would be impossible to perform scientifically meaningful analyses. In combination with language and mathematics, this linear construction of temporal experience constitutes the essence of the active mode of consciousness.

The Construction of Duration

It is duration, more than any other continuing experience, that underlies our lives. We continually experience the passage of time: We move out of the past into the future; we experience one hour passing quickly, another dragging on and on and on and on. Sometimes an entire year will pass almost without notice, especially as we age; yet some years are so event filled they seem to last forever.

Albert Einstein once jokingly explained, "When you sit with a nice girl for two hours, it seems like two minutes; when you sit on a hot oven for two minutes, it seems like two hours. That's relativity." Many psychologists, ignoring that the ordinary temporal experience is personally and relativistically constructed, have searched for an internal organ of duration rooted in one biological process or another. This postulated "organ" has been termed a *biological clock*.

This search follows from the "sensory-process" paradigm of how we experience time, used primarily by those who would try to determine the "accuracy" of our time experience in relation to the ordinary clock. Such thinking confuses, once again, a convenient construction with reality. A similar confusion was once displayed by a group of farmers in the Midwest, who opposed the introduction of daylight saving time on the grounds that the extra hour of sunlight would burn the grass.

We cannot postulate an internal biological clock as the basis of ordinary temporal experience. A multiplicity of physiological processes, such as heart rate and basal metabolism, have been suggested as *the* clock, but many experiments have shown that these processes each seem to move at different rates. No single internal process that could be the biological clock has been found. There are, of course, many internal rhythmic processes that are quite important for consciousness, but these do not necessarily relate to time as it is experienced.

We seem to *construct* our experience of duration from the filtered content of normal consciousness. When these contents are artificially restricted, as in sensory deprivation, our experience of duration shortens. Conversely, multidimensional, complex experience causes duration experience to lengthen.

That our experience varies is not, of course, a new observation. It has strong antecedents in the work of the relativity-oriented time analysts, in Einstein's little joke, and in the work of the French philosopher Henri Bergson. Bergson noticed that duration is experienced differently by different people and that it might even lengthen or shorten for one person relative to other experiences. The idea of a "sense" of time may be useful in ordinary discussion, when we might wish to compare experience to the clock, to discuss someone who is habitually not "on time," for instance, but as a scientific metaphor it had led to a search for a nonexistent organ of time experience and to an implicit acceptance of a linear real time as existing independently of our consciousness.

We can replace the "time sense" metaphor with a "construction of time" similar to our understanding of how the rest of normal consciousness is constructed. Temporal experience can then be studied without necessarily being tied to any process external to consciousness, be it a biological, chemical, or ordinary mechanical clock.

The Storage-Size Metaphor

To begin thinking about physical memories, consider the computer. If we put information into a computer and instruct it to store that information in a certain way, we can count the number of spaces in its memory that it uses to store that information. We can then relate our constructed experience of the duration of a given interval to the amount

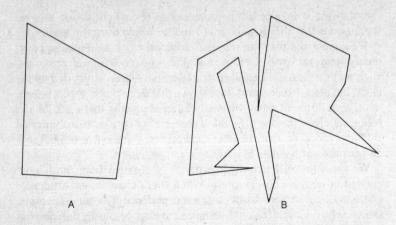

A   B

of information we remember about that interval. If more events, or more complex events, occur in that interval, the experience of duration should lengthen.

The more we experience and remember about a given situation, the longer our construction of its duration will be. Look at A in the figure above for thirty seconds, then look at B for the same time. Chances are that your experience of duration was longer for the latter figure, even though you "knew" that the experiences were equal in clock seconds. A piece of music that contains 40 events per minute is experienced as shorter than one with 80 events per minute; the latter is experienced as shorter than one with 120 events per minute. If increasingly complex figures are displayed, such as A and B in this figure, the experience of duration lengthens, as it will for tapes that contain increasingly complex sequences of sounds. But ultimately it is memory on which we construct linear time. Suppose you go on an interesting vacation. Just before you return home, the period of vacation seems quite long. After you return and become immersed once again in your daily life, the duration of the vacation suddenly seems to collapse. When away, the memory of your experience is complex: "We went to Waikiki beach, ate in that famous restaurant, listened to Dorman's orchestra, then traveled to another island, stayed here," and so on. When you are home again, this complexity collapses; you might code the experience as "I was in Hawaii for two weeks."

The psychologist J. J. Harton studied a similar phenomenon. He found that intervals containing successful events were estimated as shorter than those containing failures. He postulated that a successful experience becomes more organized in memory than a failure. With increasing organization, the storage size of the interval is smaller (as when the code is known) and the duration experience lessens. In one of my own time experiments, the more organized the memory of the shape of a line figure was, the shorter the experience of duration was.

Duration experience is a malleable construction formed from stored experience. If we can understand that "duration" is only one possible way to construct a dimension of ordinary consciousness, not a sensory process reflecting a "real" time existing independently of ourselves, we can make some sense of the vast confusion in psychological research on time and at least open up to consideration other possible ways in which our experience of time might be constructed.

Drug Experiences and Time: A Transition Between the Two Modes

Certain drugs, such as marijuana, psilocybin, LSD, and the amphetamines, including MDA, may radically alter the "reducing valve" of the normal sensory systems. If the dosage is relatively mild, the great increase in the contents of consciousness may produce an effect similar to increasing the amount of information reaching the person. Smokers of marijuana, for instance, typically report that their experience of duration lengthens during the period of intoxication and also report that they experience "more" during that interval.

But with stronger doses the effect sometimes overwhelms the linear mode of consciousness entirely and induces a nonlinear mode of experience. Very often this experience cannot be placed in linear coordinates, for it is outside this mode of operation, outside words, outside normal time. The best the verbal-logical mode can do to account for these experiences is to term them *timeless*.

For many, these experiences represent the first significant break from a normal reality and normal time. For some, the break into a new area of experience is unsupported by the remainder of their lives and their training, and they may not be able to return to normal consciousness. The very discontinuity of these experiences is difficult for many to deal with.

Nonlinear Time Experience

During each complete day, personal consciousness flows in and out of linearity. Each night we dream and enter a world in which a linear sequence of time has less meaning. Events in the dream space seem fluid. When we recall dreams and try to place them in a linear mode, we often cannot decide whether one event preceded or followed another. At other times, almost randomly, moments that are out of time come to each of us. They are moments in which there is no future, no past, merely an immediate present. Our linear, analytic world is for the moment destructured. These moments naturally do not lend themselves to analysis, for analysis and language itself is based on linearity. Often a word spoken during such a moment will be enough to return the experience to linearity, back into time as we ordinarily know it.

That we now lack a psychological framework for these nonlinear time experiences means not that they should be ignored entirely; but we must develop a new framework if we are to incorporate them into contemporary science. One tentative step in that direction might be to regard these "present-centered" moments as shifts toward a right hemisphere predominance. One approach to this problem could be in the study of the time experience of brain-damaged patients or split-brain people. It has been found, for instance, that left hemisphere damage interferes with the perception of sequence, while right hemisphere damage does not.

These "timeless" experiences are often produced by psychoactive drugs, which overwhelm the linear construction and allow "an infinite present" to exist. The receptivity and present-centeredness of these experiences are sought in meditation, which also attempts to undo deliberately the "normal" process of constructing consciousness. It is to poets that we must look for any verbal celebration of this mode of time experience. One of the most successful attempts to discuss the indescribable mode of time is found in "Burnt Norton," by T. S. Eliot:

> Words move, music moves
> Only in time; but that which is only living
> Can only die. Words, after speech, reach
> Into the silence. Only by the form, the pattern,
> Can words or music reach
> The stillness, as a Chinese jar still

Moves perpetually in its stillness.
Not the stillness of the violin, while the note lasts,
Not that only, but the coexistence,
Or say that the end precedes the beginning,
And the end and the beginning were always there
Before the beginning and after the end.
And all is always now. Words strain,
Crack and sometimes break, under the burden,
Under the tension, slip, slide, perish,
Decay with imprecision, will not stay in place,
Will not stay still. Shrieking voices
Scolding, mocking, or merely chattering,
Always assail them. The Word in the desert
Is most attacked by voices of temptation,
The crying shadow in the funeral dance,
The loud lament of the disconsolate chimera.

The detail of the pattern is movement,
As in the figure of the ten stairs.
Desire itself is movement
Not in itself desirable;
Love is itself unmoving,
Only the cause and the end of movement,
Timeless, and undesiring
Except in the aspect of time
Caught in the form of limitation
Between unbeing and being.
Sudden in a shaft of sunlight
Even while the dust moves
There rises the hidden laughter
Of children in the foliage
Quick now, here, now, always—
Ridiculous the waste sad time
Stretching before and after.

The distinction between these two modes of consciousness is well-represented in the drawing for "Moment in Time," at the beginning of this chapter. It depicts a situation that would be a linear sequence in "normal" consciousness as a unified "patterned whole."

In this mode, all action occurs in an infinite present. There is no attribution of causality or construction of sequence. All events occur simultaneously. Although linear, analytic thought forms the basis for a complex, technological society, other societies have developed around the present-centered mode. It is the conflict between these two modes of consciousness that has caused much cultural and personal misunderstanding. A Westerner may wonder what the Zen monk is talking about when he speaks of "no time" existing. We wonder why a person from India cannot seem to build a bridge on time. Yet this question is relevant only within our particular construction of reality, not in the nonlinear mode, although the ability to switch and to employ each mode in appropriate situations is quite important.

Consider the Trobrianders, a culture that Dorothy Lee reports as based on nonlinearity and on present-centeredness. To take an example similar to that of firewood and ashes: When we ordinarily view the process of the maturation of a plant (for example, a yam), we see a sequence. We experience the *same* yam turning from ripeness to overripeness in sequential time. The Zen monk does not share our view, nor does the Trobriander. The ripe yam (which in the language of the Trobriander is called *taytu*) *remains* a ripe yam. When an overripe yam appears, it is a different entity, not causally or sequentially connected with the ripe yam. It is another entity entirely and is even given another name, *yowana*. There is no temporal connection between events in the world of the Trobriander, in Lee's words, "no tense, no distinction between past and present. . . . What we consider a causal relationship in a sequence of connected events is to the Trobriander an ingredient in a patterned whole."

The temporal dimension is one key in a more complete science of consciousness. The recognition that the linear mode of time is but *one* possible construction brings to consideration other modes of temporal experience, those associated with phenomena outside the range of the normal. For us, an event is considered "paranormal" if it does not fit within the coordinates of ordinary linear time. But if linear time is but one possibility, these unusual events, unusual communications, may in fact occur, even though they cannot be charted in the coordinates of linearity. The laws that govern such experiences may not be those that govern normal consciousness: The experience of the night is not that of the day.

The nonlinear mode is a daily part of the experience of each person. It is deliberately cultivated in "mystical" traditions as a complement to ordinary consciousness. It is sometimes brought about by the administration of consciousness-altering drugs. It is the dominant cultural mode of the Trobriander and of the Hopi Indian. It is a mode associated with the intuitive, holistic side of ourselves.

THE LEGEND OF NASRUDIN

Idries Shah

A certain crafty villain was entrusted with the education of a number of orphans. Observing that children have certain strengths and weaknesses, he decided to take advantage of this knowledge. Instead of teaching them how to acquire a skill in learning, he told them that they already possessed it. Then he insisted upon their doing some things and refraining from others, and thus kept most of them blindly subject to his direction. He never revealed that his original commission had been to teach them to teach themselves.

When these children grew up, he noticed that some had detached themselves from his authority, despite all his efforts, while others remained bound to it.

He was then entrusted with a second school of orphans. From these he did not directly demand obedience and respect. Instead, he enslaved them to his will by telling them that mental culture was the sole aim of education and by appealing to their self-pride. "The mind," he told them, "will give you universal understanding."

"This must be true," thought the children. "After all, why should we not be able to solve all problems by ourselves?"

He supported the doctrine by demonstrations. "This man," he said, "is enslaved by his emotions. What a disastrous case! Only the intellect can control the emotions. That other man, however, is ruled by his intellect. How much happier he is, how free from emotional frenzy!"

He never let the children guess that there was an alternative to the choice between emotions and intellect, namely intuition, which could, however, be overcome or blurred by either of these, and always dismissed its appearance as irrelevant coincidence or guesswork. There are two kinds of "habit": one is derived from mere repetition, the other from intuition harnessed both to the emotions and to the intellect. But since intuitive habit is associated with true reality, this villainous old man simply abolished it in favour of repetitive habit.

Some of the children, nevertheless, suspected that certain miraculous aspects of life did not fit into its fragmentary pattern, and asked him whether there was not, perhaps, something else undisclosed, some secret power. He told one group of questioners, "Certainly not! Such a notion is superstitious, and due to faulty mental processes. Do not put any value on coincidence. 'Coincidence' means no more than accident, which, though perhaps of emotional interest, lacks all intellectual significance."

To another group he said, "Yes, there is more in life than you will ever know; because it cannot be acquired by honest extension of the scientific information which I gave you, or which you manage to collect under my direction."

But he took care that the two groups did not compare notes and so realize that he had given two contradictory answers. Now, from time to time, when the children reported inexplicable events to him, he consigned these to oblivion as having no scientific relevance.

He knew that, without taking stock of intuition, the children would never escape from the invisible net in which he had bound them, and that the intuitive knowledge of secrets excluded from their education could be won only when they were in a certain harmony of mind with the emotions. So he taught them to ignore variations in their mental condition; for once they discovered that powers of apprehension vary from hour to hour, they might guess how much he had concealed from them. His training confused their memory of such intuitions as they had been granted and they were willing to think along the logical lines he had prepared for them.

The children whom this villain had mistaught in his first schools were now grown up, and since he had let them come nearer to understanding the true nature of life, certain casual remarks that they made to members of the second school disturbed their faith in scientific truth. So he hastily gathered those of the first school who still remained loyal to him and sent them out to preach incomprehensible doctrines purporting to explain the hidden mechanism of life. Then he directed the attention of the second school to these teachers, saying, "Listen carefully, but never fail to use your intellect."

The intellectual children soon found that there was nothing to be learned from these doctrines and said, "They contradict logic. Only with logic are we on firm ground."

Yet some members of the first school who had broken away from the old villain's teaching reproached them, saying, "We, too, reject these doctrines, but that they fail to explain the secret mechanism of life of which you are in search does not deny its existence." They answered, "Can you, then, put the secret in logical terms?" but were told that to do so would be to deny its truth.

So they protested, "Nothing is true that cannot face the cold light of reason." A few, however, cried out, "We are ready to believe everything you tell us. We think you are wonderful." But they were as hopelessly lost as the intellectual children and the teachers of the incomprehensible doctrine, because they trusted only to a slavish credulity, not to the habit of intuition.

A state of educative chaos supervened. So many different ways of thought were current that it was often said, "I cannot trust anyone, I must find out for myself by the exercise of my supreme will."

The old villain who had bred this confusion thrived on it like a madman rejoicing in deeds of violence. Especially this cult of the intellect encouraged egotism and discord. And to those who still felt an inner uncertainty, a sense of incompleteness, or a hankering for something whole and true, he said, "Distract your minds by ambition!" He taught them to covet honours, money, possessions, sexual conquests, to compete with their neighbours, to immerse themselves in hobbies and diversions.

It is said that when a horse cannot find grass, it will accept hay. For want of the green grass of Truth they accepted the dry hay with which he filled their mangers.

The old man devised more and more distractions for them: vogues, crazes, lotteries, fashions in art, music, and literature, sporting competitions and all kinds of achievements which offered them temporary relief from this sense of lack. They were like a patient who accepts palliatives from his physician because he assures them that his disease is incurable. Or they were like the monkey and the crab-apple: he clutched the crab-apple inside a bottle, but the neck was too narrow for him to withdraw his hand and the crab-apple too. Unable to escape because hampered by the bottle, he was soon captured and put into a sack. But he proudly cried, "I still have the apple."

The fragmentary view of life forced on mankind by the old villain was now accepted; and the few people who tried to point out where Truth really lay were thought insane and readily refuted by the old argument, "If what you say is true, then prove it to us logically!"

False coin is accepted only because true coin exists, and deep in their hearts many people knew this. But they were like children born in a house from which they had never been allowed to stray, doomed to walk from one room to another without knowing that there could be another house, elsewhere, with different furnishings and a different view from its windows.

Nevertheless the tradition that true coins exist, that there is another house, and that some horses eat grass, not hay, survived in a book which was not a book, delivered by direct succession from an ancient sage to one of his descendants named Hussein. Hussein searched the world until he found the man who through craft and guile would give the teaching of this book fit expression: namely, the incomparable Mulla Nasrudin. Thereupon this book which was not a book was interpreted by the actions of a Mulla who was no Mulla; who was both wise and a fool; who was both a man and many men. And the teaching was thus brought to the attention of the children who had been misled.

Mulla Nasrudin broke out of the net which had been cast by the old villain. For how can one burn a book which is not a book? How can one name a fool who is no fool? How can one punish a man who is a multitude? How can one strike a man who is oneself?

Study the adventures of Mulla Nasrudin, plumb the depth of the subtleties! He is like a tree which has nourishment in its roots and an edible sap; whose leaves are pot-herbs, whose flowers, fruit, branches and seeds are all variously the same!

Can a tree be a man, or a man a tree?

There Is More Light Here

Someone saw Nasrudin searching for something on the ground.

"What have you lost, Mulla?" he asked.

"My key," said the Mulla. So they both went down on their knees and looked for it.

After a time the other man asked: "Where exactly did you drop it?"

"In my own house."

"Then why are you looking here?"

"There is more light here than inside my own house."

The Value of the Past

Nasrudin was sent by the King to investigate the lore of various kinds of Eastern mystical teachers. They all recounted to him tales of the miracles and the sayings of the founders and great teachers, all long dead, of their schools.

When he returned home, he submitted his report, which contained the single word "Carrots."

He was called upon to explain himself. Nasrudin told the King: "The best part is buried; few know—except the farmer—by the green that there is orange underground; if you don't work for it, it will deteriorate; there are a great many donkeys associated with it."

6

Multiple Consciousness

The Sultan Who Became an Exile

A sultan of Egypt, it is related, called a conference of learned men, and very soon—as is usually the case—a dispute arose. The subject was the Night Journey of the Prophet Mohammed. It is said that on that occasion the Prophet was taken from his bed up into the celestial spheres. During this period, he saw paradise and hell, conferred with God 90,000 times, had many other experiences—and was returned to his room while his bed was yet warm. A pot of water which had been overturned by the flight and spilled was still not empty when the Prophet returned.

Some held that this was possible, by a different measurement of time. The sultan claimed that it was impossible.

The sages said that all things were possible to divine power. This did not satisfy the king.

The news of this conflict came at length to the Sufi Sheikh Shahabudin, who immediately presented himself at Court. The sultan showed due humility to the teacher, who said: "I intend to proceed without further delay to my demonstration: for know now that both the interpretations of the problem are incorrect, and that there are demonstrable factors which can account for traditions without the need to resort to crude speculation or insipid and uninformed 'logicality.' "

There were four windows in the audience chamber. The sheikh ordered one to be opened. The sultan looked out of it. On a mountain beyond he saw an invading army, a myriad, bearing down on the palace. He was terribly afraid.

"Pray forget it: for it is nothing," said the sheikh.

He shut the window and opened it again. This time there was not a soul to be seen.

When he opened another of the windows, the city outside was seen to be consumed by flames. The sultan cried out in alarm.

"Do not distress yourself, sultan, for it is nothing," said the sheikh. When he had closed and again opened the window, there was no fire to be seen.

The third window being opened revealed a flood approaching the palace. Then, again, there was no flood.

When the fourth window was opened, instead of the customary desert, a garden of paradise was revealed—and then, by the shutting of the window, the scene vanished as before.

Now the sheikh ordered a vessel of water to be brought, and the sultan to put his head into it for a moment. As soon as he had done so the sultan found himself alone on a deserted seashore, a place which he did not know.

At this magic spell of the treacherous sheikh he was transported with fury, and vowed vengeance.

Soon he met some woodcutters who asked him who he was. Unable to explain his true state, he told them that he was shipwrecked. They gave him some clothes, and he walked to a town where a blacksmith, seeing him aimlessly wandering, asked him who he was. "A shipwrecked merchant, dependent upon the charity of woodcutters, now with no resources," answered the sultan.

The man then told him about a custom of that country. Every newcomer could ask the first woman who left the bath-house to marry him, and she would be obliged to do so. He went to the bath, and saw a beautiful maiden leaving. He asked her if she was married already: and she was, so he had to ask the next, an ugly one. And the next. The fourth was really exquisite. She said that she was not married, but pushed past him, affronted by his miserable appearance and dress.

Suddenly a man stopped before him and said: "I have been sent to find a bedraggled man here. Please follow me."

The sultan followed the servant, and was shown into a wonderful house in

one of whose sumptuous apartments he sat for hours. Finally four beautiful and gorgeously attired women came in, preceding a fifth, even more beautiful. The sultan recognized her as the last woman whom he had approached at the bath-house. She welcomed him and explained that she had hurried home to prepare for his coming, and that her hauteur was only one of the customs of the country, practiced by all women in the street.

Then followed a magnificent meal. Wonderful robes were brought and given to the sultan, while delicate music was played.

The sultan stayed seven years with his new wife, until they had squandered all her patrimony. Then the woman told him that he must now provide for her and their seven sons.

Recalling his first friend in the city, the sultan returned to the blacksmith for counsel. Since the sultan had no trade or training, he was advised to go to the marketplace and offer his services as a porter.

In one day he earned, through carrying a terrible load, only one-tenth of the money which was needed for the food of the family.

The following day the sultan made his way to the seashore again, where he found the very spot from which he had emerged seven long years before.

Deciding to say his prayers, he started to wash in the water; he suddenly and dramatically found himself back at the palace, with the vessel of water, the sheikh and his courtiers.

"Seven years of exile, evil man!" roared the sultan. "Seven years, a family and having to be a porter! Have you no fear of God, the Almighty, for this deed?"

"But it is only a moment," said the Sufi master, "since you put your head into this water."

His courtiers bore out this statement.

The sultan could not possibly bring himself to believe a word of this. He started to give the order for the beheading of the sheikh. Perceiving by inner sense that this was to happen, the sheikh exercised the capacity called Ilm el-Ghaibat: The Science of Absence. This caused him to be instantly and corporeally transported to Damascus, many days' distance away. From here he wrote a letter to the king:

"Seven years passed for you, as you will now have discovered, during an instant of your head in the water. This happens through the exercise of certain faculties, and carries no special significance except that it is illustrative of what can happen. Was not the bed warm, was not the water jar empty in the tradition?

"It is not whether a thing has happened or not which is the important element. It is possible for anything to happen. What is, however, important, is the significance of the happening. In your case, there was no significance. In the case of the Prophet, there was significance in the happening."

There is a brain and mental system that has evolved to run the body and to keep us healthy. Consciousness is the top part of the system, sensitive to transient changes in our circumstance, food supply, inner states, external threats. So there is no fixed consciousness, it is rather unstable, as it careens from one urgency to another, from emergency to necessity and back and forth. The story begins to open the mind to the possibility of the multiplicity of mental processing within. Here our normal everyday view of a single form of consciousness is effectively overwhelmed by the story, of a voyage to different places and times. All the places and times are probably within the mind, but they are not usually credited, especially by the rational part of ourselves.

Consciousness splits at times to handle multiple needs, it alters through the day, from full wakefulness to drowsiness, from active thought to the bizarre ideation of dreams. And the very delicacy of our adjustment to the world may make it easier to understand how we can have such strange experiences at times, experiences that are far from the norm.

Have you ever looked at a dressing-room mirror? You are looking full face at one image, then, all of a sudden, when you turn you suddenly see the same image, yourself, chopped-up into several bits. This is what happens to consciousness, too, when it divides.

Some experiences can only be recovered under specific conditions: a condition known as *dissociation*. Pierre Janet, a nineteenth-century psychiatrist who used hypnosis in his therapy, first introduced the term *dissociation* in 1899. He suggested to one of his patients under hypnosis that she would write letters to certain people when she came out of her hypnotic state. Later, when she was shown the letters, she had no recollection of having written them and accused Janet of forging her signature. The act of writing had been dissociated, "split off," from consciousness.

Probably all of us experience some splits in consciousness at one time or another. Have you ever felt "out of it" and just snapped back, with no recollection of the time, as if you had just lost a half hour?

When such splits become extreme or a permanent condition, a *multiple personality* may occur—in which two or more consciousnesses coexist. The consciousnesses are so well developed and distinct that they are more like separate personalities than shifting states of mood. Such people are usually unaware of the "other" personalities. Their normal consciousness is dissociated when one of the others emerges.

Daily Variations in Consciousness

Our needs for action change during the day so that our consciousness goes through numerous changes each day; we have daily changes in biological rhythms, borderline states between sleep and dreams, sleep and wakefulness, and daydreams.

The basic *biological rhythm* of human life is *circadian,* which means "about one day." Many factors keep us on a daily rhythm, the light-dark cycle, sun position, work hours, and mealtimes. When these cues are taken away, the circadian rhythm changes from a twenty-four- to a twenty-five-hour one. In a few weeks in a cueless environment, profound changes in sleep-wakefulness and body temperature occur.

One specific daily rhythm is body temperature: Every day there is a peak, a valley, and plateaus. Body temperature is related to mental activity. A person whose temperature peaks in the morning usually is more alert and capable at that time. This is a "morning person." A "night person," on the other hand, feels good-for-nothing in the morning and works best at night. Such a person's body temperature peaks in the evening.

There are extreme rhythmic variations in consciousness. One salesman suffered a severe thought disturbance every fourth day: He would get ready for work and find that he would remain in his car unable to do anything, tense and frightened. When he became conscious of the regular rhythm of this disturbance he arranged his work schedule around it. He never found out what caused the problem, but he did find out how to live with it.

Daydreaming

Everyone daydreams almost daily. Daydreams usually occur when outside events are boring, automatized, or unchanging (riding in a car, listening to a dull lecture); then our consciousness tunes out the outside world and tunes in an inside world.

Recall that we routinely simplify sensory information by tuning out unchanging events to notice novel ones. But since our mental system does not turn off when novel events are *absent, we create our own.* During daydreams we lose consciousness of the external world, and our effectiveness is diminished. Even so, daydreaming may be important. During daydreams our thoughts are more free-flowing and uncensored, making us more receptive to new courses of action and ideas, able to reflect on our faults and mistakes.

There are different kinds of daydreams. One classification divides them into four:

1. *Self-recriminating.* Daydreams prompted by the question, "What should I have done (or said)?"
2. *Well-controlled and thoughtful.* These daydreams are a form of planning—the day is organized, a party is planned, and so forth.
3. *Autistic.* In these daydreams, material usually associated with night dreams breaks through and disrupts consciousness. Seeing a horse flying through the lecture hall would be one example.
4. *Neurotic or self-conscious.* These daydreams include fantasies: "How I can score the winning point and become revered by all the fans," or "How I can be discovered by a Hollywood director."

Although parents, teachers, and bosses keep telling us not to daydream, everyone does.

Sleep

We undergo a radical and dramatic alteration in consciousness each day—sleep. The outside world is shut off; the conscious content is generated entirely from within. During sleep we continue to have conscious experience called dreams. The nature of sleep and dreams has fascinated people for millennia. Why do we sleep? Why do we dream? What do dreams mean?

Every animal sleeps, but, surprisingly, no one is sure why. Most people assume sleep is restorative, because we commonly go to sleep tired and awake refreshed. There are two kinds of tiredness, each requiring a different kind of sleep. *Physical tiredness* follows intense physical effort and is usually pleasant because of the relaxed state of the muscles. *Mental tiredness* comes after intense intellectual or emotional activity and is usually an unpleasant feeling of having been "drained."

There is little direct evidence to back up the assumption that sleep is restorative. The specific functions of sleep and dreaming remain a mystery. However, some real progress has been made in the last few years on both of these questions.

One way to figure out the functions of sleep is to deprive people of it. In 1959 a New York City disc jockey, Peter Tripp, tried to stay awake for 200 hours to benefit charity. For this marathon he was surrounded by psychologists and medical specialists; his physiological and psychological functioning were monitored continuously.

Almost from the first the overpowering force of sleepiness hit him. Constant company, walks, tests, broadcasts helped, but after about five days he needed a stimulant to keep going. . . . After little more than two days as he changed shoes in the hotel, he pointed out to [a psychiatrist] a very interesting sight. There were cobwebs in his shoes—to the eyes at least. . . . Specks on the table began to look like bugs. . . . By 110 hours there were signs of delirium. Tripp's world had grown grotesque. A doctor walked into the recording booth in a tweed suit that Tripp saw as a suit of furry worms. By about 150 hours he became disoriented, not realizing where he was, and wondering who he was. . . . Sometimes he would back up against a wall and let nobody walk behind him. Yet from 5 to 8 P.M. all his forces were mysteriously summoned, and he efficiently organized his commercials and records and managed a vigorous patter for three hours. . . . On the final morning of the final day [of the 200-hour period] a famous neurologist arrived to examine him. The doctor carried an umbrella although it was a bright day, and had a somewhat archaic mode of dress. . . . [Tripp] came to the morbid conclusion that this man was an undertaker, there for the purpose of burying him. . . . Tripp leapt for the door with several doctors in pursuit.

With some encouragement Tripp managed to get through the day, gave his broadcast, and then sank into sleep for thirteen hours. When he awakened the terrors, ghouls, and mental agony had vanished.

Sleep deprivation of 359 servicemen showed that by the third sleepless day 70 percent experienced hallucinations and 7 percent behaved abnormally. When people are deprived of sleep there can be a profound disorganization of normal mental processes. However, a good night's sleep restored all to normal.

In 1953 Eugene Aserinsky and Nathaniel Kleitman made a chance observation in the course of studying the sleep patterns of infants: Periods of eye movements and bodily activity seem to alternate regularly with periods of "quiet" sleep. These regular periods of rapid eye movements, called *REM sleep,* were observed precisely by attaching electrodes near the subjects' eyes. People of all ages experience some REM sleep every night. Whenever test subjects are awakened just after periods of REM sleep, they almost always give vivid reports of their dreams. In contrast, when awakened after other stages of sleep (collectively called "non-REM" or NREM), they report dreams only a third of the time.

William Dement has been trying to discover the relation of REM sleep to dreaming; he has produced evidence for a precise correspondence between REM sleep behavior and dream-gaze changes. One subject who showed many side-to-side eye movements reported dreaming of a tennis match!

The Stages of Sleep

Determining what stages of sleep a person is in is quite involved and requires recording of three physiological measures: EEG; the electro-oculogram, which records the movements of the eyes (EOG); and chin EMG (electromyogram, a measure of muscle tension). During the night these measures change in roughly the following way: As an experimental subject lies awake in bed before going to sleep, the EEG is likely to exhibit alpha rhythm; the EOG reveals blinks and occasional REMs; and the EMG level is relatively high. This state is called "relaxed wakefulness."

When we become drowsy, the EEG alpha rhythm is gradually replaced by the low-voltage EEG activity characteristic of "stage-one sleep." Stage-one sleep lasts only a few minutes.

Stage-two sleep is marked by *sleep spindles*. EOG activity is minimal and the EMG usually decreases still further. Gradually, high-amplitude slow waves begin to appear on the EEG. When 20 to 50 percent of the EEG record is filled with these (delta) waves, stage three is reached. Eventually, delta activity dominates the EEG. When the proportion of delta activity exceeds 50 percent, the "deepest" stage of sleep, stage four, is reached. During these stages there are no eye movements and EMG is normally low.

After about an hour and a half the sequence is reversed. By the time the EEG indicates that stage one has been reached, however, the EMG is at the lowest level of the night and REMs occur in dramatic profusion. This is "stage-one REM," or REM sleep. REM sleep is extremely curious; many contradictory phenomena occur at once. The eyes move rapidly, breathing and heart rate become irregular; erection in the male, vaginal engorgement in the female; vestibular activation.

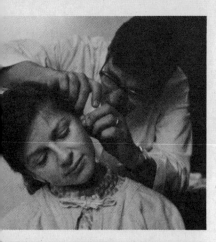

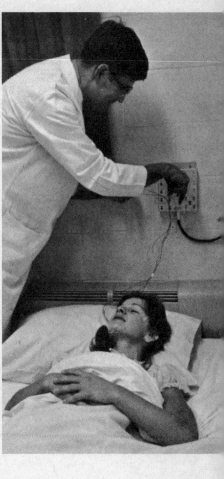

Sleep stages are studied by placing electrodes on the skull, near the eyes, and over the heart and recording the subject's brain waves, eye movements, and heart activities through the night, as in these photographs from the Dartmouth Sleep Laboratory.

STAGES OF SLEEP

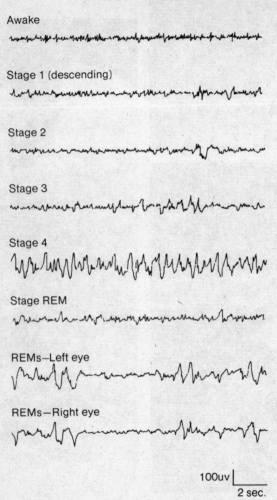

Awake

Stage 1 (descending)

Stage 2

Stage 3

Stage 4

Stage REM

REMs—Left eye

REMs—Right eye

100uv
2 sec.

The EEG from waking through the stages of sleep. Note that in REM the EEG shows high-voltage waves, indicating many rapid eye movements, but that otherwise it is similar to that of Stage 1.

However, during all this activation, *all other commands for voluntary movement emanating from the brain are blocked* from reaching the muscles at the spinal cord. For instance, you may dream that you are running, but your legs do not move. The brain, breathing, heart rate, and cerebral blood flow are all excited, but the rest of the body is momentarily paralyzed.

This happens because there is a specific activation of certain lower brain centers. Here's how it works: Immediately preceding and during REM sleep there is increased "spiking" activity in the cells of the *pontine reticular formation,* a network of cells located in the pons of the brain. These cells in turn activate eye movement neurons. At the same time, the activity in the pontine reticular formation inhibits a nearby group of cells, the *locus cerulus,* which affects muscle tone and blocks muscle movements. REM sleep lasts on average ten minutes.

The cycle of sleep stages repeats three or four times a night, although the same stage is slightly different at each occurrence. The depth of sleep decreases, there is less stage-three and stage-four sleep. Successive REM periods increase in length. And the interval between REM periods decreases from ninety minutes early in a night's sleep to as little as forty minutes.

Dreams

REM sleep provides an external indicator of the occurrence of dreaming—it was an important discovery not only for the insights it provided on sleep, but it was one of the first physiological measures psychologists and psychiatrists have been able to correlate with external experiences. Recording REM, researchers have been able to answer many basic questions about dreams. *We all dream every night, whether or not we can recall the content of our dreams.* Most people have four or five dream periods a night at about ninety-minute intervals; dream periods become longer throughout the night. Dreams are more frequently recalled if the sleeper is awakened immediately after a REM period.

The content of dreams can be influenced by outside stimuli—many people have dreamed of a loud noise only to awaken to the alarm clock. Dement and Wolpert sprayed water on subjects' faces during REM periods. When awakened, many subjects reported water imagery in their dreams.

REM sleep and the dreams it indicates might be involved in the reorganization of mental structures (schemata) to accommodate new information. People were placed in a "disturbing and perplexing" atmosphere four hours just before sleep, asked to perform difficult tasks with no explanation. During the night their REM time increased. REM sleep increases after people have had to learn complex tasks. Such a function would explain why REM sleep decreases with age: as less and less new information must be accommodated, there would be less need for REM sleep.

Divided Consciousness During Dreaming

Sometimes we know we are dreaming while we are dreaming. Some individuals claim to be able to think and act consciously while dreaming. But dreaming and wakefulness are so different that communication between the two has been thought impossible. If dreamers could signal to an observer that they *knew they were dreaming,* that would indicate a division within dreaming consciousness that could open a new channel of communication between the dreamer and the outside world.

Evidence for such "lucid" dreaming has been found. Observers in one study were able to signal to researchers that they knew they were dreaming. They had been trained to signal dreaming by moving their eyes voluntarily during dreams, producing observable effects on their polygraph records. This procedure may make possible a new approach to dream research. Such subjects might be able, for example, to mark the exact time of particular dream events. Perhaps such studies mark the beginning of "on-the-scene" reporting from the dream world.

But what might dreams mean? The most influential theory on the meaning of dreams is Freud's, presented in a brilliant book, *The Interpretation of Dreams.* Freud's analysis of the function of dreams is so complex, we note only two of the main points.

During dreams normal controls are released, allowing unconscious wishes to be expressed directly. For Freud, dreams are the "royal road to the unconscious," because dreaming is one of the few times when normally forbidden desires rise to the surface of consciousness. A hungry person might dream of food, the sexually deprived of sex. These "pent up" desires are diminished to some extent simply by being expressed in dream consciousness, and they are then less likely to disturb waking consciousness and influence behavior.

However, the expression of desires during sleep could pose problems to the sleeper. A dream about killing a rival or sleeping with a friend's spouse might be disturbing. If a dream is upsetting enough, a person may wake up. Since that rarely happens, Freud felt that dreams "guard" sleep by transforming the unconscious desires into disguised symbols. It was the aim of Freudian *psychoanalysis* to uncover what these disguised symbols meant to dreamers by encouraging them to free associate to the dream content.

A more recent and more scientific theory of dreaming is based on observations of the unique state of the brain and nervous system during REM sleep. During REM the brain stem produces neuronal "spikes," the signals to the muscles are blocked at the brain stem, and the vestibular system is stimulated; and the brain may be reshuffling schemata, as it were.

The theory is called *activation synthesis* because it assumes that the brain is *activated* in REM sleep and that dreams are a conscious *interpretation* or *synthesis* of the information in consciousness during dreams.

During wakefulness the mental operating system organizes sensory information into the simplest meaningful interpretation. Suppose the *same system* is at work during dreaming.

In dreams, therefore, mental processes attempt to organize diverse material: falling (from the vestibular activation), the inability to move (from the blocking of motor output), and the specific events of the day needing to be assimilated or accommodated. The "simplest meaningful experience" of all these events becomes the dream.

Many common dream experiences may be our *interpretation* of the brain's state: being chased, unable to avoid the pursuer, being tied up, locked up, or frozen with fright, may well be an interpretation of the blocked motor commands to our muscles during REM. Floating, flying, and falling experiences in dreams may be the interpretation of the vestibular activation; the sexual content of dreams may be an interpretation of vaginal engorgement or penile erection.

Dreams are often incoherent, even bizarre. One minute you may be speaking to your boss, the next you may be singing in a cabaret in some exotic city. Such abrupt shifts in imagery may simply be the brain's "making the best of a bad job in producing partially coherent dream imagery from the relatively noisy signals sent up . . . from the brain stem."

If activation synthesis is correct, then the experience of dreams can be understood as a product of the nature of the mental operating system when the brain is generating its own "raw" information. Of course, dreams still *may* have specific meanings, but these meanings may lie in the *interpretation* of the events.

If we are deprived of dreaming, we tend to have our dreams during the day: first as daydreams, then as hallucinations, then as more extreme difficulties. "The madman is a walking dreamer," wrote Immanuel Kant.

Sleep and dreams are certainly a most common and yet dramatic alteration of consciousness. Sleeping is almost instantaneous, and dreams are often fully orchestrated, elaborate hallucinations that *each of us experience every night*.

Hypnosis

Is hypnosis a "state" of consciousness, like dreaming? Probably not, for if one hypnotizes a person to behave and experience as if alert, then to all outward signs he will appear alert. If instructed to relax, then the signs will be as if relaxed. Hypnosis is not a unitary or consistent state like dreams.

Hypnosis indicates that we are more capable of controlling our experience and physiology than commonly thought. Hypnotized students are able to alter their skin and body temperature like yogis. Pain thresholds are raised and memory increased.

Being hypnotized enables a person to explore areas of consciousness that the normal constraints of life do not allow—a deep trance or a "mystic experience." If hypnotic controls on consciousness are developed and integrated into a coherent practice, these experiences may have further uses. If not, they remain unconnected, as were those of the king in exile in the story that begins this chapter.

It is often reported that pain thresholds are raised through hypnosis, yet for an analysis of consciousness this raises a major question: Is the pain completely inaccessible to consciousness, or, rather, is the pain not attended to as usual? The latter seems the case. In an ingenious procedure Ernest Hilgard elicited two different reports of pain experience. The first was done by ordinary verbal means and showed a consistent absence of pain. In the second, a "hidden observer," communicating by automatic writing (or by automatic talking) reported increased pain *at the same time*. This split indicates the large control we possess over consciousness, at least over our criteria for reporting events, although it is necessary for us to devise such a study to see this control. We say, for instance, that we "pay attention."

Hypnosis, like meditation, biofeedback, and autogenic training, indicates our great potential for conscious regulation. Still, even today most of us do not believe in these capacities. Our perspective is often too similar to that of the Royal College of Physicians of England in the 1850s, when Esdaile demonstrated hypnotic anesthesia for amputation of a gangrenous limb. After he had performed the operation and the patient was awake and obviously not in pain, the physicians (who possessed no reliable anesthetic) discounted the "anomalous" information in front of them. One reported that Esdaile had hired a "hardened rogue" to undergo the operation for a fee! It is difficult to change conceptions of possibility, even in the face of direct evidence.

Sensory Deprivation and Isolation

If the ordinary consciousness responds to changes in the environment, then the absence of such changes may cause it to alter. For centuries techniques to eliminate awareness of changes have been known: Mystics remove themselves to a cave or to the desert, or they perform repetitive movements or sounds.

These situations have been duplicated in isolation rooms designed to keep perceived changes to a minimum.

In early experiments in sensory deprivation, people reported unusual experiences, temporal disorientation, hallucinations, and extreme pathology. Yet those bizarre results depend on the expectations of the subjects and of the experimenter.

People try to keep the same level of stimulation going in to consciousness. It seems that different people like different "levels" of stimulation, as different people prefer their music at different loudness, or different amounts of spice in their food. Much research has been done on changing the level of sensory stimulation, since as you might expect, this would change consciousness. When a person is put into sensory deprivation, he or she will immediately try to seek stimulation. He may begin to move about, or brush his hand against his leg, or make noises vocally or with his feet. It seems that consciousness, accustomed to a supply of "news," needs its fix to keep going.

What happens when people are prevented from stimulating themselves? They rapidly become disorganized, lose intellectual ability and concentration, and their coordination declines.

For some the condition mirrors day- or night dreams: They begin to create their own world. The hallucinations, according to one report, are ". . . visual, often in vivid color and detail, or shapeless light sensations to complex objects and scenes, usually experienced in a progression from simple to complex. . . . Feelings of anxiety, irritability, boredom, restlessness, and unusual emotional lability are often reported, and paranoid-like reactions and alterations of body image are not uncommon."

However, the "disorienting" effects of sensory deprivation and isolation may be potentially beneficial. Sensory isolation has been used for relaxation and in smoking-control clinics. The radical shift in the environment may cause consciousness to change in line with expectations. There may be both pathology and benefit in boredom, depending on what we expect from it.

Subliminal Perception

As there are gradations in consciousness throughout the day, there are gradients in how conscious one is of any stimulus at any moment. Below consciousness are several "levels of awareness" and it is obviously not necessary for us to be *conscious* of everything in our world. Some things seem to seep in to the mind, indirectly, under the threshold of conscious awareness.

For example, the sleeping brain monitors the environment for meaningful sounds. We will awaken when *our* name is called but not someone else's. When sleeping people listen to recordings of names, they show a profound cortical response to their name, and, again, not to the names of others.

When some words are flashed quickly to a person, those that are "taboo" [or were, when the study was done!] take longer to recognize. *Whore* takes longer, for instance, than *shore*. Also, people tend to develop specific feelings to stimuli even though they cannot recognize them. When geometric shapes are flashed to the person faster than he can recognize them and the person is asked "How much do you like them?" he likes those figures he has seen before, while insisting the question is nonsensical!

There are many other indications that we can react to information at a level below consciousness—changes in skin resistance, heart rate, and other measures of activation. There is a growing, but still controversial, research literature showing that we may be profoundly affected by the "subliminal." The effects of these indirect stimuli are often indirect as well.

In one important series of studies, the stimulus MOMMY AND I ARE 1 was flashed to a person, who was unaware of the message. When groups who have seen this message are later tested on a variety of tasks, such as later achievement, exam scores, aspirations, all seem enhanced! These studies were done with the idea of supporting the psychoanalytic point of view that the experience of such "oneness" will enhance performance. While it is not necessary to accept such an implausible idea, certainly the phenomenon is important enough to merit a change in our ideas of the permeability and multiplicity of our consciousness.

Drug-Induced Alterations in Consciousness

One of the most popular means of inducing alterations is through the ingestion of drugs. The effects of drugs are not only pharmacological but also social. Drugs can also express one's desire for change, both for oneself and in society. But the benefits of taking drugs may pass if they are unsupported by the perspective and context provided in, say, the esoteric traditions, and the drug's negative aspects may be quite great, in terms of both physiology and psychology. The most popular drugs used in our culture are coffee, tobacco, and alcohol, with marijuana a recent addition. More exotic and more troublesome to manage in our society are the opiate narcotics such as opium, morphine, and heroin; barbiturate tranquilizers such as phenobarbitol, Librium, and methaqualone; the central stimulants such as the amphetamines; and the "psychedelic" drugs such as mescaline and LSD.

In spite of the dissimilarity of these drugs, most drug taking follows a general pattern, largely one of expectation. In most cases social and recreational drugs are introduced into a culture by an avant-garde minority who are primarily interested in their effects on consciousness. This occurred, for example, with the use of coffee in Egypt and England, with tobacco in the West (after the discovery of its use by Indians), with alcohol, with opiates, and with "psychedelics."

As Brecher points out in an excellent review in *Licit and Illicit Drugs,* the pattern is similar: The drug is first confiscated and condemned but finally coopted by the culture. Most Americans do not realize, for instance, that nicotine withdrawal, as Brecher documents, is as difficult as heroin withdrawal, and perhaps as dangerous. Yet heroin is quite illicit; cigarettes are readily available. The user of heroin must, therefore, traffic in the underworld, where many other factors influence the use of the drug. The drug may be impure and of an uncontrolled dosage; the supply may be unreliable and often unsanitary. The user may have little or no means of controlling the dosage. The drug may be quite costly and he or she may be forced to extreme means to obtain the dosage, including criminal means.

Since we are considering these drugs as they are used to *change consciousness*, the social aspects are quite relevant. As these drugs are used, they all take maximum advantage of the placebo effect. Tobacco can be either a relaxant or a stimulant, depending on the needs of the person, and depending on how the drug is ingested—it seems that short puffs increase stimulation, while deep ones relax. Each drug, of course, has a specific pharmacological action, but the drugs also all share a certain mild deautomatization of experience, which people prize.

Sedatives

Alcohol is consumed in vast quantities in most civilized countries and is used socially, recreationally, and medically—as well as for psychological support by some users. It is probably the most severely abused drug in our society. Most experts agree that "alcohol addiction, unlike morphine addiction, is utterly destructive to the human mind," and similarly to the body, through irreversible brain and liver damage. Large proportions of the arrests in the United States are for drunkenness. Still, the drug is used by most without difficulty.

Alcohol is a depressant. Yet, it often produces euphoria in small doses, probably because in small doses it primarily depresses inhibitions. As with other sedatives, alcohol displays a continuum of action.

In certain cultures throughout the world alcohol is employed in religious rituals as a "sacred" drug, although it is also the subject of prohibition. In our society it is such a standard drug that a group of researchers meeting to discuss the problems of drug abuse might well serve martinis and wine at their dinner without a second thought.

Barbiturates act in the same manner as does alcohol, and their effects add to any alcohol ingested, making the combination extremely dangerous. Like alcohol, barbiturates are commonly used in our society, and they can cause both psychological and physiological dependence. These drugs, sold under trademarked names, provide an example of the shift from internal to external control of our conscious state. In medical and quasi-medical situations these drugs have become a substitute for training to relax at will. Barbiturates are often introduced as an external tranquilizer. They often act as a placebo; many people, for instance, report relief from stress immediately after the administration of such a drug, even though it has not had time to act.

Stimulants

Coffee and tea are so widely used that it is difficult for us to consider them drugs. But they are, and have been for centuries, employed to change consciousness. These drugs have been considered of such immense value that wars have been fought to ensure their supply. The "lift" and clear thinking they supply were first used by the Sufis of Egypt to enable them to remain awake during rituals. Coffee was later banned in several countries with the same repercussions as our contemporary difficulties with marijuana. The *Encyclopaedia Britannica* quotes an early Arabic writer:

> The sale of coffee has been forbidden. The vessels used for this beverage . . . have been broken to pieces. The dealers in coffee have received the bastinado, and have undergone other ill-treatment without even a plausible excuse; they were punished by loss of their money. The husks of the plant . . . have been more than once devoted to the flames, and in several instances persons making use of it . . . have been severely handled.

Again, if a drug is given great attention, and is distributed with great expectations and with appropriate ritual, its effect on us will be great. If the same drug is routinely dispensed by vending machines in polyethylene cups at regular intervals, its effect on our experience will be lessened.

Tobacco was introduced to the West in the sixteenth century, when Columbus found Indians smoking rolled tobacco leaves and inhaling the smoke. Settlers in the New World learned to smoke, and when asked about their "disgusting habit," they replied that they found it impossible to give up. The nicotine in tobacco is physiologically addicting and is the main reason for its continued use. Tobacco use is quite widespread now, and we do not consider its effect a "drug-induced state of consciousness," again, because its use is so common.

Although caffeine and other drugs stimulate the brain and nervous system, people take the stronger stimulants, such as amphetamines, in large doses to induce a feeling of well-being or inject it into their veins for a euphoric "rush." This feeling is the primary motivation for those who use these drugs for consciousness alternation. Central stimulants heighten people's sensitivity to weak stimuli, deautomatize their awareness to some extent, and produce exhilaration for brief periods, but this is often followed by depression. The drawbacks to amphetamine use are due, again, to often extreme dosage and the method of injection, as well as to the social—often criminal—milieu of the availability of the drugs.

Opiates

Long used in east and northeast Asia to induce extraordinary, dreamlike experiences, the opiates have recently become a major drug in the West. Opium is the basic derivative of the poppy. Morphine, used primarily for pain relief, is stronger than opium; and heroin is, in turn, stronger than morphine. "Street" heroin, however, is diluted to below the strength of opium. People may use this drug for several reasons: They may be introduced to morphine as a painkiller and become addicted to it; they may be part of a subculture where its use is widespread; or they may be new "middle-class" users of a generation not part of the "underground dope scene."

The primary effect of opiate drugs on consciousness seems to be an intoxication euphoria that is especially likely when the drug is injected. However, the drawbacks of these drugs are immense. They are addicting and, much worse, they are illegal in most cases. This illegality often forces the user to enter the world of the "pusher," one in which great sums of money are needed to supply a habit; this, in turn, may force the user to follow a criminal career. This is undoubtedly the worst social effect of the drug. Most experts agree that heroin in controlled dosages does not cause any major biological damage—as does continual overdose of alcohol or tobacco—and addicts can be maintained (as in England) with little difficulty.

Psychedelics

Psychedelic means "mind expanding" or "mind manifesting." This is not a strictly descriptive term but rather is frankly promotional. It is used to describe drugs such as marijuana, LSD, psilocybin, mescaline, and so on. These drugs have attained great popularity in terms of their supposed "mystic" nature and, hence, the promotion. It is by no means clear how they work biologically, especially in the case of LSD, of which a dose of less than 100 millionths of a gram is likely to have significant psychological effects. People take these drugs exclusively to affect consciousness.

Marijuana is reported to enhance the appreciation of music and other sensory pleasures, to aid in sleep and in relaxation, and to increase appetite. At strong levels of intoxication people get easily sidetracked and forget their thoughts. Its use is spreading in western Europe and America, as a replacement for alcohol.

The effect of LSD and similar drugs, such as mescaline, is much more striking; yet, the effect seems quite dependent on the taker's expectations. These drugs are used in developed religious rituals by American Indians, and in undeveloped rituals by people seeking a radical restructuring of consciousness. Albert Hoffman, the discoverer of LSD, had no expectations and thus provides perhaps the clearest recorded summary of the experience:

> After 40 minutes, I noted the following symptoms in my laboratory journal: slight giddiness, restlessness, difficulty in concentration, visual disturbance, laughing. . . . Later: I lost all count of time, I noticed with dismay that my environment was undergoing progressive changes. My visual field wavered and everything appeared deformed as in a faulty mirror. Space and time became more and more disorganized and I was overcome by a fear that I was going out of my mind. The worst part of it being that I was clearly aware of my condition. My power of observation was unimpaired. . . . Occasionally, I felt as if I were out of my body. I thought I had died. My ego seemed suspended somewhere in space, from where I saw my dead body lying on the sofa. . . . It was particularly striking how acoustic perceptions, such as the noise of water gushing from a tap or the spoken word, were transformed into optical illusions. I then fell asleep and awakened the next morning somewhat tired but otherwise feeling perfectly well.

These drugs seem to work largely by causing a radical disruption of "normal" consciousness and perhaps unusual neuronal activity. When this is done, new insights may occasionally result, but they rarely prove of lasting use or significance, since they are brought about quickly and with little of the preparation and surrounding support that can cultivate insight into lasting change.

The Experience of Dying

Perhaps the most radical experience of all occurs when a person almost dies—there seem to be striking and consistent experiences, ones that are difficult to explain by our ordinary approaches to consciousness.

The psychologist Kenneth Ring studied 102 men and women who had "near-death experiences"—who had been very close to death or actually clinically dead and revived—and found highly interesting results. These people reported experiencing *intense feelings of peace* or *joy,* or felt that they *left their body* and *traveled through a dark tunnel.* In addition, they reported *seeing a brilliant light* or *beautiful colors.* A few reported *speaking with deceased relatives* or friends or a *"presence"* who convinced the person to return. They may also have felt that they had taken stock of their life by reviewing all or parts of it, sometimes in what they could only describe as similar to a "movie," in that they seemed to be watching their experiences from the outside.

This "core experience" seems to be ordered in five distinct stages: (1) feelings of peace and affective well-being; (2) body separation; (3) entering the darkness; (4) seeing the light; (5) entering the light. People who experienced the first stage reported a cessation of pain and intense feelings of joy, peace, or calm, usually unlike anything they had previously experienced. This has led to some speculation that endorphins are involved. In the second stage, some people reported a sense of being detached from their bodies, and some even felt they were somehow looking down at their bodies. Those who did also reported an unusual brightness of the environment.

The next stage seemed to be one of transition. People would experience moving through a dark space, sometimes described as a tunnel. At the end of the "tunnel," there was often a brilliant light. Although very bright, it did not hurt the eyes and was described as very comforting and beautiful. Finally, a very few people reported entering the light, which was somehow a different land—a field or valley, always very bright and beautiful, and indescribable.

There were other elements of the core experience: the life review; encounter with a "presence" or deceased loved ones; and making the decision to return. In the *life review,* a person may experience all or part of his or her life in the form of visual, instantaneous images. This experience is usually positive, although people report a sense of detachment, and sometimes also an ability to "edit"—to move backward or forward or to "skip" certain parts.

Twenty people in Ring's sample experienced a "presence," which was rarely seen, but that somehow communicated directly with the person, offering him or her the opportunity to go back. This presence was sometimes interpreted within a religious framework—that is, as being God or Jesus for Christians and Krishna for Hindus. Alternatively, a person may "be greeted" by the "spirits" of deceased loved ones, usually relatives, who inform the person that it is not time yet, and that he or she must go back. Generally, people felt they needed to return to help others, to be able to serve the world, not themselves.

The frequency and intensity of the core experience tended to be greatest for illness victims, moderate for accident victims, and very low for attempted suicides. Interestingly, the few attempted suicides who had core experiences did not use drugs, which may suppress the experience, but they still had fewer "transcendent" elements, and their experiences tended to differ from the nonsuicides. While not everyone in Ring's sample experienced all or any of these phenomena, *not one person had a negative experience*.

No one is really sure why some people have these experiences, or why some people have them and others do not—or at least do not remember them. (Ring reported one person whose eyewitnesses said he revived speaking of these things, but later on did not remember.) We know little about this, and it is quite controversial. There were no demographic differences (age, sex, social class, marital status, religion) in Ring's sample between experiencers and nonexperiencers. While the experiences may be interpreted within a religious framework, religiousness is unrelated to the likelihood or to the depth of the core experiences.

> "I believe in the basis of all religions. They're all connected as far as I'm concerned."
>
> "I don't think of religion as a religion any more. God is above all religions. God is the religion, so, therefore, the various religions have no effect whatsoever on me."

Finally, it did not appear to be due to suggestion; people who had *not* previously heard of this phenomenon were *more* likely to experience it.

Regardless of whether or not a person had a core experience, the experience of nearly dying almost always had a positive effect on the person's life.

Everyone who had a brush with death came away a different person. As one young man said,

> "[I had an] awareness that something more was going on in life than just the physical part of it. . . . It was just a total awareness of not just the material and how much we can buy. . . . There's more than just consuming life. There's a point where you have to *give* to it and that's real important. And there was an awareness at that point that I had to give more to myself *out* of life. That awareness has come to me."

Ring summarizes:

> The typical near-death survivor emerges from his experience with a heightened sense of appreciation for life, determined to live life to the fullest. He has a purpose in living, even though he cannot articulate just what this purpose is.

This study is, of course, exploratory. However, it indicates that our ideas about the extraordinary conscious experiences reported in mystical literature have, at least, to be reconsidered. Some psychologists think these experiences are simple hallucinations, but the common elements in the experience indicate that perhaps dying is not a terrible experience after all, hallucination or not.

But to the more receptive and open minded among us, this study, and similar ones [for it has been repeated] profoundly challenge the ideas we have about our minds, our consciousness, and ourselves. Perhaps there is another system operating inside ourselves, one that is independent of the normal machinations of minds and the divisions, dissociations, and discussions of normal life. Certainly these studies call into question some of the most deeply held assumptions of contemporary psychology and contemporary life, and they bring to mind some of the ideas of the traditions that have, for millennia, attempted to develop consciousness further, especially the saying "Die before you die."

As with the sultan who became an exile, alterations in consciousness brought about by hypnosis, fasting, drugs, sensory deprivation, dreams, or even a near-death experience may fascinate the person who experiences them. To psychologists these alterations indicate that consciousness is changeable and multiple; it alters to suit conditions daily, sometimes in a quite radical manner, such as dreams. *Yet because these radical changes occur so often, the miracle of them is lost to us, as the miracles the senses perform every instant are lost.*

For centuries, people have sought, with more or less success, to bring this multiplicity of our consciousness under some control, in one description "Die before you die." Their deliberate techniques, part of organized schools of religion, of philosophy, are in the next chapter.

LUCID DREAMING: DIRECTING
THE ACTION AS IT HAPPENS

Stephen P. LaBerge

During "lucid dreams" we are remarkably wakeful—even though still asleep. We may be able to reason clearly, remember freely, signal that we are conscious, and may even change the plot if we so choose. But it takes training.

> *I am in the middle of a riot in the classroom. Everyone is running around in some sort of struggle. Most of them are Third World Types, and one of them has a hold on me—he is huge, with a pockmarked face. I realize that I am dreaming and stop struggling. I look him in the eyes and, while holding his hands, speak to him in a loving way, trusting my intuition to supply the beautiful words of acceptance that flow out of me. The riot has vanished, the dream fades, and I awaken feeling wonderfully calm.*

We do not usually question the reality of our dreams until after we have awakened. But it is not always so. That we sometimes dream while knowing that we are dreaming has been known since the time of Aristotle. During such "lucid dreams," the dreamer's consciousness seems remarkably wakeful. The lucid dreamer can reason clearly, remember freely, and act volitionally upon reflection, all while continuing to dream vividly. As in the dream above, which I had a little more than two years ago, the dreamer may take an active hand in resolving the dream's conflict and in bringing the plot to a satisfactory conclusion.

Unlike researchers who have gotten people to change the outcome of their dreams through discussions beforehand, I have found that the dreamer can change the dream from within—while it is in progress. For example, even while I was dreaming about the thug assaulting me, I felt on another level that he represented an aspect of my own personality I was actively denying. I wanted to make peace with that part of me and was able to do so, consciously, in the course of the dream.

In a personal experiment, I discovered that it is possible to enhance one's capacity for lucid dreaming. For three years, I recorded all the lucid dreams that I could recall—a total of 389. Experimenting with a variety of autosuggestion techniques, I was able to increase the frequency of lucid dreams almost fourfold, to a peak of as many as 26 dreams a month. Because of the vagueness and inefficiency of such techniques, it took me almost two years to work out a method that was fully effective. But toward the end of my experiment, in the third year, I was able to produce lucid dreams virtually at will.

People can not only train themselves to dream lucidly but may also be able to signal laboratory researchers that they are having the dreams. My colleagues at the Sleep Research Center at Stanford University, Drs. Vincent Zarcone, William C. Dement, Lynn Nagel, and I have already demonstrated in one study that use of prearranged signals is possible. We were able to verify the occurrence of lucid dreams during rapid eye movement [REM] sleep for subjects who signaled that they knew they were dreaming. The signals consisted of particular dream actions that had observable concomitants and were performed in accordance with presleep agreements. We believe that such experiments can provide a new model for dream research. In the view of Charles Tart, a psychologist at the University of Davis, they may lead to "an era of deliberate and controlled phenomenological and scientific exploration of dreaming . . . which promises great excitement as well as great significance."

Lucid dreaming has been treated more often as a mysterious talent than as a learnable skill. What little has been written consists largely of reports of lucid dreams, with few hints on how the ability might be cultivated. One exception is the book *Creative Dreaming,* in which psychologist Patricia Garfield describes a very simple method of autosuggestion: Before going to sleep, she would tell herself, in effect, "Tonight

I *will* have a lucid dream." Garfield, who has experimented with the technique for several years, reports having had an average of four or five lucid dreams per month. Her results indicate that autosuggestion might be a starting point for a method of deliberately inducing lucid dreams.

Long before my study, I had had occasional lucid dreams. At the age of five, I can remember having a series of such dreams, which I would intentionally redream on successive nights. I vividly recall one of the dreams, in which I was underwater for too long and suddenly became fearful of drowning, but then I recalled that in the dream series, I had always been able to breathe underwater. The next lucid dream I can recall did not occur until twenty years later; for several years after that, however, I had an average of less than one a month, but I found lucid dreams sufficiently intriguing to persuade me to study the phenomenon, starting in 1977, for a Ph.D. thesis at Stanford.

During the first year and one half of the study, I experimented with Garfield's autosuggestion technique. I achieved essentially the same results she did, averaging about five dreams a month.

By the end of Phase I, I had observed two presleep psychological factors that were associated with the later occurrence of lucid dreams. The first and most obvious was motivation. During Phase I, there were two months during which I reported, respectively, two and three times more lucid dreams than the average for the rest of this period. During the first month, I was preparing a dissertation proposal in connection with the study, and during the second, I was attempting to have lucid dreams in the sleep laboratory. During both months, I was thus challenged to demonstrate the feasibility of a scientific study of lucid dreaming.

Gradually, more self-observation led to the realization of a second psychological factor: the presleep intention to *remember* to be lucid during the next dream. This clarification of intention was accompanied by an immediate increase in the monthly frequency of lucid dreams (Phase II). Further practice and procedural refinements led within a year to a method that could reliably induce lucid dreams. The method is based on our ability to remember to perform future actions. One does this by forming mental associations between what one wants to remember to do and the future circumstances in which one intends to act. The associations are most readily formed by the mnemonic device of visualizing oneself doing what one intends to remember. It is also helpful to verbalize the intention: "When such and such, do thus and so." What I call the mnemonic induction of lucid dreams (MILD) procedure goes as follows:

1. During the early morning, I awaken spontaneously from a dream.
2. After memorizing the dream, I engage in ten to fifteen minutes of reading or any other activity demanding full wakefulness.
3. Then, while lying in bed and returning to sleep, I say to myself, "Next time I'm dreaming, I want to remember I'm dreaming."
4. I visualize my body lying asleep in bed, with rapid eye movements indicating that I am dreaming. At the same time, I see myself as being in the dream just rehearsed (or in any other, in case none was recalled upon awakening) and realizing that I am in fact dreaming.
5. I repeat steps 3 and 4 until I feel my intention is clearly fixed.

Using the MILD technique (during Phase IV and the last four months of Phase II), I had an average of 21.5 lucid dreams per month, with as many as four in one night. Afterward, I discontinued regular practice of MILD during a four-month withdrawal period (Phase III), resulting in a decline that was reversed during the last two months (Phase IV), when I used MILD to produce lucid dreams for the laboratory study I will describe later.

It seemed to me that I could stimulate lucidity whenever I wanted to during REM sleep, which normally occurs about every ninety minutes, four or five times a night, and produces our richest dreams. Although I could successfully induce the dreams in the first REM period of the night, the procedure was most effective during the early morning—in the last stages of REM sleep, when dreams are copious—and after awakening from a previous dream.

Interestingly, certain waking activities during the hours of sleep have been claimed to stimulate lucid dreaming. Garfield, for example, found that in her case, "sexual intercourse during the middle of the night was often followed by a lucid dream" if she returned to sleep. Gregory Scott Sparrow, a counselor in Virginia Beach, reports having lucid dreams when he goes to sleep after meditating early in the morning. Others have told of having the dreams after reading or writing early in the morning.

The diversity of these stimuli (all of which were confirmed by my own experience) suggests it is not the particular behavior that is important but the *wakefulness* required for it.

We can probably further refine techniques for training people to dream lucidly. So far, MILD has not been tested in a formal lab setting; only three other lucid dreamers besides myself have reported using it successfully. Because it is based on a universal cognitive skill, though, I believe MILD will prove to be generally useful.

But other approaches might be profitably explored. One is the use of hypnosis. On three occasions I was hypnotized and given a posthypnotic suggestion to have a lucid dream; after going to sleep, I did indeed have such a dream two out of the three times.

Another possible method of stimulating lucid dreams might be to provide lab subjects with an external cue while they are sleeping. Other investigators have found that subjects hearing tape recordings of their own voices during REM sleep have dreams that are more assertive, active, and independent. While sleeping in the lab, I had a tape recording of my voice played during REM periods, reciting, "Stephen, you're dreaming." Both times I incorporated the sentence into dreams that I was having and became lucid, but on each occasion I awoke almost immediately.

Although many people report being able to dream lucidly, how can we prove empirically that they achieve a kind of consciousness during those dreams? In the absence of experimental data, contemporary dream researchers have questioned whether these experiences occur during sleep or during brief periods of hallucinatory wakefulness. Further, if lucid dreamers really are asleep, how can we arrange for them to signal the laboratory researcher when they are having the dreams?

We know that actions in dreams sometimes have shown good correlations with polygraphically recorded eye movements and muscle activity. For example, if a dog is chasing a ball down the street in a dream, the dreamer's eyes have been observed to move rapidly, as if he were following the action. Similarly, body movements in dreams have been known to be accompanied by electrical changes in the muscles of the dreamer. Thus, it seems plausible that lab subjects might be able to signal by carrying out particular dream actions that have observable correlates.

Previous experiments have shown that sleeping subjects are sometimes able to produce behavioral responses while dreaming. One of the most recent studies was done by Rosalind Cartwright at Rush University and Judith Brown, one of her students, who instructed groups of subjects to press microswitches if they began to dream during sleep; the researchers found that when these subjects were awakened, they were more likely to remember dreaming if they had pressed the switches.

However, since according to Cartwright the subjects were not conscious of making the responses, these studies do not provide evidence of voluntary action (and thus reflective consciousness) during sleep.

In our study at the Stanford Sleep Center, I was one of four subjects claiming proficiency as lucid dreamers who were studied for a total of 27 nights. We were all hooked up each night to standard apparatus that records eye movements, brain waves, and muscle tension in the chin as well as the wrists (for signaling). The four of us—two men and two women—attempted to follow a prearranged procedure of signaling whenever we became aware we were dreaming. A variety of signals were used, generally consisting of a pattern of upward eye movements and left and right fist clenches. Although we were allowed to perform each of the prearranged signals when the machinery was being calibrated, we did not otherwise practice while awake.

After each lucid dream we were to awaken and make a detailed report. In the course of the study, 27 lucid dreams were reported subsequent to awakening from various stages of sleep. The four of us reported signaling during 22 of the dreams. After each night's recording, the reports mentioning signals were submitted, along with the respective polysomnograms, to a judge *who was not informed of the times of the reports.* (The judge was experienced in scoring polygraph records but had no association with the experimentators.)

In 16 cases, the judge was able to select the appropriate 30-second periods on the basis of a correspondence between reported and observed signals. But what might account for the judge's lack of success in blind-matching 6 of the 22 instances of signaling? We inspected the recordings that immediately preceded each of those signals and found that in most cases, the signals were not strong enough to rise above the level of background "noise"—random activity of the muscles—in the recordings. However, the judge identified no signals from the recordings that had not, in fact, been reported by the four subjects.

The most complex signal, which I performed successfully on two occasions, consisted of a single upward eye movement, followed by a series of left (L) and right (R) dream fist clenches, in the order LLL, LRLL. This sequence is equivalent to my initials in Morse code (LLL being three dots, or S; and LRLL being a dot-dash-dot-dot sequence, or L).

Were the subjects really asleep when the signals were sent? If the criterion of being awake is whether the person perceives the external world, then the subjects were not, in fact, awake. Although we knew we were in the laboratory, that knowledge was a matter of memory, not perception; upon awakening, all four of us reported having been totally in the dream world and not in sensory contact with the laboratory environment in which we slept.

Was it possible that we were really awake but just not paying attention to the environment (as, for example, when a person is reading or absorbed in daydreaming)? All four of us tended to report that we were conscious of the *absence* of sensory input from the external world. These subjective accounts are, moreover, corroborated by the physiological measures.

The study suggests that under certain circumstances, dream cognition during REM sleep can be much more reflective and rational than was previously assumed. If further experiments confirm that it is indeed possible for lucid dreamers to intentionally signal while they dream, we may soon have a technique for exploring the timing, sequences, and content of dreams with first-hand data from within the dreamer's world itself.

In lucid dreams, the realization that one is dreaming may either be gradual or relatively sudden. In the following dream, consciousness comes slowly, under prodding by one of the characters: "I am crossing a bridge over an abyss. When I look into the depths I am afraid to continue. My companion, behind me, says, 'You know, you don't *have* to go this way. You can go back the way you came,' and he points down an immense distance. But then it occurs to me that if I became lucid I would not need to fear the height. As I realize that I *am* dreaming, I'm able to master my fear—I cross the bridge and awaken."

What happens in lucid dreams has real significance for the dreamer. Though the events that appear to take place in dreams are illusory, our *feelings* in response to dream content are real. So when we are fearful in a dream and realize that it is a dream, the fear doesn't vanish automatically. We still have to deal with it; were it not so, lucid dreams would have no useful connection with our waking lives.

We could compare the nonlucid dreamer to a small child terrified of the dark. The child really believes there are "monsters" lurking in the shadows. The lucid dreamer would perhaps be an older child—still afraid of the dark, yet no longer believing that there are monsters out there.

For the naïve dreamer, lucidity is most likely to be precipitated by anxiety. But it may also be brought on by embarrassment or delight—

or by some bizarre element that suddenly intrudes in the dream. As an example of an anomaly that clarifies the dream consciousness, here is another of my lucid dreams:

"I am walking down a street when I notice a new church—a mosque, in fact, so vast and impressive that I realize that I'm dreaming. As I approach it with great interest, its huge window blasts forth the theme from *Close Encounters of the Third Kind* in organ tones that shake the street beneath my feet. I am thrilled with the realization that it is a spaceship in disguise. Now fully lucid, with great expectation, I walk up the steps and into the blinding light of the door. But here memory fails."

Dreams have long held the reputation of being an important source of cultural, scientific, and artistic innovation. Is it not possible that the fantastic but unreliable creativity of the dreaming state could be brought under conscious control? In the following lucid dream, I seem to have played the piano much more creatively than in the waking state.

"I have not been doing too well in a high school mechanical drawing class. After it, I am sitting listening to a lecture in a large room filled with students. Somehow, as the teacher is saying something or demonstrating at the piano, I remember I'm dreaming. I get up and consider what to do. I walk up to the teacher at the piano as if I were an expected guest artist and sit down to play. I think of playing something out of a book of music, but I find that my vision is too weak. So, I improvise a fantasy in F-sharp minor, starting out prosaically enough but building up to a terrific climax. The truth of the music has, however, made most of the audience flee. But *I* feel satisfied as the dream fades with the last chord."

In contrast, the lucid dreamer's power to control dream content can sometimes become a problem—when, for instance, the person becomes just lucid enough to realize that he or she has the power to awaken or otherwise avoid an unpleasant dream experience instead of resolving the conflict. I became aware of this problem in myself in an early lucid dream:

"I am escaping down the side of a skyscraper, climbing, like a lizard, when I realize that I'm dreaming and can fly away. As I do so, the dream fades into a scene in which [a certain teacher] comments on my dream: 'It was good that Stephen realized he was dreaming and could fly, but too bad that he failed to see that since it was a dream, there was no need to escape.' "

There is an important issue that we have so far neglected to raise—the symbolic significance of lucid dreams. What does it mean to dream while knowing we are dreaming?

We may generalize from what Freud said of Hervey de Saint-Denys, a famous lucid dreamer of the nineteenth century: "It seems as though in [the lucid dreamer's] case the wish to sleep [has] given way to another . . . wish, namely to observe his dreams and enjoy them." And why not! Dreams could be the magic theater of all possibilities and a workshop of creativity and growth. Yet too often we use them to play out repetitious melodramas and confine ourselves by habit to a prison of self-limitation. Lucid dreaming presents a way out of this sleep within our sleep, allowing us to take responsibility for dream and waking lives that we have created.

But there is more significance to lucid dreaming than that. If you were asked, "Are you awake *now*?" you would doubtless reply, "Certainly." However, feeling certain that we are awake provides no guarantee that we *are* awake. When Samuel Johnson kicked a stone as if to say "We *know* what's real," he was expressing this sense of certainty. Yet Johnson could have been dreaming he kicked a stone and felt the same. The illusory sense of certainty about the completeness and coherence of our lives leads us to what William James described as a "premature closing of our accounts with reality."

Finally, in my opinion, the real significance of lucid dreams is that they guide us to higher levels of consciousness, for they suggest what it would be like to discover that we are not yet fully awake. Consider the following analogy: As the state of ordinary dreaming is to lucid dreaming, so the ordinary waking state is to the fully awakened state. Taken in this sense, the lucid dreamer's wish might be to transcend his or her level of limited awareness.

The lucid dreamer does not wish to leave the dream world by awakening but rather, to awaken within the dream itself. A slogan suggests itself: "Be *in* the dream but not *of* it."

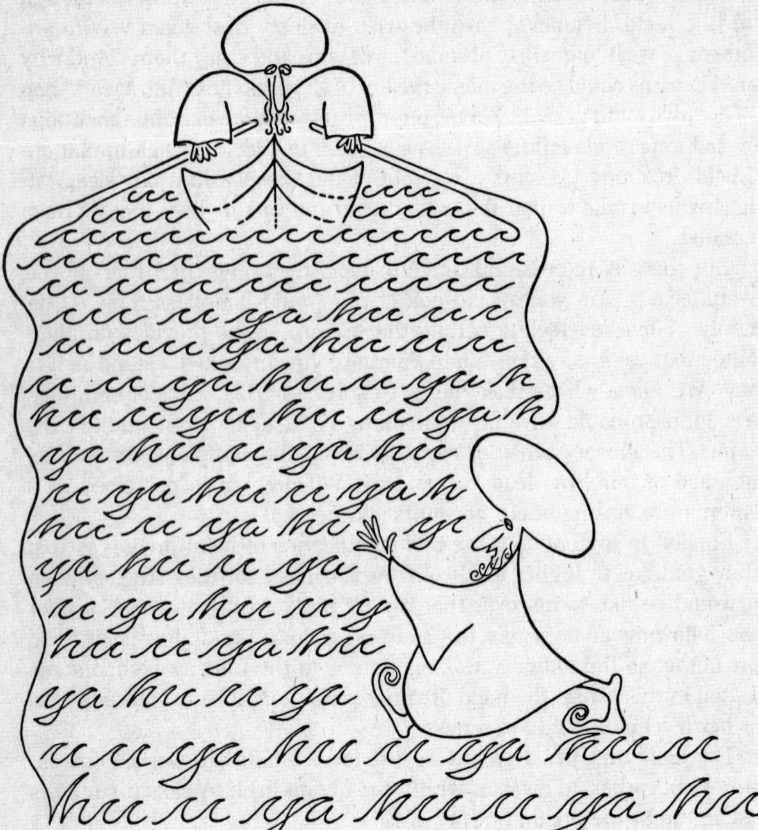

7

The Organized Systems: Changing Consciousness

The Man Who Walked on Water

A conventionally minded dervish, from an austerely pious school, was walking one day along a river bank. He was absorbed in concentration on moralistic and scholastic problems, for this was the form which Sufi teaching had taken in the community to which he belonged. He equated emotional religion with the search for ultimate Truth.

Suddenly his thoughts were interrupted by a loud shout: Someone was repeating the dervish call. "There is no point in that," he said to himself, "because the man is mispronouncing the syllables. Instead of intoning YA HU, he is saying U YA HU."

Then he realized that he had a duty, as a more careful student, to correct this unfortunate person, who might have no opportunity to be rightly guided, and was therefore probably only doing his best to attune himself to the idea behind the sounds.

So he hired a boat, and made his way to the island in midstream from which the sound appeared to come. There he found a man sitting in a reed hut, dressed in a dervish robe, moving in time to his own repetition of the initiatory phrase. "My friend," said the first dervish, "you are mispronouncing the phrase. It is incumbent on me to tell you this, because there is merit for him who gives and for him who takes advice. This is the way in which you speak it," and he told him.

"Thank you," said the other dervish humbly.

The first dervish entered his boat again, full of satisfaction at having done a good deed. After all, it was said that a man who could repeat the sacred *formula correctly could even walk on the waves: something that he had never seen, but had always hoped—for some reason—to be able to achieve.*

Now he could hear nothing from the reed hut, but he was sure that his lesson had been well taken. Then he heard a faltering U YA as the second dervish started to repeat the phrase in his old way.

While the first dervish was thinking about this, reflecting on the perversity of humanity and its persistence in error, he suddenly saw a strange sight. From the island, the other dervish was coming toward him, walking on the surface of the water.

Amazed, he stopped rowing. The second dervish walked up to him, and said, "Brother, I am sorry to trouble you, but I have come out to ask you again the standard method of making the repetition you were telling me, because I find it difficult to remember it."

Those who are intrigued by questions about the mind, consciousness, or evolution often become psychologists, philosophers, physicians, or psychiatrists. In the cultures of the Middle and Far East, those similarly intrigued by consciousness and the questions that surround it have generally entered the relevant disciplines of their society, such as Sufism. Until quite recently, the culture of the West has lacked the basic premises that could allow us to appreciate the intent and application of these kinds of psychologies, as the rugseller could not comprehend the numbers above 100.

An impersonal scientific approach, with emphasis on logic and analysis, makes it difficult for most of us even to conceive of a psychology that could be based on the existence of another mode of thought. But our normal, stable consciousness is a somewhat arbitrary personal construction. Although this construction has been a success, it is not the only way in which an external "reality" can be approached. How can anyone be thought to walk on water?

Consciousness changes through the day, is radically different at night, and can be altered quite easily in content and mode. It should not be too surprising, then, that another major mode of consciousness can appear, in each of us at times, and could be the basis for a different cultural approach to external reality. It is a mode of consciousness that is arational, predominantly spatial rather than temporal, and receptive as opposed to active, and it is this "mode of experience" that is predominantly cultivated within the esoteric traditions.

Since the unusual experiences and frames of mind that are often cultivated (and discussed in this chapter) are, by their very mode of operation, not readily accessible to causal explanation or even to linguistic exploration, many psychologists and other students of the mind have been tempted to ignore them or even to deny their existence. These traditional psychologies have been relegated to the "esoteric," or even to the "occult," the realm of the mysterious—the word most often employed is *mysticism*.

One meaning of *esoteric* is "deeply hidden, inaccessible, needing special training." There is, of course, much esotericism in modern science as well. In the past century, many scholars and researchers have become exceedingly specialized, devoting their careers to the exploration of "one approach to a part of a part of a problem." Most psychologists can no longer be fully conversant with all the research currently in the field, since it includes everything from electrochemical analyses of single cells on the retina to demographic analyses of voting patterns.

Inaccessibility, difficulty, and an elitist "professionalism" encrust the traditional psychologies as well as the modern. In each area of inquiry, a certain parochialism has tended to creep in. A scientific psychologist may be interested in the relationship of consciousness to the brain and may become an electroencephalographer, one who measures the tiny voltages that appear at the scalp and attempts to relate these signs to states of consciousness. In time, his vision may narrow to the complex problems of analysis of the EEG, and his interest may become focused on technique rather than content. A similar narrowing of vision has occurred in psychology as a discipline since the advent of behaviorism.

In the traditional psychologies, one group may find that a certain technique works well in a given situation, be it relaxation, concentration, or movement. Its members may tend to apply the technique in situations or with people for whom it is inappropriate. Because the technique works for them, they come to believe that it *ought* to work for everyone at all times. The technique becomes the end and may become an obsession.

Those who are involved in using such a technique—whether it is a particular meditation technique, a certain breathing exercise, or a training procedure—can become fixated and restricted to what the technique can offer. The adherents may set up schools to teach the "sacred" ritual, forgetting that each technique has its relevance only for a certain community at a certain time.

Instead of focusing on knowledge or human development, people often become mere adherents of an organization and do not experience the benefits of the technique. Other difficulties exist: The virtue of humility is often taken as the "end point" in the esoteric traditions and may even become a moral imperative, but this personal characteristic is to be taken not as an end in itself, but as a *technique*. "It enables a person to function in a certain manner." Similarly, specific diets developed for a certain community at one stage may be promulgated across cultures and epochs—the style may remain but the original context is lost, and the diet remains as an empty ritual. Dress, other exercises such as postures and dance can also follow this process.

The negative aspects of meditation can become overimportant. Indulgence in these exercises may lead to permanent withdrawal from life, regression from and a devaluation of intellectuality. It is certainly true that, devoid of a proper context, meditation can and has become an empty technique, food for the literal-minded who insist on the "proper" procedure but have forgotten its purpose. And yet it is the attitude and *attention* of the meditator that is important, rather than the specific form of the practice, as is emphasized in the story that begins this chapter.

As can happen with any scientific procedure that persists for too long, the original application and intent of the esoteric technique may become lost, although the surface appearance of the enterprise is well maintained. Religious organizations may construct elaborate cathedrals and design robes, just as scientists may well develop elaborate equipment and professional journals, but all too often the enterprise may be limited to a propagation of the means, with the original objective forgotten.

Within either the scientific or esoteric traditions, this sort of parochialism can lead to a disdain for those who employ another procedure, theory, or technique in an attempt to reach the same end. The very word *academic* has come to mean a distinction without significance. Within the esoteric traditions, religious arguments mirror the process. A small stylistic difference in a "sacred" prayer or a meditation may cause a schism that leads to lasting and sometimes violent disagreements. It has even been the cause of major wars.

The disdain is often greater between members of the two psychologies. Many Westerners see those of the Orient as following a path of self-indulgence, performing useless and ridiculous rituals and withdrawing from life while many starve around them. From the adherents of mysticism often come hysterical attacks on their idea of "materialism" and on the "world" of Western man as an "illusion."

On the one hand, many cultures seem unable to feed, clothe, and house their people adequately. They sometimes lack a full measure of the skills needed to organize and coordinate effort. The underdevelopment and training of a causal mode of analysis contributes to these problems. On the other hand, the development of a hyperanalytic, "rational" science, unchecked by a comprehensive understanding born of intuition, can develop into the destruction of all on the planet. This lack of an overall framework or perspective can lead to a certain sterility and irrelevance in the content of scientific inquiry. At worst, science can become the pursuit of technology for its own sake, the performance of experiments simply because they *can* be performed, or the building of a new highway simply because it *can* be built. In both cases, the imbalance contributes somewhat to major cultural problems.

For Western students of psychology and science, it is time to begin a new synthesis, to absorb some of the concepts and ideas of the traditional psychologies into modern psychological terms, to retain a lost balance. To do this, we must extend the conceptions of modern science, extend our concept of what is possible for man.

It is difficult for us to assume the correct viewpoint; the superheated and explosive economic, social, and scientific growth of the past two generations has left many who have grown up in this era convinced that a world without material limits is the norm. It has, for many, been their only experience of the world. The ideal of a perpetual and limitless expansion has shaped our marketplace, economic planning, and social life, and they inform the background of science and the humanities. Our politicians conventionally promise as much as is possible in the relief of the constancies of our condition; our scientific endeavor is unchecked by a traditional perspective; and our culture is the best-educated, wealthiest in history, and one of the most spiritually illiterate.

In an era devoted primarily to decreasing death rates, improving living conditions, and developing science, there is little time left for other considerations. Yet, in spite of this progress in our material welfare and health, we do not often note that the death rate is still 100 percent.

But there will be an end to the current "one-time" bonanza of growth and development, sooner or later; we are at a transition point. The limitless material progress, although certainly edifying to those who have it, is at a point of no real increase; we have reached the limits of our oil, and many of our natural resources are beginning to peter out. Our ideas of success, set up by the early postwar years, are beginning to fade a bit; we face blowing up the earth, we face overpopulating it.

In many areas people are beginning to feel that we have left *something* (without knowing what) out of our cultural upbringing, out of our science, medicine, education, and personal development. An alternative, more comprehensive and more secure approach is needed. Perhaps we base too many plans on the assumption of social and material progress, an assumption rooted in the seemingly limitless growth of the past two generations.

Scientists and humanist scholars are men and women of the times and share both the benefits of our culture's developments and the blindness of our collective shortsight. Their blindness and distortions render many of our otherwise most competent and educated people unequipped to judge ideas and developments in personal knowledge. Even those who are most interested often treat personal development as a less valuable side of themselves. Ideas in this area might seem "too old," associated too much with an old-fashioned, degenerated religious mysticism.

There is a large group of productive men and women who might draw from and contribute to an extended understanding of human nature, closed off from it by the strengths of their cultural training—and a second group all too eager to be told that "life is an illusion" and to join up here and climb aboard the next Kosmik Union Special, flying saucer, or Guru-of-the-Month Club.

An interested observer of the middle ground is in for some considerable discomfort, since those actively pursuing several interesting ideas have been drawn a bit over the edge. Parapsychology, to the receptive mind, is an area of research that is at least worth some serious, sober, and open-minded scientific investigation. However, one sometimes finds conversations with investigators sliding from a discussion of a single experiment to the Bermuda Triangle, unidentified flying objects, oddball encounters, or massage techniques.

People seeking "growth" find their needs for personal knowledge blunted and diverted to successful and rich institutions, with massage, sexual athletics, investment schemes, parties, incomprehensible doctrines such as those of Gurdjieff, Kahunism (a flying-saucer cult), "yoga tag," or simpleminded meditation offered as a substitute for transcendence. Such "growth centers," I fear, are to be understood more in the sense of "growth stocks" and childish self-indulgence than as anything seriously concerned with human development.

While these systems and centers might be thought to be sent to try us, and to prey on misunderstandings, in truth *it is difficult to find the change-points in human consciousness*. Many that have been tried are the result of guesswork and not a thorough analysis of what *needs* to be changed, rather than what might be changed.

For instance, many of the classical "mystical" techniques work by going against bodily desires and needs. Why? The answer lies in the nature of the controls on consciousness and our mental system—as we have seen, our consciousness must "mind" all the functions of the body. This is probably what has been meant, in more archaic terminology, that consciousness is encased in a "coil of flesh." Thus many of the attempts to "break the bounds" of human consciousness do so by trying to break the controlling links to the body. This is the basis of the almost uncountable mystical attempts to rid us of sensual or bodily desires.

For centuries, people have tried to "mortify the flesh": to free the brain from the bodily restraints on its operation. It has been done by thousands of methods—by flagellation, torture, vision walks, fasts, lotus positions, sitting on nails, denial or denigration of sexuality, power, sensuality, food, or almost anything nice!

There have countless regimes designed, in their idealistic and well-meaning way: monasteries that feature a release from all "worldly" desires, often regimes that force a restriction of diet and stimulation, all for the purpose of "freeing the conscious mind" to go elsewhere. It is indeed unfortunate that so many have had to suffer for so long, often for so little.

The systems that develop consciousness at their best, do serve to hasten the process of decentration, of awareness of a greater range of influence on us, of one's real role in life. But most of the time, their original goal becomes clouded in the search for a disconnected "higher awareness" somewhere, out there, in the wilds of experience.

The Traditional Psychologies:
Some General Remarks

Any written account of these psychologies is limited. We *can* learn from such an account while granting that it may not be complete, just as a written description of ski lifts, bindings, equipment, and intermediate ski techniques does not substitute for the experience of skiing down the slope.

One distinguishing feature of the traditional psychologies is their practicality, almost "applied psychology." These disciplines cover many aspects of life that our Western educational process often omits—*how* to breathe, *how* to care for the body, *how* to master bodily functions usually considered "involuntary." These esoteric traditions approach psychology as a practical, personal discipline and emphasize techniques that effect alterations in body states and in consciousness to obtain knowledge other than, but additional to, the intellectual.

In esoteric traditions, human life is considered one part of a larger whole, reciprocally influencing and being influenced by the "environment," as in the story "Moment in Time," which begins chapter 5. The concept of the environment in these esoteric psychologies is also much more inclusive than the Western one. It includes the importance of subtle geophysical forces, for example, the rhythmic changes that daily occur on earth, the light-dark cycle, internal and external biological rhythms, and the effects of microclimatic conditions, such as the ionization of the air. Until quite recently, these forces have not been included within the Western scientific world view.

If we can keep a wary eye on the excesses of both types of psychology, we may achieve a synthesis of the highest elements in both types, rather than of their drawbacks.

Meditation Exercises

In attempting to understand meditation, the interested student immediately discovers a bizarre and seemingly unconnected variety of techniques. Turkish dervishes spin in a circle; Buddhists concentrate on breath; yogis may gaze at a mandala or at a vase and others contemplate a meaningless phrase, such as "Show me your face before your father and mother met." What do these diverse exercises have in common in their manner of operation and in the experiences that they make possible?

Several aspects of meditation are even more confusing to the interested psychologist. What could be a state of "no mind" or of "mysterious darkness"?

People meditate to change consciousness, to bring about what is often called a mystic experience. But how do people describe this experience, and how do the meditation techniques bring it about? Is there any way that these techniques and these experiences can be integrated with a contemporary knowledge of the psychology of consciousness? What relevance do the techniques and the experiences have to contemporary psychology and to individuals?

Meditation is among the most common of the techniques of the traditional psychologies. Such techniques have been employed in almost every culture, from that of ancient Egypt to that of the contemporary Eskimo.

But remember "The Man Who Walked on Water"—these techniques are not what they seem, and the relationship between our mental attitude and what we can accomplish may surprise us!

There have been simple misinterpretations. Meditation is often considered to be a form of directed thinking, as when we say "I'll meditate on that," meaning, "I'll think about it, consider it, and come to a conclusion." If meditation is considered an exercise in reason or problem solving, then some of the statements and claims of its Indian and Japanese practitioners seem incomprehensible. But the exercises of meditation do not involve reason, and they cannot be understood by means of ordinary logic alone. They are, rather, techniques designed to cultivate a certain mode of operation of the nervous system, at a certain time, within a certain context. The mode of operation is hoped to be one beyond the ordinary biased consciousness. *This* is the use of "thinking of nothing."

A story in Philip Kapleau's *The Three Pillars of Zen* provides us with a useful point at which to begin a psychological consideration of the practices of meditation.

The importance of single-mindedness, of bare attention, is illustrated in the following anecdote:

One day a man of the people said to the Zen master Ikkyu: "Master, will you please write for me some maxims of the highest wisdom?"

Ikkyu immediately took his brush and wrote the word "Attention."

"Is that all?" asked the man. "Will you not add something more?"

Ikkyu then wrote twice running: "Attention. Attention."

"Well," remarked the man rather irritably, "I really don't see much depth or subtlety in what you have just written."

Then Ikkyu wrote the same word three times running: "Attention. Attention. Attention."

Half angered, the man demanded: "What does that word Attention mean anyway?"

And Ikkyu answered, gently: "Attention means attention."

Meditation produces an alteration in consciousness—a shift away from the active, outward-oriented mode toward a receptive and quiescent mode, and, often, a shift from an external focus of attention to an internal one. If this alteration is isolated from the context needed to support it (as when Westerners try meditating), it can be meaningless, or even disruptive. But as a first step in many of the traditional psychologies, meditation is regarded as an extremely important preparation for a more comprehensive personal knowledge. For many, it may also demonstrate that ordinary consciousness is a personal construction and can be extended to a new mode of operation.

Meditation is a technique for turning down the "brilliance" of the conscious thought of the day, so that more subtle sources of information can be perceived. It constitutes a deliberate attempt to separate oneself for a short period from the flow of daily life and to "turn off" the active mode of normal consciousness in order to enter the complementary mode of "darkness" and receptivity.

Since reliable information about the various forms of meditation has so far been rather hard to come by in the Western world, we should perhaps first set the background and review some of the general similarities of meditation exercises. Most involve separating the practitioner from daily, ongoing activities. He or she usually sits alone or with a small group in a special place (perhaps constructed) in a naturally isolated area, sometimes near a waterfall.

Generally, the meditator attempts to keep all external sources of stimulation to a minimum to avoid being distracted from the object of meditation. This isolation is felt especially necessary in modern cities, where random sounds, noises, and human voices can be distracting. In most forms of yoga and Zen, there is emphasis on the lotus position, in order to keep body movements to a minimum and therefore out of awareness during the meditation period. The straight back is said to lessen drowsiness in the reduced-stimulation setting.

Instructions for most beginning meditation exercises are similar: Attend closely and continuously to the meditation object (say, a vase). This exercise is more difficult than it sounds; most beginners lose awareness of the meditation object quite often. Each time one notices that awareness has shifted away from the object of meditation, one must return his or her attention to it. Each session of meditation lasts about half an hour and is practiced twice a day: in the morning before the day's major work and in the evening. As progress is made, more and more complicated exercises are usually given.

In terms of the psychology of consciousness, there are two general varieties of meditation: those exercises that involve restriction of awareness, focusing of attention on the object of meditation or on the repetition of a word (*concentrative meditation*); and those that involve a deliberate attempt to "open up" awareness of the external environment.

Concentrative Meditation

No matter the specific form or technique, the essence of meditation is the attempt to restrict awareness to a single unchanging source of stimulation for a definite period of time. In many traditions, the successful achievement of this is termed *one-pointedness of mind*.

If the exercise involves vision, the meditator gazes at the object of meditation continuously. If the meditation is auditory, the sound, chant, or prayer is repeated either aloud or silently. If the meditation consists in physical movement, the movement is continuously repeated. In all cases, awareness is focused on the movement or the visual object or the sound.

In Zen, as a first exercise the student is instructed to count his breaths from one to ten and repeat it. When the count is lost, as it will be by beginners, the instructions are that the count should be returned to one and begun again. After he is able to concentrate completely on his breaths, the student then begins a more advanced exercise and focuses attention on the *process* of breathing itself. He thinks about nothing but the movement of the air within, the air reaching his nose, going down into the lungs, remaining in the lungs, and finally going out again. This is a convenient way to begin meditating, since breathing is a rhythmic activity that continues whether we will it or not.

In *What the Buddha Taught*, Walpola Rahula gives these instructions:

You breathe in and out all day and night, but you are never mindful of it, you never for a second concentrate your mind on it. Now you are going to do just this. Breathe in and out as usual, without any effort or strain. Now, bring your mind to concentrate on your breathing-in and breathing-out, let your mind watch and observe your breathing in and out; let your mind be aware and vigilant of your breathing in and out. When you breathe, you sometimes take deep breaths, sometimes not. This does not matter at all. Breathe normally and naturally. The only thing is that when you take deep breaths you should be aware of its movements and changes. Forget all other things, your surroundings, your environment; do not raise your eyes and look at anything. Try to do this for five or ten minutes.

At the beginning, you will find it extremely difficult to bring your mind to concentrate on your breathing. You will be astonished how your mind runs away. It does not stay. You begin to think of various things. You hear sounds outside. Your mind is disturbed and distracted. You may be dismayed and disappointed. But if you continue to practice this exercise twice a day, morning and evening, for about five or ten minutes at a time, you will gradually, by and by, begin to concentrate your mind on your breathing. After a certain period you will experience just that split second when your mind is fully concentrated on your breathing, when you will not hear even sounds nearby, when no external world exists for you.

As the student of Rinzai Zen progresses, he or she learns to remain motionless and to sit in the lotus position. As one learns to maintain awareness of the breath successfully, one is given a more advanced meditation exercise: a riddle or a paradox, called a *koan*, to meditate on.

To many commentators, at least to those who try to fit it into a linear framework, the koan has been the subject of much misunderstanding and confusion. The question-and-answer routine has seemed to be one for the Marx Brothers. The "question" may be, "Show me your face before your mother and father met." The "answer" may be the student's slapping the questioner in the face. The master "asks" the student, "Move that boat on the lake right now with your mind"; the student stands up, runs over, and hits his head against the gong, turns a somersault, and lands in front of the master, "fully enlightened."

Since the student "answered" successfully, it is quite clear that the "answers" to the koan are not to be considered logically—as set answers to a rational problem that can be solved by the usual manner of thinking through various rational alternatives and choosing one. In fact, the lack of a rational solution is intended to demonstrate to the practitioner that the solutions in this new mode of experience are not those of the intellect. There is no text in which the meaning of life is to be found.

We might instead consider the koan exercise in the terms of the psychology of consciousness. In these terms, the koan is an extreme and compelling method of forcing intense concentration on one single thought. This is an early koan exercise:

> In all seriousness, a monk asked Joshu, "Has the dog Buddha nature or not?" Joshu retorted, "Mu!"

This koan is to be taken not verbally and logically, not as something to be worked through like a problem, but as an extreme exercise in concentration. This is confirmed in instructions given in the lectures of a contemporary Zen master, Yasutani Roshi:

> You must concentrate day and night, questioning yourself about Mu through every one of your 360 bones and 84,000 pores . . . what this refers to is your entire being. Let all of you become one mass of doubt and questioning. Concentrate on and penetrate fully into Mu. To penetrate into Mu means to achieve absolute unity with it. How can you achieve this unity? By holding to Mu tenaciously day and night! Do not separate yourself from it under any circumstances! Focus your mind on it constantly. Do not construe Mu as nothingness and do not conceive it in terms of existence or nonexistence. You must not, in other words, think of Mu as a problem involving the existence or nonexistence of Buddha-nature. Then what do you do? You stop speculating and concentrate wholly on Mu—just Mu!

Later Koan exercises involve other unanswerable questions, such as the ever-popular "What is the sound of one hand clapping?" and "What is the size of the real you?" A contemporary (Los Angeles) Zen master gives, "How can I attain enlightenment by driving on the freeway?"

Because no verbal-logical answer to the question can be found, the koan becomes a useful and demanding focus of attention over a very long period of time. The koan becomes a meditation object, day and night, a constant and compelling focusing of awareness on a single source. The lack of a rational, logical solution forces the student to go through and to discard all verbal associations, all thoughts, all solutions usually evoked by a question. He is then forced by the nature of the question itself to approach the condition known as *one-pointedness*— concentrating solely on one thing: the unanswerable koan. It is an attempt actively to destructure the ordinary lineal mode of consciousness.

The use of the koan is strongest in the Rinzai school of Zen, which emphasizes a sudden alteration of awareness *(satori)* brought about by this extreme concentration on one point over a long period of time while under stress.

Yoga

The practices of yoga are much more varied than those of Zen. Concentrative meditation in yoga is only one part of a totality of activity, each part of which contributes to alterations of consciousness. Many yoga practitioners devote their effort to attempts to regulate consciously many basic "involuntary" physiological processes—blood flow, heart rate, digestive and muscular activity, breathing, and so on. There are many popular reports of yoga masters being buried alive for long periods of time, stopping their blood flow, walking barefoot on hot coals. In a laboratory study, Anand and his associates found that some yogis could reduce oxygen consumption to levels far below normal.

A common form of yogic meditation practice involves the use of *mantra*. Mantra are often words of significance, such as names of the deity, but for the psychology of consciousness the important element is that the technique uses a word as the focus of awareness, just as the first Zen exercises make use of breathing.

The instructions are to repeat the mantram over and over again, either aloud or silently. The mantram is to be kept in awareness to the exclusion of all else; just as in the Zen breathing exercise, when awareness lapses from the object of meditation, in this case the mantram, the attention is to be returned to it. Mantra are sonorous, flowing words, which repeat easily. An example is *Om*. This mantram is chanted aloud in groups or used individually in silent or voiced meditation. Another mantram is *Om mani padme hum,* a smooth, mellifluous chant. Similar mantra have analogous sounds such as *Ayn* or *Hum,* somewhat similar in sound to *Mu* in the first Zen koan.

A form of mantra yoga, Transcendental Meditation, has become fairly well known in the West, especially in the United States. In this form of meditation, too, the practitioner is given a specific mantram and is instructed to repeat it silently over and over for about half an hour twice a day, in the morning and again in the evening. No special posture is required for the exercise; rather, one is instructed to assume a comfortable posture, such as sitting erect in a chair. The thoughts that arise during the meditation are considered to be of no significance, and as soon as one is aware that one is no longer focused on the mantra, attention is to be returned to it.

The specific mantra used in Transcendental Meditation are not given publicly, since the devotees of this technique claim that there are special effects of each word, in addition to the general effects of the concentration. But it can be noted here that these mantras are also mellifluous and smooth. The devotees of Transcendental Meditation also claim that this technique presents the essence of meditation in a form suitable for Westerners.

There is no doubt that mantra yoga, including Transcendental Meditation, is a very convenient form of a concentrative meditation; it is quite easy to produce and attend to a silent word, anywhere, at any time. Since no special posture is required, the arduous training for sitting in a lotus position is unnecessary. If the essential component of meditation involves concentration on an unchanging stimulus, then Transcendental Meditation has it, but of course it has a lot of other associated ideas as well!

Mandalas are used much like mantra. The practitioner focuses his gaze on the mandala and restricts his awareness to the visual input. Any stray thought, association, or feeling that arises is ignored; attention is withheld from the stray thought or association and returned to the mandala. Simple mandalas often employ a circular motif in which awareness is drawn to the center as one continues to contemplate, fixing the gaze more and more closely on the center.

Another visual meditation technique in yoga involves a "steady gaze" (*tratakam*) on external objects. External objects are used in meditation as a focus for a fixed point of concentration, rather than for their physical characteristics; so one can use a stone, a vase, a light, a candle, and so on.

The repetitive processes of the body, such as breathing and the beating of the heart, can serve as similar focuses for concentration in yoga. These techniques are described in Mishra's manual and in many others. Internally generated sounds (*nadam*) can also be focuses for meditation. The sounds used in meditation can be internal, imaginary, or natural. Often the yogi sits near a source of repetitive sound, such as a waterfall, wind source, or beehive, and simply listens and concentrates. When these repetitious, monotonous sounds are imagined, the technique becomes quite similar to the silent repetition of a mantra.

The creation of a meditation image can extend to visual meditation as well. Frederic Spiegelberg, in *Spiritual Practices of India*, describes the *Dharana*, or fixation of consciousness procedures, in the *Kasina* exercises:

> *The point of primary importance is that one* should really create such a meditation image to accompany him continuously; only as a secondary consideration does it matter what this particular image may be, that is, through which one of the Kasina exercises it has been produced. Instead of contemplating a disc of earth, for example, one can meditate on an evenly ploughed field seen from a distance.
>
> *Every image that remains permanently in one's consciousness and every enduring mood can be a help to this fixation of one's consciousness. As a matter of fact, every hallucination, every unappeasable hatred, every amorous attachment provides a certain power of concentration to him who cherishes it, and helps him direct the forces of his being towards a single goal.* This is of course more the case with the man who has achieved self-control and freedom from his passions, and who after having mastered his sense impulses succeeds in giving to his consciousness a definite turn of his own choosing . . . *Every activity is of equal value as a basis for a Dharana exercise.* [Emphasis added.]

Speigelberg provides the point of interest: Why would anyone bother with these meaningless exercises, when money can be made? Because most people's mental system is often uncontrolled and it is for the ultimate *control* of the mental operating system that all these exercises are done. All the fasting, prayer, renunciation are designed to defeat those well-developed schemata, designed for the purpose of survival. If "we" are running the system, rather than "them" (the desires), we may well be able to direct the mind to new directions, directions which are now called for in our survival as a race.

Religious and Mystical Experiences

When combined with other practices of traditional psychologies, meditation is intended to bring about a more "complete" consciousness. The full emergence of this experience is called the "mystical experience."

Upsets to Routine. A major precipitating event for many mystical experiences is a strong upset of normal routine: fasting; extreme physical exertion as in long-distance running; in more modern times, changes in jobs, in social situations, travel, and exposure to "shocks." It is in times of shocks and stresses that a person may be able to see himself for what he is, not what he hopes!

Deautomatization. One specific aim in both concentrative and opening-up meditation is to dismantle the automatic selectivity of ordinary awareness. One aim of the esoteric traditions is to remove "blindness," to awaken a fresh perception. The word *enlightenment* or *illumination* is often used for progress in these disciplines. The psychological term is *deautomatization,* an undoing of the normal automatization of consciousness.

The Mystical Experience. Many meditation and spiritual exercises result in what are called mystical or religious experiences. They have occurred in many cultures and religious disciplines.

In his classic *The Varieties of Religious Experience,* William James (1917) cites the analysis and description by a Canadian psychiatrist of a mystical experience, which James called "cosmic consciousness."

I was walking in a state of quiet, almost passive enjoyment, not actually thinking, but letting ideas, images, and emotions flow of themselves, as it were, through my mind. All at once, without warning of any kind, I found myself wrapped in a flame-colored cloud. For an instant I thought of fire, an immense conflagration somewhere close by in the great city; the next, I knew that the fire was within myself. Directly afterward there came upon me a sense of exultation, an immense joyousness accompanied or immediately followed by an intellectual illumination impossible to describe. Among other things, I did not merely come to believe but I saw that the universe is not composed of dead matter, but is, on the contrary, a living Presence; I became conscious in myself of eternal life. It was not a conviction that I would have eternal life, but a consciousness that I possessed eternal life then; I saw that all men are immortal; that the cosmic order is such that without any peradventure all things work together for the good of each and all; that the foundation principle of the world, of all the worlds, is what we call love, and that the happiness of each and all is in the long run absolutely certain. The vision lasted a few seconds and was gone; but the memory of it and the sense of the reality of what it taught has remained during the quarter of a century which has since elapsed. I knew that what the vision showed was true. I attained to a point of view from which I saw that it must be true. That view, that conviction, I may say that consciousness, has never, even during periods of the deepest depression, been lost.

James (1890) defines four characteristics of the mystical experience.

1. *Unity or oneness.* Experience becomes comprehensive rather than fragmented; relationships between things normally separate are seen.
2. *A sense of "realness."* The person has the sensation that the relations between things he or she experiences are closer to truth than ordinary experiences.
3. *Ineffability.* The experience is said to be impossible to communicate in ordinary words.
4. *Vividness and richness.* Events take on a glow of freshness and clarity not present in ordinary consciousness.

Conclusion: Meditation and the Relevance of "Consciousness Development"

The practice of meditation—whirling, chanting, concentrating on a non-sensical question, thinking or speaking a "sacred" prayer over and over, visualizing a cross, gazing at a vase—are not quite so exotic as some might wish; but neither are they exercises in reason or problem solving. They are exercises in attentional deployment, both those that focus on one stimulus and those that are intended to actively deautomatize ordinary consciousness.

The "mystic" experience brought about by concentrative meditation, deautomatization exercises, and other techniques is, then, a shift from the normal, analytic world containing separate, discrete objects and persons to a second mode, an experience of "unity" and holistic perception. This experience is outside the province of language and rationality, since it is a mode of simultaneity, but it is a complementary dimension of consciousness that adds to and can give comprehension to the ordered sequence of "normal" thought.

But why have people sought to develop this mode, and what value is there in a "mystic" experience? The answers to these questions are not easy. Many of the traditional replies are well known; yet some brief interpretation and comment might be useful.

First, the normal mental system cannot encompass many aspects of life that many people want to experience and understand. That these phenomena have been "ruled out" of much of Western scientific inquiry does not lessen the need that many now feel to explore these areas personally. Meditation is but one of very many attempts to develop consciousness in such a way that certain relational aspects of reality become accessible to the practitioner.

Second, the analytic mode, in which there is separation of objects, and of the self from others (which the theologian Buber has termed the I-it relationship), has proved useful in individual biological survival; yet concentration on this mode may have evolved to fit the conditions of life many thousands of years ago. The evolution of culture proceeds much more slowly than biological evolution; so the analytic mode may not be as all-important a criterion for our contemporary Western society as it once was, and we may even be said to be biologically obsolete in these terms. The awareness of this separation was a great advantage when survival threats were to the individual; for instance, one could locate and isolate an enemy animal and use it for food. This basic need for individual survival is no longer quite so basic for many in the West. Most of us now buy our food; we do not need to hunt for it. Few readers of this book are in any danger of imminent starvation.

The survival problems now facing us are *collective* rather than individual: They are problems of how to prevent a large nuclear war, pollution of the earth, overpopulation; how to relate and understand diverse and divergent ideas, doctrines, and people—all of which have constructed their own "reality." And note well that in these problems, an exclusive focus on individual consciousness and individual survival may work against, not for, a solution. A shift toward a comprehensive consciousness of the interconnectedness of life, toward a relinquishing of the "every man for himself" attitude inherent in our ordinary construction of consciousness, might enable us to take those "selfless" steps that could begin to solve our collective problems. Certainly our culture has too severely emphasized the development of only one way of organizing reality. Perhaps we can now begin to see that the complementary mode has survival value for our culture as a whole. (In a minor way, some recent cultural events can be seen in this light: I refer to the increasing awareness of the earth as one system that is part of the ecology movement and to interdisciplinary training and systems analysis, among others.)

DEAUTOMATIZATION
AND THE MYSTIC EXPERIENCE

Arthur J. Deikman

To study the mystic experience one must turn initially to material that appears unscientific, is couched in religious terms, and seems completely subjective. Yet these religious writings are data and not to be dismissed as something divorced from the reality with which psychological science is concerned. The following passage from *The Cloud of Unknowing,* a fourteenth-century religious treatise, described a procedure to be followed in order to attain an intuitive knowledge of God. Such an intuitive experience is called mystical because it is considered beyond the scope of language to convey. However, a careful reading will show that these instructions contain within their religious idiom psychological ideas pertinent to the study and understanding of a wide range of phenomena not necessarily connected with theological issues:

> Forget all the creatures that ever God made and the works of them, so that thy thought or thy desire be not directed or stretched to any of them, neither in general or in special. . . . At the first time when thou dost it, thou findst but a darkness and as it were a kind of unknowing, thou knowest not what, saving that thou feelst in thy will a naked intent unto God . . . thou mayest neither see him clearly by light of understanding in thy reason, nor feel him in sweetness of love in thy affection . . . if ever thou shalt see him or feel him as it may be here, it must always be in this cloud and in this darkness. . . . . Smite upon that thick cloud of unknowing with a sharp dart of longing love (Knowles, 1961, p. 77).

Specific questions are raised by this subjective account: What constitutes a state of consciousness whose content is not rational thought ("understanding in thy reason"), affective ("sweetness of love"), or sensate ("darkness," "cloud of unknowing")? By what means do both an active "forgetting" and an objectless "longing" bring about such a state? A comparison of this passage with others in the classical mystic literature indicates that the author is referring to the activities of renunciation and contemplative meditation. This paper will present a psychological model of the mystic experience based on the assumptions that meditation and renunciation are primary techniques for producing it, and that the process can be conceptualized as one of deautomatization . . . .

Basic Mystic Techniques

How is the mystic experience produced? To answer this question I will examine the two basic techniques involved in mystical exercises: contemplation and renunciation.

Contemplation is, ideally, a nonanalytic apprehension of an object or idea—nonanalytic because discursive thought is banished and the attempt is made to empty the mind of everything except the percept of the object in question. Thought is conceived of as an interference with the direct contact that yields essential knowledge through perception alone. The renunciation of worldly goals and pleasures, both physical and psychological, is an extension of the same principle of freeing oneself from distractions that interfere with the perception of higher realisms or more beautiful aspects of existence. The renunciation prescribed is most thorough and quite explicit in all texts. The passage that begins this paper instructs, "Forget all the creatures that ever God made . . . so that thy thought . . . be not directed . . . to any of them." In the Lankavatra Scripture one reads, "he must seek to annihilate all vagrant thoughts and notions belonging to the externality of things, and all ideas of individuality and generality, of suffering and impermanence, and cultivate the noblest ideas of egolessness and emptiness and imagelessness" (Goddard, 1938, p. 323). Meister Eckhart promises: "If we keep ourselves free from the things that are outside us, God will give us in exchange everything that is in heaven, . . . itself with all its powers" (Clark and Skinner, 1958, p. 104). In Hilton one reads, "There if you desire to discover your soul, withdraw your thoughts from outward and material things, forgetting if possible your own body and its five senses" (Hilton, 1953, p. 205). St. John calls for the explicit banishment of memory:

> Of all these forms and manners of knowledge the soul must strip and void itself, and it must strive to lose the imaginary apprehension of them, so that there may be left in it no kind of impression of knowledge, nor trace of aught soever, but rather the soul must remain barren and bare, as if these forms had never passed through it and in total oblivion and suspension. And this cannot happen unless the memory be annihilated as to all its forms, if it is to be united with God (St. John of the Cross, 1953, p. 227).

In most Western and Eastern mystic practice, renunciation also extends to the actual life situation of the mystic. Poverty, chastity, and the solitary way are regarded as essential to the attainment of mystic union. Zen Buddhism, however, sees the ordinary life as a proper vehicle for "satori" as long as the "worldly" passions and desires are given up, and with them the intellectual approach to experience. "When I am in my isness, thoroughly purged of all intellectual sediments, I have my freedom in its primary sense . . . free from intellectual complexities and moralistic attachments" (Suzuki, 1959, p. 19).

Instructions for performing contemplative meditation indicate that a very active effort is made to exclude outer and inner stimuli, to devalue and banish them, and at the same time to focus attention on the meditative object. In this active phase of contemplation the concentration of attention upon particular objects, ideas, physical movements, or breathing exercises is advised as an aid to diverting attention from its usual channels and restricting it to a monotonous focus.* Patanjali comments,

> Binding the mind-stuff to a place is fixed-attention. . . . Focusedness of the presented idea on that place is contemplation. . . . This same [contemplation] shining forth [in consciousness] as the intended object and nothing more, and, as it were, emptied of itself, is concentration. . . . The three in one are constraint. . . . Even these [three] are indirect aids to seedless [concentration] (Woods, 1914, pp. 203–208).

Elaborate instructions are found in Yoga for the selection of objects for contemplation and for the proper utilization of posture and breathing to create optimal conditions for concentration. Such techniques are not usually found in the Western religious literature except in the form of the injunction to keep the self oriented toward God and to fight the distractions which are seen as coming from the devil [*The Spiritual Exercises of St. Ignatius* (Puhl, 1962) is a possible exception].

The active phase of contemplative meditation is a preliminary to the stage of full contemplation, in which the subject is caught up and absorbed in a process he initiated but which now seems autonomous, requiring no effort. Instead, passivity—self-surrender—is called for, an open receptivity amidst the "darkness" resulting from the banishment of thoughts and sensations and the renunciation of goals and desires directed toward the world.

> When this active effort of mental concentration is successful, it is followed by a more passive, receptive state of samadhi in which the earnest disciple will enter into the blissful abode of noble wisdom (Goddard, 1938, p. 323).

> For if such a soul should desire to make any effort of its own with its interior faculties, this means that it will hinder and lose the blessings which . . . God is instilling into it and impressing upon it (Hilton, 1953, p. 380).

*Breathing exercises can also affect the carbon-dioxide content of the blood and thus alter the state of consciousness chemically.

It should not be forgotten that the techniques of contemplation and renunciation are exercised within the structure of some sort of theological schema. This schema is used to interpret and organize the experiences that occur. However, mere doctrine is usually not enough. The Eastern texts insist on the necessity for being guided by a guru (an experienced teacher), for safety's sake as well as in order to attain the spiritual goal. In Western religion, a "spiritual advisor" serves as a guide and teacher. The presence of a motivating and organizing conceptual structure and the support and encouragement of a teacher are undoubtedly important in helping a person to persist in the meditation exercises and to achieve the marked personality changes that can occur through success in this endeavor. Enduring personality change is made more likely by the emphasis on adapting behavior to the values and insights associated both with the doctrinal structure and with the stages of mystical experience.

How can one explain the phenomena and their relation to these techniques? Most explanations in the psychological and psychoanalytic literature have been general statements emphasizing a regression to the early infant-mother symbiotic relationship. These statements range from an extreme position, such as Alexander's (1931), where Buddhist training is described as withdrawal of libido from the world to be reinvested in the ego until an intra-uterine narcissism is achieved—"the pure narcissism of the sperm"—to the basic statements of Freud's (1961, XXI, 64–73) that "oceanic feeling" is a memory of a relatively undifferentiated infantile ego state. Lewin (1950, pp. 149–155) in particular has developed this concept. In recent years hypotheses have been advanced uniting the concepts of regression and of active adaptation. The works of Kris (1952, p. 302), Fingarette (1963), and Prince and Savage (1965) illustrate this approach to the mystic experience. This paper will attempt an explanation of mystic phenomena from a different point of view, that of attentional mechanisms in perception and cognition.

Deautomatization

In earlier studies of experimental meditation, I hypothesized that mystic phenomena were a consequence of a *deautomatization* of the psychological structures that organize, limit, select, and interpret perceptual stimuli. I suggested the hypotheses of sensory translation, reality transfer, and perceptual expansion to explain certain unusual perceptions of the meditation subjects (Deikman, 1966b). At this point I will try to present an integrated formulation that relates these concepts to the classical mystic techniques of renunciation and contemplation.

Deautomatization is a concept stemming from Hartmann's (1958, pp. 88–91) discussion of the automatization of motor behavior:

> In well-established achievements [motor apparatuses] function automatically: the integration of the somatic systems involved in the action is automatized, and so is the integration of the individual mental acts involved in it. With the increasing exercise of the action its intermediate steps disappear from consciousness . . . not only motor behavior but perception and thinking, too, show automatization. . . .
>
> It is obvious that automatization may have economic advantages, in saving attention cathexis in particular and simple cathexis of consciousness in general. . . . Here, as in most adaptation processes, we have a purposive provision for the average expectable range of tasks.

Gill and Brenman (1959, p. 178) developed the concept of deautomatization:

> Deautomatization is an undoing of the automatizations of apparatuses—both means and goal structures—directed toward the environment. Deautomatization is, as it were, a shake-up which can be followed by an advance or a retreat in the level of organization. . . . Some manipulation of the attention directed toward the functioning of an apparatus is necessary if it is to be deautomatized.

Thus, deautomatization may be conceptualized as the undoing of automatization, presumably by *reinvesting actions, and percepts with attention.*

The concept of psychological *structures* follows the definition by Rapaport and Gill (1959, pp. 157–158):

> *Structures are configurations of a low rate of change . . . within which, between which, and by means of which mental processes take place. . . . Structures are hierarchically ordered. . . .* This assumption . . . is significant because it is the foundation for the

psychoanalytic propositions concerning differentiation (whether resulting in discrete structures which are then co-ordinated, or in the increased internal articulation of structures), and because it implies that the quality of a process depends upon the level of the structural hierarchy on which it takes place.

The deautomatization of a structure may result in a shift to a structure lower in the hierarchy, rather than a complete cessation of the particular function involved.

Contemplative Meditation

In reflecting on this technique of contemplative meditation, one can see that it seems to constitute just such a manipulation of attention as is required to produce deautomatization. The percept receives intense attention while the use of attention for abstract categorization and thought is explicitly prohibited. Since automatization normally accomplishes the transfer of attention *from* a percept or action to abstract thought activity, the meditation procedure exerts a force in the reverse direction. Cognition is inhibited in favor of perception; the active intellectual style is replaced by a receptive perceptual mode.

Automatization is a hierarchically organized developmental process, so one would expect deautomatization to result in a shift toward a perceptual and cognitive organization characterized as "primitive," that is, an organization preceding the analytic, abstract, intellectual mode typical of present-day adult thought. The perceptual and cognitive functioning of children and of people of primitive cultures have been studied by Werner, who describes primitive imagery and thought as (a) relatively more vivid and sensuous, (b) syncretic, (c) physiognomic and animated, (d) dedifferentiated with respect to the distinctions between self and object and between objects, and (e) characterized by a dedifferentiation and fusion of sense modalities. In a statement based on studies of eidetic imagery in children as well as on broader studies of perceptual development, Werner (1957, p. 152) states:

The image . . . gradually changed in functional character. It became essentially subject to the exigencies of abstract thought. Once the image changes in function and becomes an instrument in reflective thought, its structure will also change. It is only through such structural change that the image can serve as an instrument of expression in abstract mental activity. This is why, of necessity, the sensuousness, fullness of detail, the color and vivacity of the image must fade.

Theoretically, deautomatization should reverse this development in the direction of primitive thought, and it is striking to note that the classical accounts of mystic experience emphasize the phenomenon of Unity. Unity can be viewed as a dedifferentiation that merges all boundaries until the self is no longer experienced as a separate object and customary perceptual and cognitive distinctions are no longer applicable. In this respect, the mystic literature is consistent with the deautomatization hypothesis. If one searches for evidence of changes in the mystic's experience of the external world, the classical literature is of less help, because the mystic's orientation is inward rather than outward and he tends to write about God rather than nature. However, in certain accounts of untrained-sensate experience there is evidence of a gain in sensory richness and vividness. James (1929, pp. 243–244), in describing the conversion experience, states: "A third peculiarity of the assurance state is the objective change which the world often appears to undergo, 'An appearance of newness beautifies every object.' " He quotes Billy Bray: "I shouted for joy, I praised God with my whole heart . . . I remember this, that everything looked new to me, the people, the fields, the cattle, the trees. I was like a new man in a new world." Another example, this one from a woman, "I pled for mercy and had a vivid realization of forgiveness and renewal of my nature. When rising from my knees I exclaimed, 'Old things have passed away, all things have become new.' It was like entering another world, a new state of existence. Natural objects were glorified. My spiritual vision was so clarified that I saw beauty in every material object in the universe." Again, "The appearance of everything was altered, there seemed to be as it were a calm, a sweet cast or appearance of divine glory in almost everything."

Such a change in a person's perception of the world has been called by Underhill (1955, p. 235), "clarity of vision, a heightening of physical perception," and she quotes Blake's phrase, "cleanse the doors of perception." It is hard to document this perceptual alteration because the autobiographical accounts that Underhill, James, and others cite are a blend of the mystic's spiritual feeling and his actual perception, with the result that the spiritual content dominates the description the mystic gives of the physical world. However, these accounts do suggest that a "new vision" takes place, colored by an inner exaltation. Their authors report perceiving a new brilliance to the world, of seeing everything as if for the first time, of noticing beauty which for the most part they may have previously passed by without seeing. Although such descriptions do not prove a change in sensory perception, they strongly imply it. These particular phenomena appear quite variable and are not mentioned in many mystic accounts. However, direct evidence was obtained on this point in the meditation experiments already cited (Deikman, 1963, 1966b). There, it was possible to ask questions and to analyze the subjects' reports to obtain information on their perceptual experiences. The phenomena the subjects reported fulfilled Werner's criteria completely, although the extent of change varied from one subject to the next. They described their reactions to the percept, a blue vase, as follows: (a) an increased vividness and richness of the percept—"more vivid," "luminous"; (b) animation in the vase, which seemed to move with a life of its own; (c) a marked decrease in self-object distinction, occurring in those subjects who continued longest in the experiments: "I really began to feel, you know, almost as though the blue and I were perhaps merging, or that vase and I were. . . . It was as though everything was sort of merging"; (d) syncretic thought and a fusing and alteration of normal perceptual modes: "I began to feel this light going back and forth," "When the vase changes shape I feel this in my body," "I'm still not sure, though, whether it's the motion in the rings or if it's the rings [concentric rings of light between the subject and the vase]. But in a certain way it is real . . . it's not real in the sense that you can see it, touch it, taste it, smell it or anything but it certainly is real in the sense that you can experience it happening." The perceptual and cognitive changes that did occur in the subjects were consistently in the direction of a more "primitive" organization.

Thus, the available evidence supports the hypothesis that a deautomatization is produced by contemplative meditation. One might be tempted to call this deautomatization a regression to the perceptual and cognitive state of the child or infant. However, such a concept rests on assumptions as to the child's experience of the world that cannot yet be verified. In an oft-quoted passage, Wordsworth (1904, p. 353) writes:

> There was a time when meadow, grove, and stream,
> The earth, and every common sight,
> To me did seem
> Apparelled in celestial light,
> The glory and the freshness of a dream.

However, he may be confusing childhood with what is actually a re-construction based on an interaction of adult associative capacities with the *memory* of the more direct sensory contact of the child. "Glory" is probably an adult product. Rather than speaking of a return to childhood, it is more accurate to say that the undoing of automatic perceptual and cognitive structures permits a gain in sensory intensity and richness at the expense of abstract categorization and differentiation. One might call the direction regressive in a developmental sense, but the actual experience is probably not within the psychological scope of any child. It is a deautomatization occurring in an adult mind, and the experience gains its richness from adult memories and functions now subject to a different mode of consciousness.

Renunciation

The deautomatization produced by contemplative meditation is en-hanced and aided by the adoption of renunciation as a goal and a life style, a renunciation not confined to the brief meditative period alone. Poverty, chastity, isolation, and silence are traditional techniques pre-scribed for pursuing the mystic path. To experience God, keep your thoughts turned to God and away from the world and the body that binds one to the world. The meditative strategy is carried over into all segments of the subject's life. The mystic strives to banish from awareness the objects of the world and the desires directed toward them. To the extent that perceptual and cognitive structures require the "nutriment" of their accustomed stimuli for adequate functioning, renunciation would be expected to weaken and even disrupt these structures, thus tending to produce an unusual experience (Rapaport, 1951). Such an isolation from nutritive stimuli probably occurs internally as well. The subjects of the meditation experiment quoted earlier reported that a decrease in re-sponsiveness to distracting stimuli took place as they became more prac-ticed. They became more effective, with less effort, in barring unwanted stimuli from awareness. These reports suggest that psychological barrier structures were established as the subjects became more adept (Deikman, 1963, p. 338). EEG studies of Zen monks yielded similar results. The effect of a distracting stimulus, as measured by the disappearance of alpha rhythm, was most prominent in the novices, less prominent in those of intermediate training, and almost absent in the master (Kasamatsu & Hirai, 1963). It may be that the intensive long-term practice of meditation creates temporary stimulus barriers producing a functional state of sensory isolation.* On the basis of sensory isolation experiments it would be expected that long-term deprivation (or decreased variability) of a particular class of stimulus "nutriment" would cause an alteration in those functions previously established to deal with that class of stimuli (Schultz, 1965, pp. 95–97; Solomon *et al.*, 1961, pp. 226–237). These alterations seem to be a type of deautomatization, as defined earlier— for example, the reported increased brightness of colors and the impairment of perceptual skills such as color discrimination (Zubeck *et al.*, 1961). Thus, renunciation alone can be viewed as producing deautomatization. When combined with contemplative meditation, it produces a very powerful effect.

Finally, the more renunciation is achieved, the more the mystic is committed to his goal of Union or Enlightenment. His motivation necessarily increases, for having abandoned the world, he has no other hope of sustenance.

Principal Features of the Mystic Experience

Granted that deautomatization takes place, it is necessary to explain five principal features of the mystic experience: (a) intense realness, (b) unusual sensations, (c) unity, (d) ineffability, and (e) trans-sensate phenomena.

Realness

It is assumed by those who have had a mystic experience, whether induced by years of meditation or by a single dose of LSD, that the truthfulness of the experience is attested to by its sense of realness. The criticism of skeptics is often met with the statement, "You have to ex-

---

*It has been postulated by McReynolds (1960, p. 269) that a related stimulus barrier system may be operative in schizophrenia.

perience it yourself and then you will understand." This means that if one has the actual experience he will be convinced by its intense *feeling of reality*. "I know it was real because it was more real than my talking to you now." But "realness" is not evidence. Indeed, there are many clinical examples of variability in the intensity of the feeling of realness that is not correlated with corresponding variability in the reality. A dream may be so "real" as to carry conviction into the waking state, although its content may be bizarre beyond correspondence to this world or to any other. Psychosis is often preceded or accompanied by a sense that the world is *less real* than normally, sometimes that it is more real, or has a different reality. The phenomenon of depersonalization demonstrates the potential for an alteration in the sense of the realness of one's own person, although one's evidential self undergoes no change whatsoever. However, in the case of depersonalization, or of derealization, the distinction between what is external and what is internal is still clear. What changes is the quality of realness attached to those object representations. Thus it appears that (a) the *feeling* of realness represents a function distinct from that of reality *judgment,* although they usually operate in synchrony; (b) the feeling of realness is not inherent in sensations, per se; and (c) realness can be considered a quality function capable of displacement and therefore, of intensification, reduction, and transfer affecting all varieties of ideational and sensorial contents.*

From a developmental point of view, it is clear that biological survival depends on a clear sense of what is palpable and what is not. The sense of reality necessarily becomes fused with the object world. When one considers that meditation combined with renunciation brings about a profound disruption of the subject's normal psychological relationship to the world, it becomes plausible that the practice of such mystic techniques would be associated with a significant alteration of the feeling of reality. The quality of reality formerly attached to objects becomes attached to the particular sensations and ideas that enter awareness during periods of perceptual and cognitive deautomatization. Stimuli of the inner world become invested with the feeling of reality ordinarily bestowed on objects. Through what might be termed "reality transfer," *thoughts and images become real* (Deikman, 1966, pp. 109–111).

*Paul Federn's (1955, pp. 241–260) idea that the normal feeling of reality requires an adequate investment of energy (libido) in the ego boundary, points toward the notion of a quantity of "realness." Avery Weisman (1958) has developed and extended this idea, but prefers the more encompassing concept of "libidinal fields" to that of ego boundaries.

Unusual Percepts

The sensations and ideation occurring during mystic deautomatization are often very unusual; they do not seem part of the continuum of everyday consciousness. "All at once, without warning of any kind, he found himself wrapped around as it were by a flame colored cloud" (Bucke, 1961, p. 8). Perceptions of encompassing light, infinite energy, ineffable visions, and incommunicable knowledge are remarkable in their seeming distinction from perceptions of the phenomena of the "natural world." According to mystics, these experiences are different because they pertain to a higher transcendent reality. What is perceived is said to come from another world, or at least another dimension. Although such a possibility cannot be ruled out, many of the phenomena can be understood as representing *an unusual mode of perception,* rather than an unusual external stimulus.

In the studies of experimental meditation already mentioned, two long-term subjects reported vivid instances of light and force. For example:

> Shortly I began to sense motion and shifting of light and dark and this became stronger and stronger. Now when this happens it's happening not only in my vision but it's happening or it feels like a physical kind of thing. It's connected with feelings of attraction, expansion, absorption and suddenly my vision pinpointed on a particular place and . . . I was in the grip of a very powerful sensation and this became the center (Deikman, 1966b, p. 109).

This report suggests that the perception of motion and shifting light and darkness may have been the perception of the *movement* of attention among various psychic contents (whatever such "movement" might actually be). "Attraction," "expansion," "absorption," would thus reflect the dynamics of the effort to focus attention—successful focusing is experienced as being "in the grip of" a powerful force. Another example: "when the vase changes shape . . . I feel this in my body and particularly in my eyes . . . there is an actual kind of physical sensation as though something is moving there which recreates the shape of the vase" (Deikman, 1966b, p. 109). In this instance, the subject might have experienced the perception of a resynthesis taking place following deautomatization of the normal percept; that is, the percept of the vase was being reconstructed outside of normal awareness and the *process* of reconstruction was perceived as a physical sensation. I have termed this hypothetical perceptual mode *"sensory translation,"* defining it as the perception of psychic *action* (conflict, repression, problem solving, attentiveness, and so forth) via the relatively unstructured sensations of light, color, movement, force, sound, smell, or taste (Kris, 1952; Deikman, 1966b, pp. 108–109). This concept is related to Silberer's (1951) concept of hypnagogic phenomena but differs in its referents and genesis. In the hypnagogic state and in dreaming, a *symbolic* translation of psychic activity and ideas occurs. Although light, force, and movement may play a part in hypnagogic and dream constructions, the predominant percepts are complex visual, verbal, conceptual, and activity images. "Sensory translation" refers to the experience of nonverbal, simple, concrete perceptual equivalents of psychic action.*

The concept of sensory translation offers an intriguing explanation for the ubiquitous use of light as a metaphor for mystic experience. It may not just be a metaphor. "Illumination" may be derived from an actual sensory experience occurring when in the cognitive act of unification, a liberation of energy takes place, or when a resolution of unconscious conflict occurs, permitting the experience of "peace," "presence," and the like. Liberated energy experienced as light may be the core sensory experience of mysticism.

If the hypothesis of sensory translation is correct, it presents the problem of why sensory translation comes into operation in any particular instance.

In general, it appears that sensory translation may occur when (a) heightened attention is directed to the sensory pathways, (b) controlled analytic thought is absent, and (c) the subject's attitude is one of receptivity to stimuli (openness instead of defensiveness or suspiciousness). Training in contemplative meditation is specifically directed toward attaining a state with those characteristics. Laski (1961) reports that spontaneous mystic experiences may occur during such diverse activ-

---

*Somewhat related concepts, although extreme in scope, are those advanced by Michaux (1963, pp. 7–9), who suggests that the frequent experience of waves of vibrations in hallucinogenic drug states is the result of direct perception of the "brain waves" measured by the EEG; and by Leary (1964, pp. 330–339), who suggests that hallucinogenic drugs permit a "direct awareness of the processes which physicists and biochemists and neurologists measure," for example, electrons in orbit or the interaction of cells.

ities as childbirth, viewing landscapes, listening to music, or having sexual intercourse. Although her subjects gave little description of their thought processes preceding the ecstasies, they were all involved at the time in intense sensory activities in which the three conditions listed above would tend to prevail. Those conditions seem also to apply to the mystical experience associated with LSD. The state of mind induced by hallucinogenic drugs is reported to be one of increased sensory attention accompanied by an impairment or loss of different intellectual functions (Crochet *et al.*, 1963; Watts, 1962; Michaux, 1963). With regard to the criterion of receptivity, if paranoid reactions occur during the drug state they are inimical to an ecstatic experience. On the other hand, when drug subjects lose their defensiveness and suspiciousness so that they "accept" rather than fight their situation, the "transcendent" experience often ensues (Sherwood *et al.*, 1962). Thus, the general psychological context may be described as *perceptual concentration*. In this special state of consciousness the subject becomes aware of certain intra-psychic processes ordinarily excluded from or beyond the scope of awareness. The vehicle for this perception appears to be amorphous sensation, made real by a displacement of reality feeling ("reality transfer") and thus misinterpreted as being of external origin.

Unity

Experiencing one's self as one with the universe or with God is the hallmark of the mystic experience, regardless of its cultural context. As James (1929, p. 410) puts it,

> This overcoming of all the usual barriers between the individual and the Absolute is the great mystic achievement. In mystic states we both become one with the Absolute and we become aware of our oneness. This is the everlasting and triumphant mystical tradition, hardly altered by differences of clime or creed. In Hinduism, in Neoplatonism, in Sufism, in Christian mysticism, in Whitmanism, we find the same recurring note, so that there is about mystical utterance an eternal unanimity which ought to make a critic stop and think, and which brings it about that the mystical classics have, as has been said, neither birthday nor native land. Perpetually telling of the unity of man with God, their speech antedates languages, and they do not grow old.

I have already referred to explanations of this phenomena in terms of regression. Two additional hypotheses should be considered: On the one hand, the perception of unity may be the perception of one's own psychic structure; on the other hand, the experience may be a perception of the real structure of the world.

It is a commonplace fact that we do not experience the world directly. Instead, we have an experience of sensation and associated memories from which we infer the nature of the stimulating object. As far as anyone can tell, the actual *substance* of the perception is the electrochemical activity that constitutes perception and thinking. From this point of view, the contents of awareness are homogeneous. They are variations of the same substance. If awareness were turned back upon itself, as postulated for sensory translation, this fundamental homogeneity (unity) of perceived reality—the electrochemical activity—might itself be experienced as a truth about the outer world, rather than the inner one. Unity, the idea and the experience that we are one with the world and with God, would thus constitute a valid perception insofar as it pertained to the nature of the thought process, but need not in itself be a correct perception of the external world.

Logically, there is also the possibility that the perception of unity does correctly evaluate the external world. As described earlier, deautomatization is an undoing of a psychic structure permitting the experience of increased detail and sensation at the price of requiring more attention. With such attention, it is possible that deautomatization may permit the awareness of new dimensions of the total stimulus array—a process of *"perceptual expansion."* The studies of Werner (1957), Von Senden (1960), and Shapiro (1960) suggest that development from infancy to adulthood is accompanied by an organization of the perceptual and cognitive world that has as its price the selection of some stimuli and stimulus qualities to the exclusion of others. If the automatization underlying that organization is reversed, or temporarily suspended, aspects of reality that were formerly unavailable might then enter awareness. Unity may in fact be a property of the real world that becomes perceptible via the techniques of meditation and renunciation, or under the special conditions, as yet unknown, that create the spontaneous, brief mystic experience of untrained persons.

Ineffability

Mystic experiences are ineffable, incapable of being expressed to another person. Although mystics sometimes write long accounts, they maintain that the experience cannot be communicated by words or by reference to similar experiences from ordinary life. They feel at a loss for appropriate words to communicate the intense realness, the unusual sensations, and the unity cognition already mentioned. However, a careful examination of mystic phenomena indicates that there are at least several types of experiences, all of which are "indescribable" but each of which differs substantially in content and formal characteristics. Error and confusion result when these several states of consciousness are lumped together as "the mystic experience" on the basis of their common characteristic of ineffability.

To begin with, one type of mystic experience cannot be communicated in words because it is probably based on primitive memories and related to fantasies of a preverbal (infantile) or nonverbal sensory experience.[*] Certain mystical reports that speak of being blissfully enfolded, comforted, and bathed in the love of God are very suggestive of the prototypical "undifferentiated state," the union of infant and breast, emphasized by psychoanalytic explanations of mystical phenomena. Indeed, it seems highly plausible that such early memories and fantasies might be reexperienced as a consequence of (a) the regression in thought processes brought about by renunciation and contemplative meditation, and (b) the activation of infantile longings by the guiding religious promise— that is, "that a benign deity would reward childlike surrender with permanent euphoria" (Moller, 1965, p. 127). In addition, the conditions of functional sensory isolation associated with mystic training may contribute to an increase in recall and vividness of such memories (Suraci, 1964).

A second type of mystical experience is equally ineffable but strikingly

---

[*]Schactel (1959, p. 284) regards early childhood, beyond infancy, as unrememberable for structural reasons: "It is not merely the repression of a specific content, such as early sexual experience, that accounts for the general childhood amnesia; the biologically, culturally, and socially influenced process of memory organization results in the formation of categories (schemata) of memory which are not suitable vehicles to receive and reproduce experiences of the quality and intensity typical of early childhood." It would follow that verbal structures would likewise be "unsuitable."

different—namely, a revelation too complex to be verbalized. Such experiences are reported frequently by those who have drug-induced mystical experiences. In such states the subject has a revelation of the significance and interrelationships of many dimensions of life; he becomes aware of many levels of meaning simultaneously and "understands" the totality of existence. The question of whether such knowledge is actual or an illusion remains unanswered; however, if such a multileveled comprehension were to occur, it would be difficult—perhaps impossible—to express verbally. Ordinary language is structured to follow the logical development of one idea at a time and it might be quite inadequate to express an experience encompassing a large number of concepts simultaneously. William James suggested that "states of mystical intuition may be only very sudden and great extensions of the ordinary 'field of consciousness.' " He used the image of the vast reaches of a tidal flat exposed by the lowering of the water level (James, 1920, pp. 500–513). However, mystic revelation may be ineffable, not only because of the sudden broadening of consciousness that James suggests, but also because of a new "vertical" organization of concepts.* For example, for a short while after reading *The Decline and Fall of the Roman Empire*, one may be aware of the immense vista of a civilization's history as Gibbon recreated it. That experience can hardly be conveyed except through the medium of the book itself, and to that extent it is ineffable, and a minor version of James's widened consciousness. Suppose one then read *War and Peace* and acquired Tolstoy's perspective of historical events and their determination by chance factors. Again, this is an experience hard to express without returning to the novel. Now suppose one could "see" not only each of these world views individually but also their parallel relationships to each other, and the cross connections between the individual conceptual structures. And then suppose one added to these conceptual strata the biochemical perspective expressed by *The Fitness of the Environment* (Henderson, 1958), a work which deals, among other things, with the unique and vital properties of the water molecule. Then the *vertical* interrelationships of all these extensive schemata might, indeed, be beyond verbal expression, beyond ordinary conceptual capacities—in other words, they would approach the ineffable.

---

*A similar distinction concerning "vertical" listening to music is made by Ehrenzweig (1964, pp. 385–387).

Trans-sensate Phenomena

A third type of ineffable experience is that which I have described earlier as the "trained-transcendent" mystical experience. The author of *The Cloud of Unknowing*, St. John of the Cross, Walter Hilton, and others are very specific in describing a new perceptual experience that does not include feelings of warmth, sweetness, visions, or any other elements of familiar sensory or intellectual experience. They emphasize that the experience *goes beyond* the customary sensory pathways, ideas and memories. As I have shown, they describe the state as definitely not blank or empty but as filled with intense, profound, vivid perception which they regard as the ultimate goal of the mystic path.* If one accepts their descriptions as phenomenologically accurate, one is presented with the problem of explaining the nature of such a state and the process by which it occurs. Following the hypotheses presented earlier in this paper, I would like to suggest that such experiences are the result of the operation of a new perceptual capacity responsive to dimensions of the stimulus array previously ignored or blocked from awareness. For such mystics, renunciation has weakened and temporarily removed the ordinary objects of consciousness as a focus of awareness. Contemplative meditation has undone the logical organization of consciousness. At the same time, the mystic is intensely *motivated* to perceive something. If undeveloped or unutilized perceptual capacities do exist, it seems likely that they would be mobilized and come into operation under such conditions. The perceptual experience that would then take place would be one outside of customary verbal or sensory reference. It would be *unidentifiable*, hence indescribable. The high value, the meaningfulness, and the intensity reported of such experiences suggest that the perception has a different scope from that of normal consciousness. The loss of "self" characteristic of the trans-sensate experience indicates that the new perceptual mode is not associated with reflective awareness—the "I" of normal consciousness is in abeyance.

*Ehrenzweig (1964, p. 382) proposes that mystic "blankness" is due to a structural limitation: "the true mystic orison becomes empty yet filled with intense experience. . . . This full emptiness . . . is the direct result of our conscious failure to grasp imagery formed on more primitive levels of differentiation. . . . Owing to their incompatible shapes, [these images] cancelled each other out on the way up to consciousness and so produce in our surface experience a bland 'abstract' image still replete with unconscious fantasy."

Conclusion

A mystic experience is the production of an unusual state of consciousness. This state is brought about by a deautomatization of hierarchically ordered structures that ordinarily conserve attentional energy for maximum efficiency in achieving the basic goals of the individual: biological survival as an organism and psychological survival as a personality. Perceptual selection and cognitive patterning are in the service of these goals. Under special conditions of dysfunction, such as in acute psychosis or in LSD states, or under special goal conditions such as exist in religious mystics, the pragmatic systems of automatic selection are set aside or break down, in favor of alternate modes of consciousness whose stimulus processing may be less efficient from a biological point of view but whose very inefficiency may permit the experience of aspects of the real world formerly excluded or ignored. The extent to which such a shift takes place is a function of the motivation of the individual, his particular neurophysiological state, and the environmental conditions encouraging or discouraging such a change.

A final comment should be made. The content of the mystic experience reflects not only its unusual mode of consciousness but also the particular stimuli being processed through that mode. The mystic experience can be beatific, satanic, revelatory, or psychotic, depending on the stimuli predominant in each case. Such an explanation says nothing conclusive about the source of "transcendent" stimuli. God or the Unconscious share equal possibilities here and one's interpretation will reflect one's presuppositions and beliefs. The mystic vision is one of unity, and modern physics lends some support to this perception when it asserts that the world and its living forms are variations of the same elements. However, there is no evidence that separateness and differences are illusions (as affirmed by Vedanta) or that God or a transcendent reality exists (as affirmed by Western religions). The available scientific evidence tends to support the view that the mystic experience is one of internal perception, an experience that can be ecstatic, profound, or therapeutic for purely internal reasons. Yet for psychological science, the problem of understanding such internal processes is hardly less complex than the theological problem of understanding God. Indeed, regardless of one's direction in the search to know what reality is, a feeling of awe, beauty, reverence, and humility seems to be the product of one's efforts. Since these emotions are characteristic of the mystic experience, itself, the question of the epistemological validity of that experience may have less importance than was initially supposed.

THE SUFI TRADITION

(*An Interview from* Psychology Today)

"Some Gurus Are Frankly Phonies, and They Don't Try to Hide It from Me. They Think I Am One Too."

Elizabeth Hall

ELIZABETH HALL: Idries Shah, you are the West's leading exponent of Sufism, that rich religious tradition growing out of the Middle East. Why, at a time when new cults are springing up, do you refuse to be a guru? You could easily become one.

IDRIES SHAH: There are a lot of reasons. But if we are talking about the teacher who has disciples, it's because I feel no need for an admiring audience to tell me how wonderful I am or to do what I say. If he had a sufficient outlet for his desire to be a big shot or his feeling of holiness or his wish to have others dependent on him, he wouldn't be a guru.

I got all that out of my own system very early and, consistent with Sufi tradition, I believe that those who don't want to teach are the ones who can and should. The West still has a vocation hang-up and has not yet discovered this. Here, the only recognized achiever is an obsessive. In the East we believe that a person who can't help doing a thing isn't necessarily the best one to do it. A compulsive cookie baker may bake very bad cookies.

HALL: Are you saying that a person who feels that he must engage in a certain profession is doing it because of some emotional need?

SHAH: I think this is very often the case, and it doesn't necessarily produce the best professional. Show an ordinary person an obsessive and he will believe you have shown him a dedicated and wonderful person—provided he shares his beliefs. If he doesn't, of course, he regards the one obsessed as evil. Sufism regards this as a facile and untrue posture. And if there is one consistency in the Sufi tradition, it is that man must be in the world but not of the world. There is no role for a priest-king or guru.

HALL: Then you have a negative opinion of all gurus.

SHAH: Not of all. Their followers need the guru as much as the guru needs his followers. I just don't regard it as a religious operation. I take a guru to be a sort of psychotherapist. At the very best, he keeps people quiet and polarized around him and gives some sort of meaning to their lives.

HALL: Librium might do the same thing.

SHAH: That's going a little too far. But they feel safety in numbers. They actually feel there is something wrong with what they are doing, and they feel better if they talk to somebody else who is doing it. I always tell them that I think it would be much better if they gave up the guru role in their own minds and realized that they are providing a perfectly good social service.

HALL: How do they take to that advice?

SHAH: Sometimes they laugh and sometimes they cry. The general impression is that one of us is wrong. Because I don't make the same kind of noises that they do, they seem to believe that either I am a lunatic or that I am starting some new kind of con. Perhaps I have found a new racket.

HALL: I am surprised that these gurus tell you all their secrets as freely as they do.

SHAH: I must tell you that I have not renounced the Eastern technique of pretending to be interested in what another person is saying, even pretending to be on his side. Therefore, I am able to draw out gurus and to get them to commit themselves to an extent that a Westerner, because of his conscience, could not do. The Westerner would not allow certain things to go unchallenged and would not trick, as it were, another person. So he doesn't find out the truth.

Look here, it's time that somebody took the lid off the guru racket. Since I have nothing to lose, it might as well be me. With many of these gurus it comes down to an "us and them" sort of thing between the East and the West. Gurus from India used to stop by on their way to California and their attitude was generally, let's take the Westerners to the cleaners; they colonized us, now we will get money out of them. I heard this sort of thing even from people who had impeccable spiritual reputations back home in India.

HALL: It is an understandable human reaction to centuries of Western exploitation.

SHAH: It's understandable, but I deny that it's a spiritual activity. What I want to say is, "Brother, you are in the revenge business, and that's a different kind of business from me." There are always groups that are willing to negotiate with me and want to use my name. On one occasion a chap in a black shirt and white tie told me, "You take Britain, but don't touch the United States, because that's ours." I had a terrible vision of Al Capone. The difference was that the guru's disciples kissed his feet.

HALL: Gurus keep proliferating in the United States, always with massive followings. A fifteen-year-old Perfect Master can fill the Astrodome.

See What I Mean?

Nasrudin was throwing handfuls of crumbs around his house.
   "What are you doing?" someone asked him.
   "Keeping the tigers away."
   "But there are no tigers in these parts."
   "That's right. Effective, isn't it?"

SHAH: Getting the masses is the easy part. A guru can attract a crowd of a million in India, but few in the crowd take him seriously. You see, India has had gurus for thousands of years, so they are generally sophisticated about them; they take in the attitude with their mother's milk. This culture just hasn't been innoculated against the guru. Let's turn it around. If I were fresh off a plane from India and told you that I was going to Detroit to become a wonderful automobile millionaire, you would smile at me. You know perfectly well the obstacles, the taxes, the ulcers that I face. Well, the Indian is in the same position with the automobile industry as the American with the guru. I'm not impressed by naïve American reactions to gurus; if you can show me a guru who can pull off that racket in the East, then I will be surprised.

HALL: Before we go any further, we'd better get down to basics and ask the obvious question. What is Sufism?

SHAH: The most obvious question of all is for us the most difficult question. But I'll try to answer. Sufism is experience of life through a method of dealing with life and human relations. This method is based on an understanding of man, which places at one's disposal the means to organize one's relationships and one's learning systems. So instead of saying that Sufism is a body of thought in which you believe certain things and don't believe other things, we say that the Sufi experience has to be provoked in a person. Once provoked, it becomes his own property, rather as a person masters an art.

HALL: So ideally, for four million readers, you would have four million different explanations.

SHAH: In fact, it wouldn't work out like that. We progress by means of *nashr,* an Arabic word that means scatter technique. For example, I've published quite a number of miscellaneous books, articles, tapes and so on, which scatter many forms of this Sufi material. These two thousand different stories cover many different tendencies in many people, and they are able to attach themselves to some aspect of it.

HALL: I noticed as I read that the same point would be made over and over again in a different way in a different story. In all my reading, I think the story that made the most profound impression on me was "The Water of Paradise." Afterward, I found the same point in other stories, but had I not read "The Water of Paradise" first, I might not have picked it up.

SHAH: That is the way the process tends to work. Suppose we get a group of twenty people past the stage where they no longer expect us to give them miracles and stimulation and attention. We sit them down in a room and give them twenty or thirty stories, asking them to tell us what they see in the stories, what they like, and what they don't like. The stories first operate as a sorting-out process. They sort out both the very clever people who need psychotherapy and who have come only to put you down, and the people who have come to worship. In responsible Sufi circles, no one attempts to handle either the sneerers or the worshippers, and they are very politely detached from the others.

If a Pot Can Multiply

One day Nasrudin lent his cooking pots to a neighbor, who was giving a feast. The neighbor returned them, together with one extra one—a very tiny pot.

"What is this?" asked Nasrudin.

"According to law, I have given you the offspring of your property which was born when the pots were in my care," said the joker.

Shortly afterwards Nasrudin borrowed his neighbor's pots, but did not return them.

The man came round to get them back.

"Alas!" said Nasrudin, "they are dead. We have established, have we not, that pots are mortal?"

HALL: They are not fertile ground?

SHAH: They have something else to do first. And what they need is offered abundantly elsewhere. There's no reason for them to bother us. Next we begin to work with people who are left. In order to do this, we must cool it. We must not have any spooky atmosphere, any strange robes or gongs or intonations. The new students generally react to the stories either as they think you would like them to react or as their background tells them they should react. Once they realize that no prizes are being given for correct answers, they begin to see that their previous conditioning determines the way they are seeing the material in the stories.

So, the second use of the stories is to provide a protected situation in which people can realize the extent of the conditioning in their ordinary lives. The third use comes later, rather like when you get the oil to the surface of a well after you have burnt off the gases. After we have burnt off the conditioning, we start getting completely new interpretations and reactions to the stories. At last, as the students become less emotional, we can begin to deal with the real person, not the artifact that society has made him.

I Know Her Best

People ran to tell the Mulla that his mother-in-law had fallen into the river. "She will be swept out to sea, for the current is very fast here," they cried.

Without a moment's hesitation Nasrudin dived into the river and started to swim upstream.

"No!" they cried, "downstream! That is the only way a person can be carried away from here."

"Listen!" panted the Mulla, "I know my wife's mother. If everyone else is swept downstream, the place to look for her is upstream."

HALL: Is this a very long process?

SHAH: You can't predict it at all. With some people it is an instant process; with others, it takes weeks or months. Still others get fed up and quit because, like good children of the consumer society, they crave something to consume and we're not giving it to them.

HALL: You say that conditioning gets in the way of responses to Sufi material. But everyone is conditioned from birth, so how does one ever escape from his conditioning?

SHAH: We can't live in the world without being conditioned. Even the control of one's bladder is conditioned. It is absurd to talk, as some do, of deconditioned or nonconditioned people. But it is possible to see why conditioning has taken place and why a person's beliefs become oversimplified.

Nobody is trying to abolish conditioning, merely to describe it, to make it possible to change it, and also to see where it needs to operate, and where it does not. Some sort of secondary personality, which we call the "commanding self," takes over man when his mentation is not correctly balanced. This self, which he takes for his real one, is in fact a mixture of emotional impulses and various pieces of conditioning. As a consequence of Sufi experience, people—instead of seeing things through a filter of conditioning plus emotional reactions, a filter which constantly discards certain stimuli—can see things through some part of themselves that can only be described as not conditioned.

HALL: Are you saying that when one comes to an awareness that he is conditioned, he can operate aside from it? He can say, "Why do I believe all this? Well, perhaps it is because . . ."

SHAH: Exactly. Then he is halfway toward being liberated from his conditioning—or at least toward keeping it under control. People who say that we must smash conditioning are themselves oversimplifying things.

HALL: A number of years ago an American psychologist carried out an interesting experiment. He had a device that supplied two things, one to each eye. One image was a baseball player, the other was a matador. He had a group of American and Mexican schoolteachers look through this device. Most of the Americans saw a baseball player and most of the Mexicans saw the matador. From what you have said, I gather that Sufism might enable an American to see the matador and a Mexican to see the baseball player.

SHAH: That is what many of the Sufi stories try to do. As a reader, you tend to identify with one of the people in the story. When he behaves unexpectedly, it gives you a bit of a jolt and forces you to see him with different eyes.

HALL: When one reads about Sufism, one comes upon conflicting explanations. Some people say that Sufism is pantheistic; others that it is related to theosophy. Certainly there are strains in Sufism that you can find in any of the major world religions.

SHAH: There are many ways to talk about the religious aspects of Sufism. I'll just choose one and see where it leads. The Sufis themselves say that their religion has no history, because it is not culture-bound. Although Sufism has been productive in Islam, according to Sufi tradition and scripture, Sufis existed in pre-Islamic times. The Sufis say that all religion is evolution, otherwise it wouldn't survive. They also say that all religion is capable of development up to the same point. In historical times, Sufis have worked within all recognized religions: Christianity, Judaism, Islam, Vedanta, Buddhism and so on. Sufis are in religion but not of it.

Early to Rise

"Nasrudin, my son, get up early in the mornings."

"Why, Father?"

"It is a good habit. Why, once I rose at dawn and went for a walk. I found on the road a sack of gold."

"How did you know it was not lost the previous night?"

"That is not the point. In any case, it had not been there the night before. I noticed that."

"Then it isn't lucky for everyone to get up early. The man who lost the gold must have been up earlier than you."

HALL: What is the Sufi attitude toward mysticism and the ecstatic experience?

SHAH: Sufis are extraordinarily cautious about this. They don't allow a person to do spiritual exercises unless they are convinced that he can undergo such exercises without harm and appreciate them without distraction. Spiritual exercises are allowed only at a certain time and a certain place and with certain people. When the ecstatic exercises are taken out of context, they become a circus at best and unhinge minds at worst.

HALL: So the ecstatic experience has its place but only at a certain time at a certain stage of development?

SHAH: Yes, and with certain training. The ecstatic experience is certainly not required. It is merely a way of helping man to realize his potential.

HALL: Many of the great Sufi teachers seem to regard the ecstatic experience as only a way station.

SHAH: Oh, yes. The ecstatic experience is absolutely the lowest form of advanced knowledge. Western biographers of the saints have made it very difficult for us by assuming that Joan of Arc and Theresa of Avila, who have had such experiences, have reached God. I am sure that this is only a misunderstanding based on faulty storage and faulty retrieval of information.

HALL: Sufis also seem to take extrasensory perception as a matter of course and as not very interesting.

SHAH: Not interesting at all. It is not more than a by-product. Let me give you a banal analogy. If I were training to be a runner and went out every day to run, I would get faster and faster and be able to run farther and farther with less fatigue. Now, I also find that I have a better complexion, my blood supply is better, and my digestion has improved. These things don't interest me; they are only by-products of my running. I have another objective. When people I am associated with become overwhelmed by ESP phenomena, I always insist that they stop it, because their objective is elsewhere.

HALL: They are supposed to be developing their potential; not attempting to read minds or move objects around. Do you think that researchers will one day explain the physical basis of ESP, or do you think it will always elude them?

SHAH: If I say it will elude the scientists, it will annoy the people who are able to get enormous grants for research into ESP. But I think, yes, a great deal more can be discovered, providing the scientists are prepared to be good scientists. And by that I mean that they are prepared to structure their experiments successively in accordance with their discoveries. They must be ready to follow anomalies and not hew doggedly to their original working hypothesis. And they will certainly have to give up their concept of the observer being outside of the experiment, which has been their dearest pet for many years. And another thing, as we find constantly in metaphysics, people who are likely to be able to understand and develop capacities for ESP are more likely to be found among people who are not interested in the subject.

HALL: Is that because disinterest is necessary to approach the subject properly?

SHAH: Something like that. Being disinterested, you can approach ESP more coolly and calmly. The Sufis say, "You will be able to exercise these supernatural powers when you can put out your hand and get a wild dove to land on it." But the other reason why the people who are fascinated by ESP or metaphysics or magic are the last who should study it is that they are interested for the wrong reasons. It may be compensation. They are not equipped to study ESP. They are equipped for something else: fear, greed, fate, or love of humanity.

HALL: Often they have a desperate wish to prove that ESP is either true or false.

SHAH: Yes, that's what I call heroism. But it's not professionalism and that's what the job calls for.

HALL: You've also written a couple of books on magic: *Oriental Magic* and *The Secret Lore of Magic,* an investigation of Western magic. Today there's an upsurge of interest in astrology and witchcraft and magic. You must have speculated somewhat about magic in those books.

SHAH: Very little. The main purpose of my books on magic was to make this material available to the general reader. For too long people believed that there were secret books, hidden places, and amazing things. They held on to this information as something to frighten themselves with. So the first purpose was information. This is the magic of East and West. That's all. There is no more. The second purpose of those books was to show that there do seem to be forces, some of which are either rationalized by this magic or may be developed from it, which do not come within customary physics or within the experience of ordinary people. I think this should be studied, that we should gather the data and analyze the phenomena.

We need to separate the chemistry of magic from the alchemy, as it were.

HALL: That's not exactly what the contemporary devotees of witchcraft and magic are up to.

SHAH: No. My work has no relevance to the current interest whatever. Oh, it makes my books sell, but they were written for cool-headed people and there aren't many of those around.

HALL: Most of the people who get interested in magic seem to be enthusiasts.

SHAH: Yes, it's just as with ESP. There's no reason why they shouldn't be enthusiasts, but having encouraged them—which I couldn't help— I must now avoid them. They would only be disappointed in what I have to say.

You know, Rumi said that people counterfeit gold because there is such a thing as real gold, and I think that's the situation we are in with Sufi studies at the moment. It is much easier to write a book on Sufism than it is to study it. It is much easier to start a group and tell people what you want them to do than it is to learn first.

The problem is that the spurious, the unreal, the untrue is so much easier to find that it is in danger of becoming the norm. Until recently, for example, if you didn't use drugs in spiritual pursuits, you were not considered genuine. If you said, "Look, drugs are irrelevant to spiritual matters," you were regarded as a square. Their attitude is not at all a search for truth.

HALL: Many people seem to use drugs as an attempt to get instant enlightenment.

SHAH: People want to be healed or cured or saved, but they want it now. It's astonishing. When people come here to see me, they want to get something, and if I can't give them higher consciousness, they will take my bedspreads or my ashtrays or whatever else they can pick up around the house.

HALL: They want something to carry away.

SHAH: They are thinking in terms of loose property, almost physical. They are savages in the best sense of the word. They are not what they think they are at all. I am invited to believe that they take bedspreads and ashtrays by accident. But it never works the other way; they never leave their wallets behind by mistake. One thing I learned from my father very early: Don't take any notice of what people say, just watch what they do.

HALL: Let's get back to your main work. What is the best way of introducing the Sufi way of thinking to the West?

SHAH: I am sure that the best way is not to start a cult, but to introduce a body of literary material that should interest people enough to establish the Sufi phenomenon as viable. We don't plan to form an organization with somebody at the top and others at the bottom collecting money or wearing funny clothes or converting people to Sufism. We view Sufism not as an ideology that molds people to the right way of belief or action, but as an art or science that can exert a beneficial influence on individuals and societies, in accordance with the needs of those individuals and societies.

HALL: Does Western society need this infusion of Sufi thought?

SHAH: It needs it for the same reason that any society needs it, because it gives one something that one cannot get elsewhere. For example, Sufi thought makes a person more efficient. A watchmaker becomes a better watchmaker. A housewife becomes a better housewife. When somebody said as much in California last year, 120 hippies got up and left the hall. They didn't wait to hear that they weren't going to be forced to be more efficient.

HALL: But there must be more than efficiency to it.

SHAH: Of course. I wouldn't try to sell Sufism purely as a means to efficiency, even though it does make one more effective in all kinds of ways. I think Sufism is important because it enables one to detach from life and see it as near to its reality as one can possibly get. Sufi experience tends to produce the kind of person who is calm not because he can't get excited, but because he knows that getting excited about an event or problem is not going to have any lasting effect.

HALL: Would you say that it might give a person an outlook on the problems of this time similar to the outlook he might presently have on the problems of the sixteenth century?

SHAH: Very much so. And such an outlook takes the heat out of almost every kind of contention. Instead of becoming the classical Oriental philosopher who says "All reality is imagination. Why should I care about the world," you begin to see alternative ways of acting. For example, some of the finest people in this country spend a great deal of their time jumping up and down in Trafalgar Square waving banners that condemn the various dirty beasts of the world. Such behavior makes the dirty beasts delighted at the thought that they are so important and the jumpers are so impotent. If the Trafalgar Square jumpers had an objective view of their behavior, they would abandon it. First, they would see that they were only giving aid and comfort to the enemy, and second, they would be able to see how to do something about the dirty beasts—and if it were necessary to do *anything* about them.

HALL: In other words, Sufism might help us solve some of the enormous social, political and environmental problems that face us.

SHAH: People talk about Sufism as if it were the acquisition of powers. Sufi metaphysics has even got a magical reputation. The truth is that Sufi study and development gives one capacities one did not have before. One would not kill merely because killing is bad. Instead, one would know that killing is unnecessary and, in addition, what one would have to do in order to make humanity happier, and able to realize better objectives. That's what knowledge is for.

HALL: When I read your books, the message came through very clearly that you are not interested in rational, sequential thought—in what Bob Ornstein calls left hemisphere activity.

SHAH: To say that I am not interested in sequential thinking is not to say that I can exist without it. I have it up to a certain point, and I expect the people I meet to be able to use it. We need information in order to approach a problem, but we also need to be able to see the thing whole.

HALL: When you speak of seeing the thing whole, you're talking about intuitive thought, where you don't reason the problem out but know the answer without knowing how you got it.

SHAH: Yes. You know the answer and can verify that it is an answer. That is the difference between romantic imagining and something that belongs to this world.

HALL: Ornstein, who seems to have been profoundly influenced by Sufi thought, has suggested that most people today tend to rely on logical, rational, linear thought and that we tend to use very little of the intuitive, nonlinear thought of the brain's right hemisphere. Would you say that Sufism can teach one to tap right hemisphere thought?

SHAH: Yes, I would. Sufism has never been overimpressed by the products of left hemisphere activity, although it's often used them. For instance, Sufis have written virtually all the great poetry of Persia, and while the inspiration for a poem may come from the right hemisphere, one must use the left hemisphere to put the poem down in proper form. I think that the behavior and products of Sufism are among the few things we have that encourage a holistic view of things. I don't want to discuss Sufism in Ornsteinian terms, however, because I'm not qualified to do so. I can only say that insofar as there is any advantage in these two hemispheres acting alternately or complementing one another, then Sufi material undoubtedly is among the very little available material that can help this process along.

HALL: Why are the traditional Western ways of study inappropriate for the study of Sufism?

SHAH: They are inappropriate only up to a point. Both the Western and the Middle Eastern methods of study come from the common heritage of the Middle Ages, when one was regarded as wise if he had a better memory than someone else. But some of the teaching methods that Sufis use do seem rather odd to the Westerner. If I were to say to you that my favorite method of teaching is to bore the audience to death, you would be shocked. But I have just received the results of some tests, which show that English schoolchildren, when shown a group of films, remembered only the ones that bored them. Now this is consistent with our experience, but it is not consistent with Western beliefs.

Another favorite Sufi teaching method is to be rude to people, sometimes shouting them down or shooing them away, a technique that is not customary in cultivated circles. By experience we know that by giving a certain kind of shock to a person, we can—for a short period—increase his perception. Until recently I wouldn't have dared speak about this, but I now have a clipping indicating that when a person endures a shock he produces theta rhythms. Some people have associated these brain rhythms with various forms of ESP. No connection has been made yet, but I think we may be beginning to understand it.

HALL: Recent studies of memory indicate that unless adrenaline is present, no learning takes place, and shock causes adrenaline to flow. We also know from experience that when you find yourself in a situation of grave danger, you tend to notice some very small detail with great clarity.

SHAH: Exactly. Concentration comes in on a strange level and in an unaccustomed way. But using this knowledge has traditionally given Sufi teachers a reputation for having bad manners. The most polite thing they say about us is that we are irascible and out of control. Some people say that a spiritual teacher should have no emotions or be totally balanced. We say that a spiritual teacher must be a person who *can be* totally balanced, not one who cannot help but be balanced.

HALL: People in the United States seem to be looking for leaders, whether spiritual or political, and they keep complaining because there are no leaders to follow.

SHAH: People are always looking for leaders; that does not mean that this is the time for a leader. The problems that a leader would be able to resolve have not been identified. Nor does the clamor mean that those who cry out are suitable followers. Most of the people who demand a leader seem to have some baby's idea of what a leader should do. The idea that a leader will walk in and we will all recognize him and follow him and everybody will be happy strikes me as a strangely immature atavism. Most of these people, I believe, want not a leader, but excitement. I doubt that those who cry the loudest would obey a leader if there was one. Talk is cheap, you know, and a lot of the talk comes from millions of old washerwomen.

HALL: If so, the washerwomen are spread throughout the culture.

SHAH: They're not called washerwomen, but if we test them, they react like washerwomen. For example, if you are selling books and you send a professor of philosophy something written in philosophical language, he will throw it away. But if you send him a spiel written for a washerwoman, he will buy the book. At heart he is a washerwoman. Intellectuals don't understand this, but business people do because their profits depend upon it. You can learn much more about human nature on Madison Avenue than you will from experts on human nature, because on Madison Avenue one stands or falls by the sales. Professors in their ivory towers can say anything because there's no penalty attached. Go to where there is a penalty attached and there you will find wisdom.

HALL: That's a tough statement. You sound as if you are down on all academics.

SHAH: Well, in the past few years I have given quite a few seminars and lectures at universities, and I have become terrified by the low level of ability. It is as if people just aren't trying. They don't read the books in their fields, don't know the workings of them, use inadequate approaches to a subject, ask ridiculous questions that a moment's thought would have enabled them to answer. If these are the cream, what is the milk like?

HALL: Are you talking about undergraduates, graduate students, or professors?

SHAH: The whole lot. Recently I've been appalled at the low levels of articles in learned journals and literary weeklies. The punctuation gone to hell, full of non sequiturs, an obvious lack of background knowledge, and so on. I went to a newspaper library and looked up the equivalent articles from the 1930s. A great change has taken place. Forty years ago there were two kinds of articles: very, very good and terribly bad. There seemed nothing in between. Now everything is slapdash and mediocre. Why are so many famous persons in hallowed institutions now so mediocre?

HALL: Critics like Dwight Macdonald have said for years that as education becomes widespread and people become semiliterate, the culture at the top is inevitably pulled down. But you're not really hostile to all academics, are you?

SHAH: No, some of my best friends are academics.

HALL: That is no way to get out of it.

SHAH: Of course, I'm not hostile to all academics. There are some great thinkers. But I do not believe that it is necessary for us to have eighty percent blithering idiots in order to get twenty percent marvelous academics. This ratio depresses me. I think that the good people are unbelievably noble in denying that the rest of them are such hopeless idiots. Privately they agree with you, but they won't rock the boat. For the sake of humanity, somebody has got to rock the boat.

HALL: For the sake of humanity, what would you like to see happen?

SHAH: What I really want, in case anybody is listening, is for the products of the last fifty years of psychological research to be studied by the public, by everybody, so that the findings become part of their way of thinking. At the moment, people have adopted only a few. They talk glibly about making Freudian slips and they have accepted the idea of inferiority complexes. But they have this great body of psychological information and refuse to use it.

There is a Sufi story about a man who went into a shop and asked the shopkeeper, "Do you have leather?" "Yes," said the shopkeeper. "Nails?" "Yes." "Thread?" "Yes." "Needles?" "Yes." "Then why don't you make yourself a pair of boots?" That story is intended to pinpoint this failure to use available knowledge. People in this civilization are starving in the middle of plenty. This is a civilization that is going down, not because it hasn't got the knowledge that would save it, but because nobody will use the knowledge.

MYSTERIES IN THE WEST: STRANGE RITES

Idries Shah

> In an instant, rise from time and space. Set the world aside and become a world within yourself.
>
> Shabistari, *Secret Garden*

It is the night of Saturday, especially consecrated to a ritual which is awesome to us, faithfully followed by the devotees of a certain cult.

Two groups of twelve, dressed in colorful costumes, carry out complicated movements within an enclosed space. They at times respond to musical stimuli applied through a primitive instrument by a man of seeming authority who, with a few assistants, supervises their activity. Entirely surrounding the area devoted to the ritual, a congregation gives its responses. At times the people sing, sometimes they shout, sometimes they are silent. Some wield an instrument which gives forth a strange sound.

Much care has evidently gone into the planning of the geometrically designed arena. Around it are colorful insignia, flags, banners, decorations probably designed to raise the emotional pitch of the individual and the group. The atmosphere is eerie partly because of the abrupt changes in emotion. Their reaction to the ecstatogenic processes being enacted in their midst is so explosive at times that one wonders why they do not spill over into the sacred enclosure. Both joy and sorrow are manifested among the votaries.

We are observers at a floodlit association football game. What is missing from the observer's account is a knowledge of what is actually happening, and why. If we have this knowledge, we can identify the players, crowd, referee, the use of the chalked lines. If we do not, we continue: Here a man writhes on the ground, another grimaces, sweat pouring from his face. One of the audience strokes himself, another his neighbor. The totem rises into the air, and is hailed by an awesome roar from the assembly. . . . Then we see that blood has been shed.

Other forms of ritual are subject to a similar approach by those who have not been through the experiences which precede their staging. Even more important, very many rituals of one kind or another have undergone alteration throughout the ages, the original intention or force being lost. When this happens, there is a mechanical or associative substitution of other factors. The ritual is distorted, even though there may be apparent reasons for its every aspect. This development is what we can call the dereliction of cult behavior.

Here, now, is an externalist account of a dervish ritual, in which events are described from the point of view of the observer alone. The author is the Reverend John Subhan, of the Methodist Episcopal Church, who was present at this event in India:

> Tonight is Thursday night, the night which is specially sacred to the Sufi. Come, let us visit some shrines and see for ourselves what strange religious rites are practiced almost at our very doors.
>
> We enter a dimly lighted room where a number of men are gathered. As we do so a signal is given by a man who appears to be the leader of the assembly, and the doors are shut. There is a hush as twelve men form into two parallel lines in the center of the room. The glimmer of a solitary hurricane lamp falls on dark faces in which only the eyes seem to live. The rest of us fall back to the sides of the room. The Dhikr is about to begin.
>
> With a startling clap of the hands the leader starts swaying from right to left. Very slowly he begins, and the men fall into the rhythm of his swaying. Every time they sway to the left they call "Hu!" in chorus, "Hu . . . Hu . . . Hu."

The dervish ritual is not of the same nature of the football game—far from it. Since, however, it is not symbolic but concerned with an interior activity, the advantages of describing such an event in this out-of-context manner are few.

8

The Perils of the "Journey": A Report from the Mind Field

The Value of the Past

Nasrudin was sent by the King to investigate the lore of various kinds of Eastern mystical teachers. They all recounted to him tales of the miracles and the sayings of the founders and great teachers, all long dead, of their schools.

When he returned home, he submitted his report, which contained the single word "Carrots."

He was called upon to explain himself. Nasrudin told the King: "The best part is buried; few know—except the farmer—by the green that there is orange underground; if you don't work for it, it will deteriorate; there are a great many donkeys associated with it."

Since most of the mind is devoted to helping its owners survive, there are many difficulties in developing and extending consciousness to encompass anything that does not concern immediate requirements.

Many vendors cry out to serve different needs: There is psychotherapy; there are emotional, social and other skill training sessions; you can go on tours to shrines of ancient civilizations and get a "Tibetan pen pal" or someone like that.

Our scientists seem to have the same problem. It is currently possible to attend scientific conferences on Eastern psychologies. Usually they have distinguished faculties who occupy the time discussing ideas far beyond their training. One recent series presented papers on "Wound Healing in Acupuncture," "Shivering Thermogenesis in Nepal," and many other topics that were rarely discussed in graduate school. Since there are no real standards (as might be in neurosurgery), there are uncritical articles chronicling the lure of the possibility of studying the secrets of "Monks who can raise their body temperatures," or control their heartbeat, change heat flow in the body, and more. Exciting, surely!

But do the scientists ever stop and consider whether it is worth the effort to find these "secrets" out? We do not live in a society in which these skills are *needed!* We have central heating and skills such as increasing body heat by arduous methods would seem to have little to recommend them, except as museum pieces.

It often seems like meeting fossil hunters. It seems that the archeological, social, and excitement value of everything—*"Did you know that Swami X can pick his nose without moving?"*—has gotten confused with the scientific value. It produces a kind of hash; it is neither science nor does it have much to do with the individual's spiritual development, or any other kind. There is a new synthesis here, but what a one! It is the Science of the East and the Spirituality of the West, rather than the other way around.

There is a parallel to the attempt to integrate Eastern Medicines— acupuncture, herbal treatments, et cetera—with those of Modern Medicine. Now, there is no question that there is a great need for physicians to consider the role of the whole person in health, life situation, psychological reactions, mental and brain state, as well as response to challenge, sense of coherence, and many, many other factors. But most of the interest is on picturesque and exotic techniques like sticking needles in a person.

But these intriguing and exotic disciplines evolved in much more primitive times. That itself is not a criticism, for it has been shown again and again by Robin Horton that the thought processes of "primitive peoples" are the same as our very own cherished ones—they have the same mental operating system!

But these exotic and ancient systems of health were designed to be used for those who could not get any medical assistance; developed before there was any possibility of intervening in the internal workings of the body. Certainly during those epochs the best thing to do would be to try to *prevent any disorder* by any means possible—diet, social networks, family assistance, mental regimes.

Modern medicine is primarily a disease-care system, and we have much to learn about preventing disorders, rather than concentrating on helping people after they get sick. But our enthusiasts of the exotic commit the mistake in reverse: Once someone has a serious disorder, using many techniques of the primitive medicines is about as useful as putting a seat belt on a person already injured in a car accident.

To return to our two kinds of psychology, it is the very esotericism of *both* systems that is an obstacle to this process. The language and procedures of the traditional psychologies are difficult to comprehend, let alone practice. So is the language of contemporary science. Our own tendency demands conclusive proof at once in our own verbal, logical, and causal terms. If for instance a man reports experiences that we consider "paranormal," we naturally want him to perform them in *our* laboratory under *our* strict conditions in *our* time scale.

Suppose we tell an illiterate peasant from India: "Human beings can construct space vehicles that can take you to the distant planets up there in the sky." He may at first simply dismiss the possibility from his mind, then later, if we say it often or compellingly enough, allow it some credence. He may become excited, since it greatly extends his possibilities. He now believes that human beings are capable of building a "magical spaceship."

We inform him: To accomplish planetary travel, he must first learn an entirely new language, English, and then a new discipline, mathematics. After learning the basics of English grammar he will need advanced training in the language. Only then can he study technical manuals. He will also need the cooperation of many other similarly trained people who have interlocking skills and who wish to assist in such a complex project. There is also the question of money, and countless other considerations.

Our peasant is ignorant of this. He cannot see why, if it is indeed *possible* for man to fly to the planets, he cannot do it *now* in his own terms. If we try to be helpful and give him a first book on English in order to allow him to make the necessary first step, he may be either offended or incredulous. "What do these stupid marks on paper have to do with the grandeur of a flight to the planets?" he may ask.

If he does not follow our advice, he may attempt to fly to Venus by prayer, or by wooden wings. He may take along some friends who are similarly excited with the idea. When his group fails, he will likely come to believe that spaceflight is really an impossibility and that anyone who claims it to be possible is simply gullible, "unscientific," or even a liar.

As Western students of psychology, we may need to overcome similar tendencies in ourselves when investigating an area that is so new, so spectacular, and so unknown to us. And the problem for us is indeed great, for there is no other area of human experience, save perhaps sexuality, about which so much garbage has been written. The Sufi poet Rumi noted this process when he wrote, "Counterfeiters exist only because there is real gold."

We are not about to write off science merely because, in some cases, it has committed excesses; so we should not ignore "Eastern science" because of its imbalances or because of the misinterpretations heaped around it.

We should note the very serious difficulties many of these psychologies have encountered in their own social and cultural areas. The source of their problems has been quite similar to that of contemporary Western psychology.

Each system of religious instruction or meditation tends to cling to specific techniques whose original purpose has been forgotten. In the traditional esoteric psychologies, for example, a balanced development of intellectuality and intuition is usually sought. Since many who become interested in these traditions are well developed intellectually, the exercises usually stress the development of an extended perspective on human nature and human life.

The specific techniques employed for this purpose sometimes come to be considered all-important. Then the intellect may become devalued, cast aside, ignored, in an overreaction against it. This may happen with an individual and even within an entire discipline, leading to an "official" devaluation of the intellect and the preaching of an incomprehensible doctrine. A similar process, although entirely reversed in content, has occurred within contemporary science and has led to an unbalanced development of an "objective" approach. The original aim may become forgotten, but techniques persist.

For instance, it has been found useful for *certain people* of a culture different from our own at *certain periods* of their study to renounce sexual practice, largely to free up their consciousness from all the biases we have discussed so far—body needs, desires, et cetera. But such "renunciation" has often been extended far beyond these bounds, leading in the Hindu tradition, for instance, to people who withdraw entirely from sexuality and who consequently distort those of the opposite sex as "temptation."

A comic instance of such distortion occurred recently when a Hindu holy man visited the United States. Upon arrival at the airport, he had to be shielded by his aides, for even seeing a woman was forbidden by his religious practices; he had remained shielded from women for his entire life in India. The television news showed various women's liberation demonstrators attempting to crash through the barricade and stand in front of this exponent of "higher consciousness." Even when the rejection of normal sexuality is not so extreme, many lesser distortions occur.

Similarly, the achievement of a transitory state of receptivity and quiescence through meditation may lure the practitioner into withdrawing completely from continuing cultural life, leading him or her to ignore serious personal and social problems, considering them "illusory." Although the corrective to such a withdrawal is often applied within these traditions, it is not often heard.

In the influential book *Thinkers of the East* the commentator Ustad Hilmi writes: "Traditions about monasticism and isolation are reflections of short-term processes of training or development, monstrously misunderstood and grotesquely elaborated by those who want to stay asleep." "Asleep" is one of the terms used to describe our normal state of mind, one focused on the highly selected and limited "everyday survival" part of reality.

Our approaches are often faulty, and we most often do not know how to evaluate the diverse and often bizarre practices, some of which are culturally specific, some of which are outmoded, some of which evolved for a different purpose than that for which they are now being used.

For many people, the first experiences of an extended consciousness have come from newly organized groups. Some of these groups are resolutely commercial, others clannish and secretive. In considering both types of groups, we encounter again the difficulties of understanding and conveying an advanced knowledge of human capacities. In observing how these "franchised mysticism groups" promote and maintain themselves, we can note how the original knowledge seems to shrink to fit commercial requirements.

Many people have been associated with both psychotherapy and parapsychology for many years. The advent of trademarked franchised mystic cults, however, is a more recent development. Some people seize upon them as the latest stage in their own continual self-preoccupation and indulgence; others seek new "experiences" for themselves.

Such forms of meditation and awareness training are usually met with immediate and continued disdain from professional psychologists and educators, sometimes justified, sometimes for the wrong reasons. Along with our cultivation of intellectual skills, and the increasing prominence of those skills in education and professional life (with attendant specialization of function), there has been an almost complete abdication of learning and teaching about the nature of the person being taught and the development of wisdom and self-knowledge. The trademarked awareness systems have moved into an area of "applied psychology" that has been abdicated by the educational professions.

It's fun to attend the weekends listening to the "trainers" describe how unique and important each "special technique" is, and how the founder, usually a car salesman (honest!) discovered each one. The systems offer either one special technique or a synthetic amalgam of techniques drawn from many sources. These techniques, in spite of the opinion of most academics, may not be entirely worthless; they may contain many needed personal skills lost in this culture, lost in the changes in family life and in the nature of specialized education.

In a society in which, as *Esquire* magazine headlines, "Success" is the "Religion of the 80s," where and when can a person learn to experience and understand the phenomenon we have been describing throughout this book—that one's very immediate experience of the world is so limited—let alone begin to develop an intuitive wisdom of the purpose of life?

The existence of "instant weekend" and simpleminded meditation training systems tells us more about what is missing from contemporary education, even at a rudimentary level, than any amount of professional criticism could do—we are a society of spiritual illiterates, suckers for a quick answer. Many have turned to the showmen/salesmen to make up for the basic shortcomings of our education—and at great, and often unnecessary, cost.

. . .

Although the benefits of the cults may be of some use, they are often perverted. The real benefit goes to the leader. The process is similar to the bureaucratic encrustation of an innovative government program— the original impetus is lost. Money that is supposed to benefit poor people instead goes to increased pensions for the bureaucrats themselves. If quite important traditional teachings about the person and conscious evolution have fallen into the hands of the contemporary guru-superstar industry, then we have to look at the lacking elements in our society as a whole. After all, if one is denied normal food one will search out alternatives, even food that makes one sick.

We are lax in the training of personal knowledge. We may spend years perfecting our tennis stroke, yet precious little training is offered on the nature of our bodies or the personal dimensions of our own experience. The research described in chapters 2 and 3 that shows our ordinary consciousness to be a one particular "best guess" about the nature of reality is rarely, if ever, taught to students in psychology or education classes.

If we have a mental operating system that is selected for immediate actions that ensure our biological survival, we should know that our judgements will always be biased this way: Sex and the family are very important priorities, for instance; they comprise a large portion of our mind. "Academic" learning is rather determinedly kept in one sphere, with its own professionals and hierarchy, "applied" training in another. Rarely does the academic become involved in training people, and rarely does the "applied" psychologist or educator make any dent in mainstream academic thinking.

The new, franchised self-improvement courses are neither the instant self/transcendence/fantastic/enlightenment panaceas supposed, nor are they, as most academics contend, lacking *any* phenomena of interest. They provide some of the rudiments of an understanding of consciousness. In the absence of anything more highly developed, such programs impress their followers and yield great benefits to their leaders—after all, a simple tape recorder might be enough to convince a primitive tribe that the bearer was a representative of the deity.

If you had never heard of an automobile, you might be excited to be offered for $150,000 a vehicle that actually "ran without horses." Such a vehicle might be made of the fenders of a 1921 Ford, the engine of a

1926 Hispano-Suiza, the transmission of a contemporary Mercedes, seats from a Chevrolet pickup truck, the rear body from an Austin.

You might be further impressed by the sacrifices and the submission you and many volunteers would need to keep such a vehicle on the road. If no one else of your acquaintance had ever heard of an automobile, you might well become famous as the person *"Who Gave It All Up for the Vehicle That Could Move Itself."* Yet even the most humble contemporary economy car would be an improvement.

From one system, one can learn to relax; from a second, to relate; from a third, to respond. Converts are made by classic methods: Program leaders offer either a minor service to the inexperienced (say, getting a personal *mantram*); or they offer a severe initiation/conversion experience, as in the large-scale awareness-training systems. Particular systems come and go, inspired by a given site or the particular style or technique of a leader, yet their successes and excesses remain fairly constant.

The Experience of the Exotic

The practices of meditation as developed in various cultures of the world and in various cultural eras are quite diverse: whirling, chanting, singing; concentration on breath, on specially posed questions, or on an internal sound. Meditation practices have many, many diverse functions, depending on the nature of the students and of the society.

But the primary function of the diverse techniques of meditation is to begin to answer the basic questions of life, such questions as go unanswered in ordinary social or educational interaction. For instance, one might ask, "What is the purpose of existence?" or "What is death?" in the same verbal analytic mode as one might ask, "What is the size of that building?"

Most of us are trained to ask questions this way. However, the traditional psychologists contend that personal questions about the nature of existence *cannot be answered in the same rational, verbal manner as can questions about the nature of the physical or even social environment*. The practices, then, are "a-logical," intended to *defeat* the ordinary sequential and analytic approach to problem solving in situations where this approach is not appropriate.

There is an old, probably untrue, story about this, but it is useful to repeat for the pattern contained in it. A Japanese academic who wished to "understand" Zen more fully went to a monastery to submit himself to the koans. He was asked "What is *mu?*" A good scholar, he proceeded to look up the syllable in Japanese and other Oriental dictionaries to determine a potential root meaning and habitual usage. He presented his findings to the Master, who immediately sent him away.

Our scholar next considered whether the question was more subtle and tried to analyze the tonal component of the syllable in every language of the Chinese group. He again presented his findings to the Master, who now thought it was time to convince this poor scholar of the seriousness of his situation, that it was not a question of another academic excursion. "I will give you one more chance," he said, "and if you do not solve the riddle, I will cut off your leg."

Now, even in the most extreme arguments or thesis examinations of the academic world, things usually don't become this rough. But the threat did frighten the scholar "out of this wits," so to speak. He completely concentrated upon the syllable itself, and in the process of concentration itself he achieved the result. The question had a nonanalytic effect, and a nonverbal result as well. Those who are not privy to the extreme concentration brought about by the Zen Master's exercise, or the scholar's reply, might not realize that many of the most important and compelling questions that face us cannot be looked up in an encyclopedia or dictionary. There is no place where the meaning of one's life is "written up."

Continual concentration upon any object produces certain biological results. Among them is a loss of contact with the external world—which may be interpreted differently by a person merely amusing himself by staring at a crack in the wall, or by a person in a psychological experiment, or by one who performs these actions at the beginning of serious practice in esoteric tradition.

TM (Trademark)

One particular form known by its trademarked name as "Transcendental Meditation" is in fact the most elemental and least transcendent form of meditation of all. Indeed, Transcendental Meditation, quite popular in the United States and Western Europe, has offered many their first idea of what these traditions are about—unfortunately, too often in the form of a goofy, giggling, gassing guru and a highly developed slick brochure promotion program of scientific "validation."

Descriptions of the "efficacy" of Transcendental Meditation are displayed in brochures and on posters stuck on Laundromats and pizza parlors from Spokane to Boca Raton: "Improves levels of rest, aids natural changes of breath rate, cardiac output, relaxation, restful alertness, brain wave synchrony, faster reaction time, increased perceptual ability, learning ability, academic performance, productivity, job satisfaction, job performance, self-actualization, inner control, mental health, psychology," and so on.

It is claimed by the proselytizers of TM that it is the "answer to all your problems." Common to many of the franchised systems are these commercial claims to improve every aspect of human life. This is a mark of a cult system. Participants believe they have in their grasp a technique good for everyone at all times—not one that might have selective benefits and detriments.

In the case of TM, the bulk of its claimed scientific "validations" are usually marked "submitted for publication"—or are published by the movement's own Maharishi International University Press. TM is promoted as a "synthesis of East and West," which means, presumably, that Western science is at last considered able to investigate practices of the East. If there *is* a synthesis here, it is an unfortunately comic one—the lack of scientific rigor in the East joined with the lack of spiritual advancement of the West.

The claims debase both science and meditation. Here, science is employed to document improvements in personality or bodily changes, with no consideration given to whether such changes are in fact due to meditation, and what the significance of the change really is.

The mere report of an alteration in the electroencephalogram means almost nothing by itself. The EEG alone is quite variable and rigorous controls are needed to ensure that any "brain waves" recorded actually relate to significant brain activity. Recording an EEG might be compared to placing a heat sensor over a computer and trying to understand the computer's program.

The innumerable brochures and posters that promote the TM movement often go beyond scientific evidence. "Increased synchrony" of the brain EEG is often claimed as a result of TM. This is supposed to connote to those versed neither in meditation nor in brain research a measure of the mind's "increased harmony"—that both hemispheres are working together. In truth, such "synchrony" (a finding largely unrepeated) derives from the fact that the brain may produce more alpha rhythm in times of quiescence, and thus the correlation of the two hemispheres of the brain is increased.

Similarly, a time-displaced frequency (Fourier) analysis is sometimes displayed. The implication is that the mind is "calm" during meditation, probably because the graphs have an appearance of regularity—the use of fancy computers to impress the audience. Someone might point out that the electroencephalogram of an epileptic seizure looks like a coherent pattern on a frequency analysis. The same is true of relaxation measures, and the various additional studies. It is still garbage in, garbage out.

The fallacy here seems to be: If any psychological or physiological measure alters during their practice of the concentrative "transcendental" meditation, then (a) it must be due, exclusively, to this wonderful practice; and (b) the changes must be "good."

The brochures and posters are a continuous barrage of displays of implied measures of increased Goodness and decreased Badness, during and after the practices.

Here's how this "almost science" process works. Anyone could perform a physiological experiment that will yield positive results, and that could be repeated (or, rather, performed for the first time) in any physiological laboratory in the world. They could also draw the same conclusions as do the TM merchandisers from their experiments.

Suppose that reading was not developed in our society; proponents might claim that reading "sacred" literature, such as the Bible, not only leads to increased Goodness, but that it *actually causes physiological changes*. Imagine the following experiment—physiological measures are taken on selected subjects before reading, while reading, and after reading; eye movement is chosen for the physiological validation of our experiment.

Before reading, physiological activity was at a low level, but during reading it dramatically increased, then returned to baseline afterward. If we wanted to continue the research, we could undoubtedly record alterations in Regional Cerebral Blood Flow (RCBF) to the left hemisphere, changes in Galvanic Skin Resistance (GSR), et cetera. We could use the latest techniques such as positron-emission tomography and measure the changes in metabolism deep within the brain itself, but this would still be "garbage in, garbage out." *Our experiment would not explain how an arbitrary measure, such as eye movement, relates to the supposed benefits of reading, or whether, for instance, other types of reading would show similar effects on the eye-movement measure.*

The research attempts to validate meditation exploit science to sell a product; it uses promotionalism similar to the drug company television commercials that show one product entering the bloodstream faster than others. Instead of the promotion, the research question should be: What are the real effects of meditation? Popular forms of meditation are, most likely, a quite reduced and sanitized form of a more advanced exercise, no more useful than repeating the words *Coca-Cola* or *money* over and over for relaxation. This exercise is not at all useless in itself, but as it is packaged it is *quicksand* to someone seeking extended knowledge.

Hucksters are to be expected when so few people are sufficiently acquainted with the intention, possibility, and range of human conscious development. The primary purpose of meditation is not physiological. No one meditates to attain "synchrony of electrical activity of the brain hemispheres" or "a long period of pure, high-amplitude, single-frequency theta waves." Could anyone really care about that? Meditation is undertaken to increase one's capacity for experience and self-understanding; glimpses of potential control over one's consciousness; a chance to observe, firsthand, our own habitual mental activity.

There are a myriad of potential consciousness-alteration techniques. As our culture is opened up to the East, various immigrants have entered with techniques borrowed across cultures.

However, although there are many techniques available, *most people are not in a position to choose which is most appropriate for them*. We have no real tradition to draw upon.

"Experts" who have little experience of spirituality offer instant-weekend self-improvement courses that promote the particular amalgam chosen by the expert himself. They often involve a little meditation, a little indoctrination, a little Scientology, and a little "validation," with the audience softened up (as in brainwashing) by fatigue, fasting, and fatuous insults. Such courses bear the same relationship to a real spiritual teaching as the techniques of a sex manual have to the experience of love.

The instant-enlightenment-weekend approach can be produced by several means: the proper use of jewelry; fasting; dancing to exhaustion; sensory deprivation or overload. Such an upset of ordinary activities and consciousness can yield something startling: a deautomatizing "first experience" that the world is different from what one had thought, that our everyday experience is, after all, a construction. We are likely to misinterpret its significance, just as people often overvalue their first sexual experience.

The franchised weekends take just such an advantage of the gap in our education. Popular mysticism claims "converted" adherents for an understanding that should be part of our basic education. Its enthusiasts take an exercise meant for one community and generalize it to everyone and offer the same mass indoctrination or initiation to everyone.

The systems are artificial and need be kept going with much effort and activity. Social gratification begins to substitute for the development of the mental system, with parties, mixers, investment clubs, phone solicitation, uniform dress, and jargon designed to create an elite in-group. Continual reminders are given to stragglers by mass mailings, letters and phone calls, Christmas gifts, solicitations of service to the head of the organization.

The noncommercial secretive societies are unfortunately similar to the well-advertised consciousness systems. The degeneration of a true religious tradition in the West has left those high-minded "metaphysical people" prey to those who substitute an ancient fragmentary teaching for a unified whole. David Pendlebury describes the current situation:

"Sobriety" and "intoxication" are of course not intended literally; nor are they merely flowery metaphors: these are technical terms denoting twin poles of human awareness, each in its own way indispensable to balanced development. A man has to see the true reality of his situation; he has to take a very sober look at himself. Equally, though, he needs a taste of another condition in which his latent possibilities are recognized. Taken on its own, either pole is sterile, developmentally speaking. There are plentiful examples all around us of such imbalances. Perhaps you too had a Calvinist great-uncle who died heartbroken, having succeeded in convincing himself (a) that "the grace of God" was essential, and (b) that such "grace" had been withheld from him. Perhaps you, too, have friends whose Ouspensky-orientated understanding of Gurdjieff has left them eternally bewailing the (obvious) facts that "man is asleep," "man cannot remember himself," "man cannot do," etc. Or other friends who have chosen to "freak out," to "blow their minds"; and are astonished, in rare moments of lucidity, to find themselves inhabiting a "behavioural sink" or "terminal sewer." Or other friends, perhaps, who inform you in and out of season that: "I was hopelessly at sea, until (name and address supplied) showed me the answer."

Pendlebury mentions the Caucasian "mystic" George Gurdjieff, whose followers present the fragmentation of much of contemporary esoteric studies. Although by many accounts Gurdjieff seemed to awaken a sense of life and action in his associates, his work has become the captive of his most doctrinaire and severe followers. Half the time you hear them shout "I must wake up" while walking into a lamppost! The sad students search each new sage for the secret that will send them away from ceaseless self-preoccupation and experience the wholeness of life.

This kind of esoteric school serves to *promote* abnormality, not an increased self-knowledge. The continuous search for spiritual knowledge leads to teachings inappropriate for our time and culture. Outmoded books on alchemy, ancient mysticism, commentaries on Gurdjieff and other mystics are all scoured by the devout in their hope of finding "the key" that will unite all.

In this they make a sad mistake: They sell themselves short, for the mind brain system in everyday life possesses the capacity to shift gears and perceive things differently; it does not need a pathetic search for something sacred.

One of Gurdjieff's teachers describes this process to one who sought out the teachings of the East: "You are scrabbling about in the sands, looking for bits of mica to piece together to make a mirror, not realizing that the sand *itself* is capable of being transformed into the purest glass."

The sand may represent the enormity of the mind, the bits of glass, the few isolated experiences prized by cult members—while there is a more profound development possible.

There is an important and somewhat blunt distinction to be made. It is between the high-profile end of the spiritual traditions, the esotericizers, who "search the depths of their souls" for bits of knowledge, and those more sober, quiet, and serious people who attempt genuine self-observation leading to a deeper understanding of themselves and of the nature of life.

Reductionism in science is bad enough, but now we have metaphysical inflation. Innumerable books written in effulgent and selfdenigratory terms about an outmoded cosmology are no more relevant to the real development of human knowledge than are psychiatric theorizing or the double-talk of commercial awareness-training groups. I think it is no wonder that the whole idea is repugnant to normal, successful, constructive people. But recall Rumi's "Counterfeiters exist because there is true gold."

"Sight" and Learning

Earlier we discussed a man who recovered from blindness—this kind of experience may provide a parallel to the issues we are discussing. A blind person accustomed to hearing inflated exaltations of the joys of sight may not be prepared when someone introduces medical procedures useful in an eye operation. "What are these cold hard things I touch?" he may exclaim of the surgical instruments. "What is their relationship to the grandeur of green grass, or to a sunset, of which I have heard so many wondrous descriptions?"

Why many people of differing specializations may need to be involved in the task of surgery; why there is a need for antisepsis, a need for someone to have studied the physiology of the eye; would escape someone who does not understand the complexity of the operation and the underlying condition. Similarly those who are interested in the analogous kind of *seeing* are often deflected to developing expertise on "the Dimensions of Spiritual Experience," or "the Wisdom of the East." Such a person wishes for more availability of *descriptions* of sight. What kind of deal is that?

However, current literature, travel writings, and scientific facts all *can* help. If properly presented, they can convey to the interested student the rudiments of "sight," and can aid in developing a more comprehensive awareness of himself and of life. This can occur even though the literature may not directly mention cosmology, God, mysticism, or any of the things most usually associated with mystical experience.

One specialist explained the function of the literature that he used:

> Literature is the means by which things which have been taken out of the community, such as knowledge, can be returned.
> The similitude is as of a seed, which may be returned to the earth long after the plant from which it grew is dead, with perhaps no trace of it remaining.

The learned may be millers of the grain-seed, but those whom we call the Wise are the cultivators of the crop.

Take heed of this parable, for it contains the explanation of much irreconcilability of attitudes in the two classes of students.

But the students usually cannot determine what they are trying to do. Many people keep trying to somehow "save" themselves by these cults. The whole problem could well be avoided if the priority system that exists in consciousness were better understood. If someone is unfulfilled in marriage, in work, in self-concept, *they are much better off trying to first get the fulfillment and stability they need, rather than term it spiritual or conscious development.* If you are hungry, you will seek food in any environment, and if you need recognition, praise, et cetera, you will do so as well.

People often try to make any organization into a heirarchy, and try to locate their own status in it. For those situations with no heirarchy, it gives the student a chance to observe the feelings and actions that take place in his own mind, somewhat like the old psychoanalytic idea of projection. Therefore, people will say, in discussing their interest in one group or another, things about their autonomy, or their "power," or their status, closeness to whomever they perceive as the head.

The difficulty is that people always try to use their *already-developed schemata,* so useful in dealing with society and the outside world, when they try to do something else. In modern society these discussions about power and status and obtaining recognition are the equivalent of the hunger pangs monks must have felt in the Middle Ages, when they were taken off rich meals and given a simple diet.

Consciousness and the Misplaced Schemata

In attempting this kind of mental development people have to do something quite difficult: give up the "worldly schemata." One approach involves the students' learning to be *flexible* enough to organize themselves around a concern, no matter what its apparent aim; attend to the job they are asked to do, and not to personalities. They are often given very many different kinds of jobs in different circumstances; as soon as one seems to be going it changes.

This kind of practice, in a situation close to their ordinary experience, is difficult, more difficult than abandoning home and leaving all possessions, but it is what helps them adapt to the *real instability and the constant changes in the world*. Through all the different experiences, the student can develop some internal stability, detachment.

This effort isn't often called *The Work* for nothing—most people say it is very difficult! The people involved need to organize themselves to be able to get beyond their current ideas and perceive something larger.

We are a very adaptable animal and we can do many different things: We are emotional, we can paint, we have arguments, we think, we are sometimes rational—but learning how to develop consciousness does not necessarily entail giving up these aspects of our nature, but *organizing them*.

On this rests a fundamental insight of both the modern and traditional psychologies, an insight that has not reached many of its students: Our mental operating system is not one designed to act rationally in business, in our social and emotional life, so it does not allow us to simply "transcend" our material nature immediately; we must carry it along. We have many mental abilities, but they are basically designed for immediate surviving in a chaotic world.

It is a matter of understanding *which* of our needs needs be satisfied at any one time, and *which* of our mental routines is useful at any moment. Certainly no one needs give up those reactions useful to survival and the "normal" social conditioning that we need to get along in any society. *It is a matter of selecting and connecting them in the right way, each for the right kind of thinking.*

Our minds are multiple, and we find it difficult to control the diverse mental abilities within. This ability to choose and direct the mental system is the most often unrealized aim of "conscious development." How it might be realized is the subject of the next and last chapter.

THE TEACHING-STORY: OBSERVATIONS ON THE FOLKLORE OF OUR MODERN THOUGHT

Idries Shah

There is no nation, no community without its stories. Children are brought up on fairy tales, cults and religions depend upon them for moral instruction: They are used for entertainment and for training. They are usually catalogued as myths, as humorous tales, as semi-historical fact, and so on, in accordance with what people believe to be their origin and function.

But what a story can be used for is often what it was originally intended to be used for. The fables of all nations provide a really remarkable example of this, because, if you can understand them at a technical level, they provide the most striking evidence of the persistence of a consistent teaching, preserved sometimes through mere repetition, yet handed down and prized simply because they give a stimulus to the imagination or entertainment for the people at large.

There are very few people nowadays who are able to make the necessary use of stories. Those who know about the higher level of being represented by stories can learn something from them, but very little. Those who can experience this level can teach the use of stories. But first of all we must allow the working hypothesis that there may be such a level operative in stories. We must approach them from the point of view that they may on that level be documents of technical value: an ancient yet still irreplacable method of arranging and transmitting a knowledge which can not be put in any other way.

In this sense such stories (because *all* stories are not technical literature), such stories may be regarded as part of a curriculum, and as valid a representation of fact as, for instance, any mathematical formula or scientific textbook.

Like any scientific textbook or mathematical formula, however, stories depend for their higher power upon someone to understand them at the higher level, someone who can establish their validity in a course of study, people who are prepared to study and use them, and so on.

At this point we can see quite easily that our conditioning (which trains us to use stories for amusement purposes) is generally in itself sufficient to prevent us from making any serious study of stories as a vehicle for higher teaching. This tendency, the human tendency to regard anything as of use to man on a lower level than it could operate, runs through much of our studies, and has to be marked well.

Yet traditions about stories do in fact linger here and there. People say that certain stories, if repeated, will provide some sort of "good luck"; or that tales have meanings which have been forgotten, and the like. But what would be called in contemporary speech the "security aspect" of stories is almost complete in the case of the genre which we call "teaching stories" because of another factor.

This factor is the operation of the law that a story, like a scientific industrial formula, say, can have its developmental or teaching effect only upon a person correctly prepared for its understanding. This is why we must use stories in a manner which will enable us to harvest their value for us in a given situation.

There is another problem which has to be appreciated when dealing with stories. Unlike scientific formulae, they have a whole series of developmental effects. In accordance with the degree of preparation of an individual and a group, so will the successive "layers" of the story become apparent. Outside of a proper school where the method and content of stories is understood, there is almost no chance of an arbitrary study of stories yielding much.

But we have to go back to an even earlier stage in order to ground ourselves, prepare ourselves, for the value of the story. This is the stage at which we can familiarize ourselves with the story and regard it as a consistent and productive parallel or allegory of certain states of mind. Its symbols are the characters in the story. The way in which they move conveys to the mind the way in which the human mind can work. In grasping this in terms of men and women, animals and places, movement and manipulation of a tale, we can put ourselves into a relationship with the higher faculties possible to the mind, by working on a lower level, the level of visualisation.

Let us examine a story or two from the foregoing points of view. First, take a story of the Elephant in the Dark.* This has actually been published as a children's book. It appears in the books of Rumi and Sanai. We have made it the subject of a commercial film, *The Dermis Probe*. This story, on the lowest possible level, makes fun of the scientists and academics who try to explain things through the evidence which they *can* evaluate, and none other. In another direction, on the same level, it is humorous in as much as it makes us laugh at the stupidity of people who work on such little evidence. As a philosophical teaching it says that man is blind and is trying to assess something too great for as-

---

*A number of blind people, or sighted people in a dark house, grope and find an elephant. Each touches only a part; each gives to his friends outside a different account of what he has experienced. Some think that it was a fan (the ears of the animal); another takes the legs for pillars; a third the tail for a rope, and so on.

sessment by means of inadequate tools. In the religious field it says that God is everywhere and everything, and man gives different names to what seem to him to be separate things, but which are in fact only parts of some greater whole which he cannot perceive because "he is blind" or "there is no light."

The interpretations are far and high as anyone can go. Because of this, people address themselves to this story in one or more of these interpretations. They then accept or reject them. Now they can feel happy; they have arrived at an opinion about the matter. According to their conditioning they produce the answer. Now look at their answers. Some will say that this is a fascinating and touching allegory of the presence of God. Others will say that it is showing people how stupid mankind can be. Some say it is anti-scholastic. Others that it is just a tale copied by Rumi from Sanai—and so on. Because none of these people can taste an inner content, none will even begin to imagine that one exists. As I say these words the ordinary mind will easily be able to dispose of them by thinking that this is just someone who has provided a sophisticated explanation for something which cannot be checked.

But we are not here to justify ourselves. We are here to open the door of the mind to the possibility that stories might be technical documents. We are here to say that there is a method of making use of these documents. Especially we are here to say that the most ancient and most important knowledge available to man is in part contained in these documents. And that this form, however primitive or old-fashioned it may seem, is in fact almost the only form in which certain teachings can be captured, preserved and transmitted. And, too, that these stories are conscious works of art, devised by people who knew exactly what they were doing, for the use of other people who knew exactly what could be done with them.

It may take a conventional thinker some time to understand that if he is looking for truth and a hidden teaching, it may be concealed in a form which would be the last, perhaps, which he would consider to be applicable to his search.

But, in order to possess himself of this knowledge, he must take it from where it *really is,* not from where he imagines it might be.

There is plenty of evidence of the working of this method, that of the story deliberately concocted and passed down, in all cultures. We do not have to confine ourselves to Eastern fables. But it is in stories of Eastern origin that we find the most complete and least deteriorated forms of the tradition. We therefore start with them. They lead us, naturally, to the significant documents in the Western and other branches of the tradition.

In approaching the study of stories, then, we have to make sure that we reclaim the information that stories contain, shall we say, a message. In this sense we are like people whose technology has fallen into disuse, rediscovering the devices used by our ancestors as we become fitted for it. Then we have to realise that we have to familiarise ourselves with certain stories, so that we can hold them in our minds, like memorising a formula. In this use, the teaching story resembles the mnemonic or formula which we trot out to help us calculate something: like saying: "one kilo equals 2.2 pounds in weight"; or even "thirty days hath September."

Now we have to realise that, since we are dealing with a form of knowledge which is specific in as much as it is planned to act in a certain way under certain conditions, those conditions must be present if we are to be able to use the story coherently. By coherently I mean here, if the story is to be the guide whereby we work through the various stages of consciousness open to us.

This means that we must not only get to know certain tales; we must study them, or even just familiarise ourselves with them, in a certain order. This idea tends to find opposition among literate people who are accustomed to doing their own reading, having been led to believe that the more you read the more likely you are to know more. But this quantitative approach is absurd when you are dealing with specific material. If you went to the British Museum library and decided to read everything in it in order to educate yourself, you would not get very far. It is only the ignorant, even in the formal sense, who cannot understand the need for particular kinds of specialisation. This is well exemplified by the club porter who once said to me, in all seriousness "You are a college man, Sir, please explain football pool permutations to me."

It is in order to get some possibility of right study that I continually say things like "Let us get down out of the trees and start to build."

So far, however, we have not been saying much more than this:

1. A special, effective and surpassingly important teaching is contained in certain materials. In this case the materials are stories.

2. We must accept the possibility before we can begin to approach the study of this knowledge.
3. Having accepted, even as a working hypothesis, the foregoing contentions, we have to set about the study in an efficient manner. In the case of the tales, the efficient manner means to approach the right stories, in the right manner, under the right circumstances.

Failure to adhere to these principles will make it impossible for us to function on the high level needed. If, for example, we settle for merely knowing a lot of stories, we may become mere raconteurs or consumers. If we settle for the moral or social teaching of the story, we simply duplicate the activities of people working in that domain. If we compare stories to try to see where the higher level is, we will not find it, because we do not know unless guided which are the ones to compare with each other, under what conditions, what to look for, whether we can perceive the secret content, in what order to approach the matter.

So the story remains a tool as much as anything else. Only the expert can use the tool, or produce anything worthwhile with it.

Having heard and accepted the above assertions, people always feel impatience. They want to get on with the job. But, not knowing that "everything takes a minimum time," or at any rate not applying this fact, they destroy the possibility of progress in a real sense.

Having established in a certain order the above facts, we have to follow through with a curriculum of study which will enable us to profit by the existence of this wonderful range of material. If you start to study what you take to be teaching-stories indiscriminately, you are more than likely to get only a small result, even with the facts already set out. Why is this?

Not only because you do not know the conditions under which the study must take place, but because the conditions themselves contain requirements of self-collection which seem to have no relationship to the necessities for familiarising oneself with a literary form.

We must, therefore, work on the mind to enable it to make use of the story, as well as presenting it with the story. This "work" on the mind is correctly possible only in the living situation, when certain people are grouped together in a certain manner, and develop a certain form of rapport. This, and no other, is the purpose of having meetings at which people are physically present.

If read hurriedly, or with one or other of the customary biases which are common among intellectuals but not other kinds of thinkers, the foregoing two paragraphs will be supposed to contain exclusivistic claims which are not in fact there.

This is itself one of the interesting—and encouraging—symptoms of the present phase of human intellectual folklore. If a tendency can readily be seen manifesting itself, whether in physics, scholasticism or metaphysics, one may be approaching its solution. What is this tendency?

The tendency is to demand a justification of what are taken to be certain claims *in the language in which the demand is made*. My stressing, for instance, that meetings at which people are present who have been grouped in a certain manner, may easily (and incorrectly) be supposed to state that the kind of learning to which I am referring can take place in no other manner. The intention of the paragraph, however, was simply to refer to one concrete manner in which what I have called "a living situation" can come about. A meeting of a number of people in a room is the only form of such a situation familiar to any extent to an average reader of such materials as this.

I have used the word "folklore" to refer to a state of mind of modern man closely similar to that of less developed communities. But there is a great difference between the two folklores. In what we regard as ingenuous folklore, the individual may believe that certain objects have magical or special characteristics, and he is more or less aware of what these are claimed to be.

In modern man's folklore, he believes that certain contentions must be absurd, and holds on to other assumptions, without being aware that he is doing so. He is motivated, in fact, by almost completely hidden prejudices.

To illustrate the working of such preconceptions, it is often necessary to provide a "shock" stimulus.

Such a stimulus occurs both in the present series of contentions about the teaching-story (because, and only because, certain information about it is lost to the community being addressed) and exists equally strongly within the frameworks of such stories themselves, when one can view them in a structural manner.

This train of thought itself produces an illustration of the relative fragmentation of contemporary minds. Here it is:

Although it is a matter of the everyday experience of almost everyone on this planet, irrespective of his stage of culture or his community, that any one thing may have a multiplicity of uses, functions and meanings, man does not apply this experience to cases which—for some occult reason—he regards as insusceptible to such attention. In other words, a person may admit that an orange has colour, aroma, food value, shape, texture and so on; and he will readily concede that an orange may be many different things according to what function is desired, observed or being fulfilled. But if you venture to suggest that, say, a story has an equal range of possible functions, his folkloric evaluating mechanism will make him say: "No, a story is for entertainment," or else something almost as byzantine: "Yes, of course. Now, are you talking about the psychological, social, anthropological or philosophical uses?"

Nobody has told him that there are, or might be, categories of effective function of a story in ranges which he has not yet experienced, perhaps not yet heard of, perhaps even cannot perceive or even coherently discuss, until a certain basic information process has taken place in his mind.

And to this kind of statement the answer is pat and hard to combat. It is: "You are trying to be clever." This, you may recall is only the "yaa-boo" reaction of the schoolchild who has come up against something which it cannot, at least at that moment, rationalise away or fully understand.

The Magic Horse

This tale is of great importance because it belongs to an instructional corpus of mystical materials with inner content but—beyond entertainment value—without immediate external significance.

The teaching-story was brought to perfection as a communication instrument many thousands of years ago. The fact that it has not developed greatly since then has caused people obsessed by some theories of our current civilisations to regard it as the product of a less enlightened time. They feel that it must surely be little more than a literary curiosity, something fit for children, the projection, perhaps, of infantile desires, a means of enacting a wish-fulfillment.

Hardly anything could be further from the truth of such pseudo-philosophical, certainly unscientific, imaginings. Many teaching-stories *are* entertaining to children and to naive peasants. Many of them in the forms in which they are viewed by conditioned theorists have been so processed by unregenerate amateurs that their effective content is distorted. Some apply only to certain communities, depending upon special circumstances for their correct unfolding: circumstances whose absence effectively prevents the action of which they are capable.

So little is known to the academics, the scholars, and the intellectuals of this world about these materials, that there is no word in modern languages which has been set aside to describe them.

But the teaching-story exists, nevertheless. It is a part of the most priceless heritage of mankind.

Real teaching-stories are not to be confused with parables; which are adequate enough in their intention, but still on a lower level of material, generally confined to the inculcation of moralistic principles, not the assistance of interior movement of the human mind. What we often take on the lower level of parable, however, can sometimes be seen by real specialists as teaching-stories; especially when experienced under the correct conditions.

Unlike the parable, the meaning of the teaching-story cannot be unravelled by ordinary intellectual methods alone. Its action is direct and certain, upon the innermost part of the human being, an action incapable of manifestation by means of the emotional or intellectual apparatus.

The closest that we can come to describing its effect is to say that it connects with a part of the individual which cannot be reached by any other convention, and that it establishes in him or in her a means of communication with a non-verbalised truth beyond the customary limitations of our familiar dimensions.

Some teaching-stories cannot now be reclaimed because of the literary and traditionalistic, even ideological, processing to which they have been subjected. The worst of such processes is the historicising one, where a community comes to believe that one of their former teaching-stories represents literal historical truth.

This tale is given here in a form which is innocent of this and other kinds of maltreatment.

Once upon a time—not so very long ago—there was a realm in which the people were exceedingly prosperous. All kinds of discoveries had been made by them, in the growing of plants, in harvesting and preserving fruits, and in making objects for sale to other countries: and in many other practical arts.

Their ruler was unusually enlightened, and he encouraged new discoveries and activities, because he knew of their advantages for his people.

He had a son named Hoshyar, who was expert in using strange contrivances, and another—called Tambal—a dreamer, who seemed interested only in things which were of little value in the eyes of the citizens.

From time to time the king, who was named King Mumkin, circulated announcements to this effect:

"Let all those who have notable devices and useful artifacts present them to the palace for examination, so that they may be appropriately rewarded."

Now there were two men of that country—an ironsmith and a woodworker—who were great rivals in most things, and each delighted in making strange contraptions. When they heard this announcement one day, they agreed to compete for an award, so that their relative merits could be decided once and for all, by their sovereign, and publicly recognized.

Accordingly, the smith worked day and night on a mighty engine, employing a multitude of talented specialists, and surrounding his workshop with high walls so that his devices and methods should not become known.

At the same time the woodworker took his simple tools and went into a forest where, after long and solitary reflection, he prepared his own masterpiece.

News of the rivalry spread, and people thought that the smith must easily win, for his cunning works had been seen before, and while the woodworker's products were generally admired, they were of occasional and undramatic use.

When both were ready, the king received them in open court.

The smith produced an immense metallic fish which could, he said, swim in and under the water. It could carry large quantities of freight over the land. It could burrow into the earth; and it could even fly slowly through the air. At first the court found it hard to believe that there could be such a wonder made by man: but when the smith and his assistants demonstrated it, the king was overjoyed and declared the smith among the most honoured in the land, with a special rank and the title of "Benefactor of the Community."

Prince Hoshyar was placed in charge of the making of the wondrous fishes, and the services of this new device became available to all mankind.

Everyone blessed the smith and Hoshyar, as well as the benign and sagacious monarch whom they loved so much.

In the excitement, the self-effacing carpenter had been all but forgotten. Then, one day, someone said: "But what about the contest? Where is the entry of the woodworker? We all know him to be an ingenious man. Perhaps he has produced something useful."

"How could anything possibly be as useful as the Wondrous Fishes?" asked Hoshyar. And many of the courtiers and the people agreed with him.

But one day the king was bored. He had become accustomed to the novelty of the fishes and the reports of the wonders which they so regularly performed. He said: "Call the woodcarver, for I would now like to see what he has made."

The simple woodcarver came into the throne-room, carrying a parcel, wrapped in coarse cloth. As the whole court craned forward to see what he had, he took off the covering to reveal—a wooden horse. It was well enough carved, and it had some intricate patterning chiselled into it, as well as being decorated with coloured paints but it was only . . . "A mere plaything!" snapped the king.

"But father," said Prince Tambal, "let us ask the man what it is for . . ."

"Very well," said the king, "what is it for?"

"Your majesty," stammered the woodcarver, "it is a magic horse. It does not look impressive, but it has, as it were, its own inner senses. Unlike the fish, which has to be directed, this horse can interpret the desires of the rider, and carry him wherever he needs to go."

"Such stupidity is fit only for Tambal," murmured the chief minister at the king's elbow; "it cannot have any real advantage when measured against the wondrous fish."

The woodcarver was preparing sadly to depart when Tambal said: "Father, let me have the wooden horse."

"All right," said the king, "give it to him. Take the woodcarver away and tie him on a tree somewhere, so that he will realise that our time is valuable. Let him contemplate the prosperity which the wondrous fish has brought us, and perhaps after some time we shall let him go free, to practise whatever he may have learned of real industriousness, through true reflection."

The woodcarver was taken away, and Prince Tambal left the court carrying the magic horse.

Tambal took the horse to his quarters, where he discovered that it had several knobs, cunningly concealed in the carved designs. When these were turned in a certain manner, the horse—together with anyone mounted on it—rose into the air and sped to whatever place was in the mind of the person who moved the knobs.

In this way, day after day, Tambal flew to places which he had never visited before. By this process he came to know a great many things. He took the horse everywhere with him.

One day he met Hoshyar, who said to him: "Carrying a wooden horse is a fit occupation for such as you. As for me, I am working for the good of all, towards my heart's desire!"

Tambal thought: "I wish I knew what was the good of all. And I wish I could know what my heart's desire is."

When he was next in his room, he sat upon the horse and thought: "I would like to find my heart's desire." At the same time he moved some of the knobs on the horse's neck.

Swifter than light the horse rose into the air and carried the prince a thousand days' ordinary journey away, to a far kingdom, ruled by a magician-king.

The king, whose name was Kahana, had a beautiful daughter called Precious Pearl, Durri-Karima. In order to protect her, he had imprisoned her in a circling palace, which wheeled in the sky, higher than any mortal could reach. As he was approaching the magic land, Tambal saw the glittering palace in the heavens, and alighted there.

The princess and the young horseman met and fell in love.

"My father will never allow us to marry," she said; "for he has ordained that I become the wife of the son of another magician-king who lives across the cold desert to the east of our homeland. He has vowed that when I am old enough I shall cement the unity of the two kingdoms by this marriage. His will has never been successfully opposed."

"I will go and try to reason with him," answered Tambal, as he mounted the magic horse again.

But when he descended into the magic land there were so many new and exciting things to see that he did not hurry to the palace. When at length he approached it, the drum at the gate, indicating the absence of the king, was already beating.

"He has gone to visit his daughter in the Whirling Palace," said a passer-by when Tambal asked him when the king might be back; "and he usually spends several hours at a time with her."

Tambal went to a quiet place where he willed the horse to carry him to the king's own apartment. "I will approach him at his own home," he thought to himself, "for if I go to the Whirling Palace without his permission he may be angry."

He hid behind some curtains in the palace when he got there, and lay down to sleep.

Meanwhile, unable to keep her secret, the Princess Precious Pearl had confessed to her father that she had been visited by a man on a flying horse, and that he wanted to marry her. Kahana was furious.

He placed sentries around the Whirling Palace, and returned to his own apartment to think things over. As soon as he entered his bed-chamber, one of the tongueless magic servants guarding it pointed to the wooden horse lying in a corner. "Aha!" exclaimed the magician-king. "Now I have him. Let us look at this horse and see what manner of thing it may be."

As he and his servants were examining the horse, the prince managed to slip away and conceal himself in another part of the palace.

After twisting the knobs, tapping the horse and generally trying to understand how it worked, the king was baffled. "Take that thing away. It has no virtue now, even if it ever had any," he said. "It is just a trifle, fit for children."

The horse was put into a store-cupboard.

Now King Kahana thought that he should make arrangements for his daughter's wedding without delay, in case the fugitive might have other powers or devices with which to try to win her. So he called her to his own palace and sent a message to the other magician-king, asking that the prince who was to marry her be sent to claim his bride.

Meanwhile Prince Tambal, escaping from the palace by night when some guards were asleep, decided that he must try to return to his own country. His quest for his heart's desire now seemed almost hopeless. "If it takes me the rest of my life," he said to himself, "I shall come back here, bringing troops to take this kingdom by force. I can only do that by convincing my father that I must have his help to attain my heart's desire."

So saying, he set off. Never was a man worse equipped for such a journey. An alien, travelling on foot, without any kind of provisions, facing pitiless heat and freezing nights interspersed with sandstorms, he soon became hopelessly lost in the desert.

Now, in his delirium, Tambal started to blame himself, his father, the magician-king, the woodcarver, even the princess and the magic horse itself. Sometimes he thought he saw water ahead of him, sometimes fair cities, sometimes he felt elated, sometimes incomparably sad. Sometimes he even thought that he had companions in his difficulties, but when he shook himself he saw that he was quite alone.

He seemed to have been travelling for an eternity. Suddenly, when he had given up and started again several times, he saw something directly in front of him. It looked like a mirage: a garden, full of delicious fruits, sparkling and almost, as it were, beckoning him towards them.

Tambal did not at first take much notice of this, but soon as he walked, he saw that he was indeed passing through such a garden. He gathered some of the fruits and tasted them cautiously. They were delicious. They took away his fear as well as his hunger and thirst. When he was full, he lay down in the shade of a huge and welcoming tree and fell asleep.

When he woke he felt well enough, but something seemed to be wrong. Running to a nearby pool, he looked at his reflection in the water. Staring up at him was a horrible apparition. It had a long beard, curved horns, ears a foot long. He looked down at his hands. They were covered with fur.

Was it a nightmare? He tried to wake himself, but all the pinching and pummelling had no effect. Now, almost bereft of his senses, beside himself with fear and horror, thrown into transports of screaming, racked with sobs, he threw himself on the ground. "Whether I live or die," he thought, "these accursed fruits have finally ruined me. Even with the greatest army of all time, conquest will not help me. Nobody would marry me now, much less the Princess Precious Pearl. And I cannot imagine the beast who would not be terrified at the sight of me—let alone my heart's desire!" And he lost consciousness.

When he woke again, it was dark and a light was approaching through the groves of silent trees. Fear and hope struggled in him. As it came closer he saw that the light was from a lamp enclosed in a brilliant starlike shape, and that it was carried by a bearded man, who walked in a pool of brightness which it cast around.

The man saw him. "My son," he said, "you have been affected by the influences of this place. If I had not come past, you would have remained just another beast of this enchanted grove, for there are many more like you. But I can help you."

Tambal wondered whether this man was a fiend in disguise, perhaps the very owner of the evil trees. But, as his sense came back he realised that he had nothing to lose.

"Help me, father," he said to the sage.

"If you really want your heart's desire," said the other man, "you have only to fix this desire firmly in your mind, not thinking of the fruit. You then have to take up some of the dried fruits, not the fresh, delicious ones, lying at the foot of all these trees, and eat them. Then follow your destiny."

So saying, he walked away.

While the sage's light disappeared into the darkness, Tambal saw that the moon was rising, and in its rays he could see that there were indeed piles of dried fruits under every tree.

He gathered some and ate them as quickly as he could.

Slowly, as he watched, the fur disappeared from his hands and arms. The horns first shrank, then vanished. The beard fell away. He was himself again. By now it was light and in the dawn he heard the tinkling of camel bells. A procession was coming through the enchanted forest.

It was undoubtedly the cavalcade of some important personage, on a long journey. As Tambal stood there, two outriders detached themselves from the glittering escort and galloped up to him.

"In the name of the Prince, our lord, we demand some of your fruit. His celestial Highness is thirsty and has indicated a desire for some of these strange apricots," said an officer.

Still Tambal did not move, such was his numbed condition after his recent experiences. Now the Prince himself came down from his palanquin and said:

"I am Jadugarzada, son of the magician-king of the East. Here is a bag of gold, oaf. I am having some of your fruit, because I am desirous of it. I am in a hurry, hastening to claim my bride, Princess Precious Pearl, daughter of Kahana, magician-king of the West."

At these words Tambal's heart turned over. But, realising that this must be his destiny which the sage had told him to follow, he offered the Prince as much of the fruit as he could eat.

When he had eaten, the Prince began to fall asleep. As he did so, horns, fur and huge ears started to grow out of him. The soldiers shook him, and the Prince began to behave in a strange way. He claimed that *he* was normal, and that *they* were deformed.

The councillors who had accompanied the party restrained the prince and held a hurried debate. Tambal claimed that all would have been well if the prince had not fallen asleep. Eventually it was decided to put Tambal in the palanquin to play the part of the prince. The horned Jadugarzada was tied to a horse with a veil thrown over his face, disguised as a serving-woman.

"He may recover his wits eventually," said the councillors, "and in any case he is still our Prince. Tambal shall marry the girl. Then, as soon as possible, we shall carry them all back to our own country for our king to unravel the problem."

Tambal, biding his time and following his destiny, agreed to his own part in the masquerade.

When the party arrived at the capital of the West, the king himself came out to meet them. Tambal was taken to the princess as her bridegroom, and she was so astonished that she nearly fainted. But Tambal managed to whisper to her rapidly what had happened, and they were duly married, amid great jubilations.

In the meantime, the horned prince had half recovered his wits, but not his human form, and his escort still kept him under cover. As soon as the feasting was over, the chief of the horned prince's party (who had been keeping Tambal and the princess under a very close watch) presented himself to the court. He said: "O just and glorious monarch, fountain of wisdom; the time has now come, according to the pronouncements of our astrologers and soothsayers, to conduct the bridal pair back to our own land, so that they may be established in their new home under the most felicitous circumstances and influences."

The princess turned to Tambal in alarm, for she knew that Jadugarzada would claim her as soon as they were on the open road—and make an end of Tambal into the bargain.

Tambal whispered to her, "Fear nothing. We must act as best we can, following our destiny. Agree to go, making only the condition that you will not travel without the wooden horse."

At first the magician-king was annoyed at this foible of his daughter's. He realised that she wanted the horse because it was connected with her first suitor. But the chief minister of the horned prince said: "Majesty, I cannot see that this is anything worse than a whim for a toy, such as any young girl might have. I hope that you will allow her to have her plaything, so that we may make haste homeward."

So the magician-king agreed, and soon the cavalcade was resplendently on its way. After the king's escort had withdrawn, and before the time of the first night-halt, the hideous Jadugarzada threw off his veil and cried out to Tambal:

"Miserable author of my misfortunes! I now intend to bind you hand and foot, to take you captive back to my own land. If, when we arrive there, you do not tell me how to remove this enchantment, I will have you flayed alive, inch by inch. Now, give me the Princess Precious Pearl."

Tambal ran to the princess and, in front of the astonished party, rose into the sky on the wooden horse with Precious Pearl mounted behind him.

Within a matter of minutes the couple alighted at the palace of King Mumkin. They related everything that had happened to them, and the king was almost overcome with delight at their safe return. He at once gave orders for the hapless woodcarver to be released, recompensed and applauded by the entire populace.

When the king was gathered to his fathers, Princess Precious Pearl and Prince Tambal succeeded him. Prince Hoshyar was quite pleased, too, because he was still entranced by the wondrous fish.

"I am glad for your own sakes, if you are happy," he used to say to them, "but, for my own part, nothing is more rewarding than concerning myself with the wondrous fish."

And this history is the origin of a strange saying current among the people of that land, yet whose beginnings have now been forgotten. The saying is: "Those who want fish can achieve much through fish, and those who do not know their heart's desire may first have to hear the story of the wooden horse."

The Story of Tea

In ancient times, tea was not known outside China. Rumours of its existence had reached the wise and the unwise of other countries, and each tried to find out what it was in accordance with what he wanted or what he thought it should be.

The king of Inja ("here") sent an embassy to China, and they were given tea by the Chinese Emperor. But, since they saw that the peasants drank it too, they concluded that it was not fit for their royal master:

and, furthermore, that the Chinese Emperor was trying to deceive them, passing off some other substance for the celestial drink.

The greatest philosopher of Anja ("there") collected all the information he could about tea, and concluded that it must be a substance which existed but rarely, and was of another order than anything then known. For was it not referred to as being a herb, as water, green, black, sometimes bitter, sometimes sweet?

In the countries of Koshish and Bebinem, for centuries the people tested all the herbs they could find. Many were poisoned, all were disappointed. For nobody had brought the tea-plant to their lands, and thus they could not find it. They also drank all the liquids which they could find, but to no avail.

In the territory of Mazhab ("Sectarianism") a small bag of tea was carried in procession before the people as they went on their religious observances. Nobody thought of tasting it: Indeed, nobody knew how. All were convinced that the tea itself had a magical quality. A wise man said: "Pour upon it boiling water, ye ignorant ones!" They hanged him and nailed him up, because to do this, according to their belief, would mean the destruction of their tea. This showed that he was an enemy of their religion.

Before he died, he had told his secret to a few, and they managed to obtain some tea and drink it secretly. When anyone said: "What are you doing?" they answered: "It is but medicine which we take for a certain disease."

And so it was throughout the world. Tea had actually been seen growing by some, who did not recognize it. It had been given to others to drink, but they thought it the beverage of the common people. It had been in the possession of others, and they worshipped it. Outside China, only a few people actually drank it, and those covertly.

Then came a man of knowledge, who said to the merchants of tea, and the drinkers of tea, and to others: "He who tastes, knows. He who tastes not, knows not. Instead of talking about the celestial beverage, say nothing, but offer it at your banquets. Those who like it will ask for more. Those who do not, will show that they are not fitted to be tea-drinkers. Close the shop of argument and mystery. Open the teahouse of experience."

The tea was brought from one stage to another along the Silk Road, and whenever a merchant carrying jade or gems or silk would pause to rest, he would make tea, and offer it to such people as were near him, whether they were aware of the repute of tea or not. This was the beginning of the Chaikhanas, the teahouses which were established all the way from Peking to Bokhara and Samarkand. And those who tasted, knew.

At first, mark well, it was only the great and the pretended men of wisdom who sought the celestial drink and who also exclaimed: "But this is only dried leaves!" or: "Why do you boil water, stranger, when all I want is the celestial drink?" or yet again: "How do I know what this is? Prove it to me. Besides the colour of the liquid is not golden, but ochre!"

When the truth was known, and when the tea was brought for all who would taste, the roles were reversed, and the only people who said things like the great and intelligent had said were the absolute fools. And such is the case to this day.

Drinks of all kinds have been used by almost all peoples as allegories connected with the search for higher knowledge.

Coffee, the most recent of social drinks, was discovered by the dervish sheikh Abu el-Hasan Shadhili, at Mocha in Arabia.

Although the Sufis and others often clearly state that "magical drinks" (wine, the water of life) are an analogy of a certain experience, literalist students tend to believe that the origin of these myths dates from the discovery of some hallucinogenic or inebriative quality in potations. According to the dervishes, such an idea is a reflection of the investigator's incapacity to understand that they are speaking in parallels.

This tale is from the teachings of the Master Hamadani (died 1140), teacher of the great Yasavi of Turkestan, as it appears in *Caravan of Dreams* by Idries Shah.

The Tale of the Sands

A *stream*, from its source in far-off mountains, passing through every kind and description of countryside, at last reached the sands of the desert. Just as it had crossed every other barrier, the stream tried to cross this one, but it found that as fast as it ran into the sand, its waters disappeared.

It was convinced, however, that its destiny was to cross this desert, and yet there was no way. Now a hidden voice, coming from the desert itself, whispered: "The wind crosses the desert, and so can the stream."

The stream objected that it was dashing itself against the sand, and only getting absorbed: that the wind could fly, and this was why it could cross a desert.

"By hurtling in your own accustomed way you cannot get across. You will either disappear or become a marsh. You must allow the wind to carry you over, to your destination."

But how could this happen? "By allowing yourself to be absorbed in the wind."

This idea was not acceptable to the stream. After all, it had never been absorbed before. It did not want to lose its individuality. And, once having lost it, how was one to know that it could ever be regained?

"The wind," said the sand, "performs this function. It takes up water, carries it over the desert, and then lets it fall again. Falling as rain, the water again becomes a river."

"How can I know that this is true?"

"It is so, and if you do not believe it, you cannot become more than a quagmire, and even that could take many, many years; and it certainly is not the same as a stream."

"But can I not remain the same stream that I am today?"

"You cannot in either case remain so," the whisper said. "Your essential part is carried away and forms a stream again. You are called what you are today because you do not know which part of you is the essential one."

When he heard this, certain echoes began to arise in the thoughts of the stream. Dimly, he remembered a state in which he—or some part of him, was it?—had been held in the arms of a wind. He also remembered—or did he?—that this was the real thing, not necessarily the obvious thing, to do.

And the stream raised his vapour into the welcoming arms of the wind, which gently and easily bore it upwards and along, letting it fall softly as soon as they reached the roof of a mountain, many, many miles away. And because he had had his doubts, the stream was able to remember and record more strongly in his mind the details of the experience. He reflected, "Yes, now I have learned my true identity."

The stream was learning. But the sands whispered: "We know, because we see it happen day after day: and because we, the sands, extend from the riverside all the way to the mountain."

And that is why it is said that the way in which the Stream of Life is to continue on its journey is written in the Sands.

This beautiful story is current in verbal tradition in many languages, almost always circulating among dervishes and their pupils.

It was used in Sir Fairfax Cartwright's *Mystic Rose from the Garden of the King,* published in Britain in 1899.

The present version is from Awaa Afifi the Tunisian, who died in 1870, as it appears in *Tales of the Dervishes* by Idries Shah.

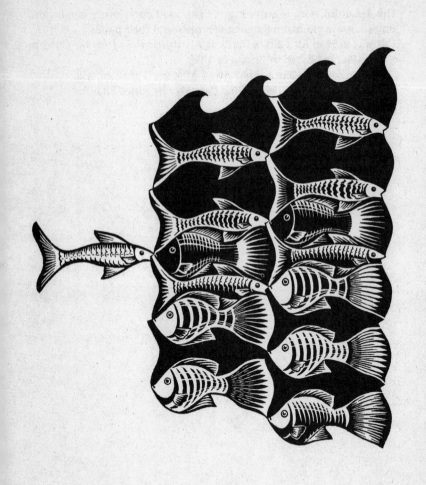

9

On the Development of Consciousness: An Important "Way"

Fishes and Water

Fishes, asking what water was, went to a wise fish. He told them that it was all around them, yet they still thought that they were thirsty.

It isn't difficult to see why many intelligent people concerned with their own and other's welfare don't see much relevance in consciousness. But what remains after the woolly ideas is important to us, both as individuals and for the survival of human beings. It is much like the situation of the fishes and water: What people are trying to understand is so well hidden because it is obvious and all around them!

There *is* an understanding of "Reality Beyond the Norm," and this understanding exists at a *"higher level."* Keep the fishes and water in mind and this statement is not as hazy as it might seem. People who read some of the wilder ideas may come away rather firmly convinced of nuttiness alone. After all, talk of "another world" or an "alternate reality". . . .

It oftens seems like some kind of hazy, gossamer world reached by a few souls after years of deprivation and subjugation. When something like this is said, "You are part of a Greater World and you are unconscious of it," further fervid notions tend to follow . . . our minds, formed in part by the cinema, may well imagine something out of *Dune.* The sports or financial pages look quite good after a discussion like that.

But the financial or sports pages aren't that far off. Suppose you knew nothing about money—how it is printed; how goods are valued; how millions of transactions make up macroeconomics. And suppose a Wall Street Guru (as they are called) tells you that your actions have effects on something only discussed among the initiates—this hazy, complex and higher level "Financial World." You buy things, you sell them, et cetera, but you need not be *conscious* of the higher-order world of macroeconomics to be a part of it—you are inseparable from it.

And your consciousness about this "mysterious world" can be *"raised"*— you can read about money matters; you can go to seminars and training programs; you can learn to understand the hazy concepts of interest and exchange rates, taxation, investment and consumption patterns, even the Gross National Product! Then you realize that this "Alternate Reality" does indeed coexist, and is not just part of the mumbo-jumbo of the financial gurus. You also may note that this "higher-order reality" *always did exist,* and you and your actions, along with the rest of humanity, were a part of it anyway. Then you become Financially Enlightened.

These perceptions described refer to a different structure to reality, one in which individual actions combine into something more organized—the way players in a team create something greater than their individual efforts, or the way people in a company can do the same. The concept of these "levels" of human reality should not really be so strange, we are used to acting in it when we say "I've always liked the way this company thinks." or "I've been a Forty-niner fan for twenty-five years."

In the same way, according to experts in the development of cognition and consciousness, there is another kind of reality of which you are already a part and can play a conscious part. If your thoughts immediately go loopy, you will deprive yourself of the action-knowledge, as it is called by the representatives of the modern Sufi tradition. It is closer to your life than you may well think. You might even be swimming in it!

A story about the Middle-Eastern joke figure Mulla Nasrudin helps picture the situation:

> Time and again Nasrudin passed from Persia to Greece on donkey-back. Each time he had two panniers of straw, and trudged back

without them. Every time the guards searched him for contraband.
They never found any.

"What are you carrying, Nasrudin?"

"I am a smuggler."

Years later, more and more prosperous in appearance, Nasrudin
moved to Egypt. One of the customs men met him there.

"Tell me, Mulla, now that you are out of the jurisdiction of Greece
and Persia, living here in such luxury—what was it that you were
smuggling when we could never catch you?"

"Donkeys."

Understanding the nature of the relationship of these multiple worlds
has caused dismay, misunderstanding, and confusion in philosophical,
religious, and esoteric "schools," and worse in the popular mind, where
it has caused much destruction of lives. The questions people ask about
this relationship are often strange, at best a non sequitur like "What is
this arm [of a shopper] going to buy at the sale next Christmas?" Or
"Does a car know where it is going?"

There is a discussion about some of the common questions people
ask in the interesting book *Journeys with a Sufi Master* by B. M. Dervish
that is important to quote:

The dichotomy between "us and them," or "you and me" and so
on is mainly caused by human training and is deliberately emphasized in a large number of human institutions. At the same
time there is also a certain interest in ordinary life in the idea of
"breaking down barriers," and "sharing experience" and so on.
Such procedures carry with them certain pleasures and advantages. These include, for instance, a sense of belonging to a
community.

The Sufis, however, have made this subject a special study, and
their results are striking and widespread. Rumi and many others
constantly speak of the value, the need even, for breaking down
the barriers between people ("all humanity are essentially one")
and even the barriers between "now" and "then," between life and
death, between man and the beyond.

The exercises which they use for this purpose lead to the capacity
to dissolve the distinctions between one and many, between past,

present, and future. Such experiences, involving the state of being concurrently at different places or in various times, even of being a whole and also parts of it, have been referred to by mystics and even magicians but seldom specifically.

This condition of merging is brought about by "removing the veil" where even the distinction between the perceiver and the perceived disappears. That this can take place means that there is an objective reality which the Sufis call Truth and where there are *none of the distinctions into which our familiar senses split perception.* [Emphasis added.]

We all are a part of several "realities" at once; they may be individual, familial, social; political, financial, and others. Just as you need *specific and professional instruction* to reliably approach an understanding of finance or politics, you need it in the development of consciousness.

There have been two general approaches to these "two worlds" in philosophical, religious, and "esoteric" schools.

First: The ordinary world we live in is the source of evil and should be shunned, and in this way, the true reality that exists beyond will be reached. This is a Gnostic approach and is responsible for the vows of poverty, chastity, and other regimes, such as fasting, monastery life, et cetera. By ridding the mind of the constraints of survival, it is thought, it can soar beyond.

Second: The world should be worked *through* to perceive the deeper reality beyond; there is a reality to the ordinary everyday world of survival but we must see deeper into it. This is a variety of Neoplatonism, in which the surface appearance of things is taken as an indication of the depths beyond. So people contemplate vases or flowers in order that they see in that one object the chance to reach toward an "essential form," thence to return to the "real world." In Zen, the saying "Before I meditated, mountains were mountains. When I began, mountains were no longer mountains. Now [after enlightenment] mountains are mountains," is intended to convey this sentiment. Better yet,"After enlightenment, the laundry, stuffing envelopes, and washing up."

Since this is no philosophical treatise, I do not feel it necessary to go through the difficulties of such approaches. It is enough to say that many people have been prevented from living full lives, *in either world,* or in either "system of reality," because of such ideas.

·   ·   ·

So, after all this, where's the obvious and easy answer to all the problems? This is the end of the book, isn't it? Obviously, there is none such, for if it were easy to write down a formula applicable to all in the way medical remedies are applicable, someone quite wise would have done so. Instead of a grand tour of all the "ways," contemporary and obsolete, I am going to discuss one extraordinary and quite important approach to the problem of understanding and developing human consciousness. I don't claim any authority on this or any exclusivity in presenting this approach, but I simply present some ideas and methods in detail.

If one states that there are ways to grasp a reality beyond the norm, a reality *worth* viewing, the immediate reaction is either: "Well, tell me all about it, then." Or, "Give me the [coherent] formula for doing so."

But as the " 'Blind' need eyes, not light," it is preferable that materials designed to *introduce a new range of thinking and perceiving* avoid trying to be prematurely coherent. Many find this the stumbling point, for people who think well have schemata well-developed for the straight explanation.

There is a problem in trying to be coherent at any cost. In one experiment people were shown a scene that was blurred. It was brought into focus in full view. Some people were asked to make guesses about the scene when it was quite blurred; some were not. As the scene came more clearly into view, everyone was asked to identify the scene. *Those who were asked to guess when the scene was blurred did much worse than those who did not guess.*

It seems that early hypotheses seem to take on a life of their own and interfere with later ability to perceive. I am sure that much of the writing in the metaphysical area is both the product of such early blurred glimpses, and the cause of further misunderstandings. It is for this reason that many of the current writings that I am discussing do not describe metaphysical reality, the nature of the seeker and the universe, et cetera— so that the student cannot prematurely organize it according to his own limited principles.

A Brief Summary and an Introduction to a Contemporary Approach

A new synthesis is in process within modern psychology—it combines the concerns of the esoteric traditions with the research methods and technology of modern science. In complement to this process a contemporary approach to the problems of consciousness is arising from the traditions themselves.

When we refer to these traditions, we refer largely to teachers, exercises, and techniques of the past. The Buddha formulated his techniques for those in India 2,600 years ago. Mohammed's school and teaching were formulated for the Middle East 1,300 years ago. But although he was speaking primarily to those of his own time and place, and many of his statements applied to those of his time, Mohammed made many statements that apply to many teachers of these traditions, independent of their situation. One that is relevant to this discussion was "Speak to those in accordance with their understanding."

So, for today, the questions addressed need be contemporary, not those relevant to an earlier era and then imported across time and culture. Our cultures have changed drastically since the time of Mohammed, and any formulation must undergo a fresh adaptation. Such a new formulation is currently being presented by Idries Shah. His work employs current technology when appropriate and draws from contemporary research in psychology and philosophy. This modern synthesis is coupled with the special form of literature that he has recently reintroduced to this culture, a contemporary version of an oral tradition, using material freshly translated into modern idiom. We have become familiar with these stories throughout this book, for they introduce the chapters. Sufi literature is so useful as psychological documents that the stories also can be used to summarize this book.

Consciousness is selective and limited. Concepts of the possible limit personal consciousness and scientific thought. We constantly ask ourselves "Is there any number higher than 100?" We limit our awareness and our possibilities. Throughout much of the day, we act like the double-seeing son and confuse our personal construction with external reality.

There is a second mode of consciousness that exists on many levels— cultural, personal, and biological. On the biological level, two cerebral hemispheres of the cortex are specialized for different modes of information processing. The left hemisphere operates primarily in the verbal, sequential mode; the right hemisphere primarily in a spatial and simultaneous mode. This right hemisphere mode is often devalued by the dominant, verbal intellect. Since you have not learned grammar, "half your life has been wasted," said the pedagogue to the boatman. This second mode often appears inelegant, lacking formal reasoning and polish of the intellect. It is more involved in space than in time, more involved in intuition than in logic and language.

It is a mode often forgotten and ignored, especially within the scientific community, but one that may prove important for science, and even for our own survival. "Have you ever learned to swim?" asks the boatman of the pedagogue. Since it is nonlinear, this second mode is not involved in the "ordinary" realm of cause and effect that underlies so much of our personal and intellectual life. It is a mode in which all occurrences exist as a "patterned whole," as in the drawing that accompanies "Moment in Time."

The two major types of psychology have each predominantly investigated one mode of human consciousness. Modern science is primarily verbal-logical; esoteric traditions have specialized in the tacit holistic mode, one largely inaccessible to language and reason. These two modes are portrayed in the story of the blind men and the elephant. One mode of consciousness approaches the elephant by piecemeal investigation; the other attempts to develop a perspective of the whole organism.

The techniques of these esoteric traditions are often thought to involve deliberately exotic and mysterious training, such as the use of special, mysterious "magic words" in meditation. However, the essence of meditation is the focusing of awareness on a single, unchanging source of stimulation. It is the attitude, not the specific form, that is primary. If the exercise is performed correctly, a new set of capacities may emerge, symbolically portrayed in "The Man Who Walked on Water." The techniques of meditation, the dishabituation exercises, and other special exercises are designed to cause a shift from the ordinary analytic consciousness to the holistic.

We do not often realize that we may possess the separate pieces of a complete consciousness, until Nasrudin in his role points it out to us. As a guide, he may ask, "Why don't you make a pair of boots out of the material at hand?" And yet, like Mulla Nasrudin, we have often been looking for the key to understanding ourselves in the brilliance of the day. But it may not be there. It lies within, in our dark side, a side often forgotten because "there is more light here."

When consciousness is changed, many begin to worship experiences or states. Yet these experiences may occur and still be meaningless, as happened to the sultan who was in exile. Since we construct our ordinary world around the limited input from our sensory systems, we remain largely unaware of much of our immediate environment, either because we lack the receptive organs or because the phenomena change slowly. But although fish are unaware of the medium in which they live, we need not remain unaware of our own geophysical ocean. Under certain conditions, this additional comprehensive awareness can be developed.

A Contemporary Approach

A fresh approach will have to defeat the systematizing nature of the modern mind, including the tendency to organize prematurely, and yet fit modern life. No one in the twentieth century will return to the thought and development of a previous era, except as escapism. People do not follow a fixed authority anymore, so the canonical approach of the church is not likely to suit a new development. The basic necessities of life are now met in a pluralistic society, not to mention thousands of other needs and wishes. So, the entertainment, social, and welfare functions of classical religion are no longer necessary. The ideas can be put into the open market.

Don't expect to have all your work done for you, or to have it all explained. I, for one, couldn't do it if I tried, but in the past twenty years many papers, documents, and articles have appeared in many journals throughout the world. They may well give people who have this "natural interest" the chance to follow it further. Here is one sampler of these documents, which will close our examination of the psychology of consciousness.

The distinguished commentator Chawan Thurlnas spells out one of the current methods quite explicitly:

Their Work Enterprises

The Sufi approach to professional, vocational and business activities resembles that of other communities, but the similarity serves also to conceal dramatic differences. Sufi disciples will cooperate in what seem to be almost every kind of activity: ranging from the arts, through commerce to academic and other undertakings in the world of learning. A number of seekers will associate together to pursue a project, because the successful completion of a mundane activity is often regarded as an index of the necessary harmonization of the group. In other words, if the project works, the members of the group are in the kind of alignment which will enable them to profit from the subtle, spiritual impulses which the Sufi work is offering.

This kind of pattern is familiar in all groups with a common interest. Both religious and other groupings, of short or long duration, can be found working together in a wide variety of areas throughout the world. The difference comes when one examines the theory and mechanism of the Sufi and the other groupings.

In the case of the Sufis, a project is devised and an attempt is made to carry it out. If this succeeds (that is, if the shop, factory, artistic atelier and so forth) flourishes within a reasonable period of time, the group concerned is accepted with its membership as eligible for special exercises and instructions which are believed to be able to operate through this "organism" with extraordinary rapidity and effectiveness. The group need not be money-oriented: some groups are charitable, others devised for entertainment, still others work in the fields of planning, design, agriculture or even certain spheres of diplomacy. But, while there need not be financial aim in the undertaking, if it is one which ordinarily yields a profit, then the index of its success always includes profit: and the entire yield is always made available to the Sufi Path. The Sufi teacher ordinarily authorizes the experiment and may give it the time-scale in which it is to succeed. If the project does not progress sufficiently well, the harmonization of its individual members is considered to be at fault, and the effort must be stopped. Many such entities fall into the hands of people who "capture" them and milk them for their own profit. This is not only regarded as reprehensible: it also has a positive side—the entire group and the operation itself is deemed to have gone sour. The positive advantage has been that the unsuitable members have been identified. Henceforth, the Work, as it is called, can insulate itself from this "diseased" limb.

The application of the doctrine that "the exterior is an indicator of the interior" strikingly emphasises the belief that harmony brings about coherent ("organic") growth; and, in contradistinction, that the imposition of patterns upon groups will never succeed in developing anything. From this it can be seen why so many Sufis are on record as working so vehemently against imposed structure. It also gives a clue as to why Sufis (other than those who imagine that they are Sufis) will never subject *everyone* from the communities to the same exercises, or even to the same range of ideas.

It is, however, true that the Sufi organism as a *whole* constitutes one single body. But this unity is one which is understood and worked with only by the "realised" Sufi. The unity is invisible at ground level, as it were.

The vast miscellaneity of some Sufi masters' activities, from this viewpoint, makes—if not sense—at least a distinction between repetitious and limited activity and the whole complicated structure within which the teacher works.

An important and highly-respected Sufi teacher in the Middle East, when asked his reactions to what we often think of as truly Sufi groups, with attentive disciples clustered around a teacher who gives out invocations and encourages unusual dress and talks all the time of "unity," "self-realization" or "unification" with the Absolute" (instead of carrying out a comprehensive programme), said: "I constantly see such people, both here and in Europe and America. Everyone thinks that they are Sufis except the Sufis themselves. Whenever I meet these circuses I go home to have a good laugh."

Other elements are found in two stories:

Service

"How," said a seeker to a well-known Sufi, "can one do even the minimum service towards helping the Teaching?"

"You have already done it," he said, "for to ask how to serve is already a contribution towards service."

Duty

A Certain Sufi was asked:

"People come for companionship, discourses and teaching. Yet you plunge them into activity. Why is this?"

He said:

"Though they—and you—may believe that they come for enlightenment, they mainly desire engagement in something. I give them engagement, so that they shall realize the limitations of engagement as a means of learning.

"Those who become totally engaged are they who sought only engagement, and who could not profit by self-observation of themselves so uselessly engaged. It is, therefore, not the deep respectors of activity who become illuminated."

The questioner said:

"Who, then, is it who does become illuminated?"

The Sufi replied:

"The illuminated are those who perform duties adequately, realizing that there is something beyond."

"But how is that 'something beyond' to be reached?"

"It is always reached by those who perform adequately. They need no further instruction. If you were doing your duty adequately, and were neither neglectful nor fanatically attached to it, you would not have had to ask the question."

Part of the complexity of the problem is that human beings are not simple creatures—we have multiple facets—and our multiplicity makes each one a quite different individual. At each mating a single male and female could produce 64 *trillion* unique individuals. The genetic complement differs, our upbringing differs, and our cultures have different strengths and weaknesses. Personalities differ, intelligence differs, experiences differ, and most importantly, circumstances differ. If you take into account these differences then you will teach different people very differently.

But this can make the organizers of such enterprises (or those responsible for spiritual learning) seem to lack a coherent and systematic basis, and the writings and principles can seem "jumpy." *"Why do you give different answers to the same question?"* might be asked (with the implication that you should always do so, if you were a Real Thinker). But just suppose a child asked you that same question after hearing several people, throughout the day, ask you, "What time is it?"

But there are coherent elements. Since a contemporary teaching is like the fishes in water, many students are oblivious to what is happening to them when they are introduced to the ideas—like the customs man missing the donkey. Many hardworking people may puzzle over what they are asked to do; they can seem almost offended that they are asked to do little things. "I am interested in higher consciousness and he asks me to bake cookies," they, in effect, say. It is very much like the person who wishes to have his blindness removed, asking about the relevance of the surgical procedures and other administrative details.

However, this kind of interchange allows one to observe what the person is really doing: Here he or she is simply demonstrating that he is *unable to place his trust in the instruction, even in doing something as simple and harmless as baking cookies when asked.* Them ol' schemata, well-developed in society, business, and school learning, die hard!

A recent question-and-answer exchange with Idries Shah speaks to this situation:

> Q: Must a student always occupy himself with trivialities, as are often mentioned in Sufi writings?
> A: There is a saying: If you seek small things to do, and do them well, great things will seek you, and demand to be performed."

The same difficulties have, apparently, been faced in classical forms of learning about "higher consciousness."

Bahaudin Naqshband on Discipleship and Development

I was mystified for many months by my esteemed mentor's giving me things to speak, to think and do which did not seem to satisfy my craving for the spiritual life. He told me many times that the craving which I felt was not for spirituality at all, and that the materials which he was giving me were the nutritions which I needed. It was only when I was able to still my maniac desires that I was able to listen to him at all. At other times I said to myself, "I have heard all this before, and it is highly doubtful," or else, "this is no spiritual man," or, further, "I want to experience, not to listen or to read."

The wonderful thing was this, that my teacher continually reminded me that this was my state of mind, and although I was outwardly trusting him and serving him in everything, I was not able to trust him to the necessary extent, nor in the vital direction. Looking back, I realized later that I was willing at that time to yield far more far-reaching parts of my sovereignty than were needed; but I was not prepared to yield the minor ones which alone were the pathways to my understanding.

I refer to this because it is by rehearsal of the experience of others that people at a similar stage in the Path may be able to recognize their own state and profit by it.

.   .   .

Once the supposed students find out it is no picnic, there are many reasons why they might not participate—they may try to get a sample of "higher" knowledge before they give of their time, money, or effort. This kind of a system, if it is to allow people to really change, probably can't work that way. I was once watching a television program about such seekers, one of whom said "If I don't get higher consciousness soon, I'm going to kill somebody!" At an early stage, the student must be able to be humble—to admit that he or she doesn't have any real knowledge of what "higher consciousness" or this form of learning and teaching is about, how it works, and how it is administered.

He or she may wonder: "What is the meaning of life? Do I have a soul? Is there existence after death? Is there a connection between human life and other, perhaps, superior, forms of life? What does a Sufi teacher know? . . ." and so on, but the student has no real knowledge of what the appropriate knowledge is, let alone where to find it. One of the problems of participation arises due to the failure of the student to admit, completely, that he knows nothing of the entire enterprise. Then he may have a vague *idea* of what learning means in this area.

But then he may say, "This activity/lecture/cookie/company/publishing/typing work/jam making . . . is *not* it—it's just too boring and trivial!" After all, the person may think, I've got an MBA! Is there really anything to learn from doing these kinds of things. But this is why it becomes so impossible and so confusing: If we did know the "answers" to the questions posed above we would have no need of the system devised by the teacher. If we do not, then we are not qualified to say this is not it. As Chawan Thurlnas mentioned earlier, the activity is not visible at "ground level."

It becomes a matter of trust and obedience—and it is difficult, for the student either accepts that there is a pattern beyond his grasp, someone who does know the "reality beyond," and he works to grasp it by participating in activities that do not seem to make a sensible connection with his questions; or he does not.

In participating in these activities, people also have a chance to become more "normal" about the rest of their life. Many people have been driven abnormal due to the inability to find a developed and professional range of instruction about consciousness in their society. When they do contact "The Teaching" they still suffer: They bring to it their own personal obsessions and paranoias, which they have developed in dealing with the rest of society—their survival schemata. These can be dropped when they find the right range of materials but this is surprisingly difficult and takes time and work. When one has already entered the house, one can stop knocking on the door.

While working, people so engaged may be able to discern how well they are able to cooperate even at the least complex level. The successful cooperation allows them to see patterns in their lives that may have eluded them in less subtle, but seemingly similar, circumstances. Does he or she concentrate only on his or her part in things and miss the overall operation? Are there personal characteristics that are standing in the way? A "Work Situation" allows these tendencies to become visible in the person. His normal tendencies can come out, and he can see them. A healthy attitude to work activities may be able to attract other healthy individuals.

The association in work enterprises offers a chance to correct some attitudes that interfere, those in which the ordinary schemata are brought forward. Instead of the average everyday critical concentration on other people's failures and flaws, a student has the chance to reorient his thinking and to consider how different people's skills can come together in a larger, emergent unit, one that can work in what has been described as "harmony." In such associations, one has the chance to become part of something superior, not defeated by the normal social attitudes.

Getting rid of the normal schemata and learning to be flexible is quite difficult for most people, especially since they are often asked to do so in situations close to their normal life and work, not in a quiet monastery. One aspect of this "superior association" in groups is whether one can learn to inhibit one's normal social ("commanding") self, the self that has as its aim the dominance of others. This is in many ways the embodiment of the schemata designed for survival.

Since the student may have an interest in "higher" matters, although he is unable to discuss them, there must be a means in which he can remain in contact with the teacher. Viable work activities can provide this means, where the teacher and student can associate until there is an opportunity for a further step to be taken. Not every moment is ripe for this kind of instruction—since people are individuals, each person will get the "feedback" he needs, but the situations have to occur in order that the barriers in the student can be observed and then pointed out. It may take a charity to bring out the lack of generosity of some, it may take a business to point out the lack of thoroughness of others, and other tendencies may only occur under stress, or war, and so on.

In describing many of these different kinds of activities, one contemporary exponent of Sufism said: "The profit is the sanity test!" This is far from a rejection of contemporary life. The profit, to businessmen as well as spiritual men, shows that the enterprise is working and the people are able to organize themselves into a functioning whole. It is important to be able to give the right effort of oneself, in the right amount, at the right time, for anything to be done.

Cooking by Candle

Nasrudin made a wager that he could spend a night on a nearby mountain and survive, in spite of ice and snow. Several wags in the teahouse agreed to adjudicate.

Nasrudin took a book and a candle and sat through the coldest night he had ever known. In the morning, half-dead, he claimed his money.

"Did you have nothing at all to keep you warm?" asked the villagers.

"Nothing."

"Not even a candle?"

"Yes, I had a candle."

"Then the bet is off."

Nasrudin did not argue.

Some months later he invited the same people to a feast at his house. They sat down in his reception room, waiting for the food. Hours passed.

They started to mutter about food.

"Let's go and see how it is getting on," said Nasrudin.

Everyone trooped into the kitchen. They found an enormous pot of water, under which a candle was burning. The water was not even tepid.

"It is not ready yet," said the Mulla. "I don't know why—it has been there since yesterday."

From this viewpoint work on mundane organizations in groups has several functions: the opportunity to exercise the right kind of effort and the right intensity at the right time; the opportunity to learn to inhibit less-desirable characteristics; to learn to give everything the master asks the right kind of attention and obedience.

These allow the formation of a larger association, be it a business, an atelier, a service or other kind of organization, an enterprise to enable those involved to become qualified for "higher" activities. But how do these mundane groupings coalesce into something larger? How do individuals become part of a more comprehensive understanding?

One startling point of spiritual writings, contained in those of contemporary Sufism, is that the individual, alone, is *not the "unit" of enlightenment, or higher understanding.* It is the group, correctly organized, that has this possibility, not a person alone. Our history records the achievements of certain famous individuals, like the Buddha, Jesus, and others. What may well be left out, it is tempting to speculate, is that these individuals were the public face of a larger group. The necessity for the right kind of effort to achieve something beyond the range of an individual is the subject of some recently published tales. Here are two:

The More the Better

There was once a mosquito who decided to kill a proud horse. She said to the horse; "If anyone could kill you, the most powerful beast anywhere, would such an individual be even greater than you?"

The horse answered: "Certainly. But, of course, there is no way of killing me!"

Then the mosquito stung him. But this was nothing but a pinprick to the horse. The mosquito was ambitious, but could not think what next to do. "I'll go to the hare," she said to herself, "because he is wise and people say that he knows how to help one attain his desire."

The hare, when questioned, said: "Band all your mosquitos together, act in unison, sting again and again, and you are bound to succeed."

So the insect called all her friends, and they listened to the wise words of the hare, and were inspired to attain the desire of overcoming the horse. They set out in an enormous swarm, found the horse, and stung him to death.

Naturally, the mosquitos were delighted at their success. They went back to the hare and told him, and all the other animals surrounding the hare at his daily court were equally impressed, and many enrolled themselves as his disciples. Nobody, of course, thought to ask what had been achieved in reality.

Now each of the mosquitos imagined himself to be a champion. They dispersed in all directions and stung everything in sight. From that day to this they have never managed to kill anything by means of their sting alone. Now and again a cloud of mosquitos kills some animal, and this keeps the legend alive, in some circles, that there is something to be gained by stinging, and that the mosquito is the greatest thing in creation—after the hare, which advised it in the first place.

The Necessity for the Teaching

Maruf, son of Zayd, was asked:

"Why is the Teaching not offered to the people of so many countries where, through their material advancement, the people could help the progress of the Work?"

He said:

"Where a people have no capacity, and where the activity has not teacher, there is no advantage in material or other advancement. You can make no swords where there is no iron.

"One day, you will recall from the Munaqib, Muinudin requested Maulana Rumi to give his son 'special mystical training by projection.' Rumi answered, 'The load which forty men pull—cannot be sustained by one.'

"The mystical force can be perceived by men, and not by a man alone. Where there is no quantity, there can be no sharing.

"If you had a camel-load of halwa, you would need the exact number of boxes to put it in before you discharged your load."

The questioner was not pleased with this answer and he said:

"The sage has failed to note that we are not merchants of halwa!"

The sage, however, said, gently, "If you were, you would understand what I mean."

Altering and Deepening Consciousness

For millennia, some people have realized that human consciousness is short-term and geared to transience—the needs and desires of the moment. One route to an extended consciousness has been (historically) through defeating bodily "desires." Therefore, many schools of thought have required fasting, vision-quests, extremes of obedience and denial of desire, such as sexual. Other approaches, such as meditation, emphasize a withdrawal from the external world to an interior mental world where new ideas, thoughts, and actions can be considered. It is an attempt to undo the automatic nature of our normal consciousness.

Such meditation exercises include "just sitting" in Zen Buddhism, and a similar form in Yoga. In one study of Zen meditation no disturbance showed up in the EEG recordings when loud sounds occurred outside. A normal person would show disturbance.

But these extreme measures of deprivation are not always necessary. *An extended consciousness can be brought about by more subtle and consistent methods.* In almost all cultures, this "deepened understanding" of life is conveyed through stories, myths, and legends, in which man's place in the world is explained and conveyed from generation to generation.

Recently, these important "teaching stories" from all the world's literature have been researched, collected, compared, and published by the distinguished Afghan author Idries Shah. He points out that these stories allow a person to experience different kinds of events and to become familiar with them, as the story is read over and over again. These stories, part of almost every culture, are universal in that they contain actions, events, and situations that are unusual and serve to extend consciousness, as a somewhat legendary wise "Old Man" who has seen things before can often predict what is going to happen. These stories often have multiple meanings. See, for instance, "The Teaching Story" herein.

One leading figure in these teaching stories and a familiar figure in Middle Eastern literature is the jokester Nasrudin. In one story, he is interested in learning to play the lute. He searches out the lute master and asks "How much do you charge for the lessons?" The lute master replies, "Ten gold pieces for the first month, one gold piece for the succeeding months." "Excellent," says Nasrudin, "I shall begin with the second month." In another story, mentioned earlier, Nasrudin was walking on the main street of a town throwing out breadcrumbs. His neighbors asked, "What are you doing, Nasrudin?" "Keeping the tigers away." "But there have not been tigers in these parts for hundreds of years." "Exactly. Effective, isn't it?"

There is currently quite serious concern about the nature of human consciousness and our ability to adapt to the modern world. Many people feel that the development of their own consciousness is of high priority because humans now have a greatly increased ability to control and manipulate the earth, an ability far beyond anything we had during the long millennia of our biological evolution. The destruction of the entire earth is no longer an impossibility. In this view, there may be no more human biological evolution without *conscious evolution*, as it is often called.

Nasrudin allows us to see our situation in this modern tale, through the lens of humor, summing up much of what is known about the inflexibility of the normal human consciousness and the current need to change thinking. Nasrudin is taking a plane from a Middle Eastern country to London along with his flock of followers. The four-engine plane takes off and all is well for a while. Then one engine fails, and the captain says, "Do not worry, we will be late into London, by a half hour." Everyone is calm. The second engine fails, and Nasrudin's flock gets worried. The captain says that they will be two hours late. Nasrudin is soothing, everything is all right. Then the third engine fails, and the captain says that the plane will limp along and will be several hours late to the destination. Nasrudin, in this story the fountain of conventional thinking, says: "Let us pray that the fourth engine does not fail!

For if it does, we'll be up here all day!"

References

Akishige, Y. 1968. *Psychological studies on Zen*. Bulletin of the Faculty of Literature of Kyushu University, Japan, no. 5.

Anand, B.; Chhina, G.; and Singh, B. 1961. Some aspects of electroencephalographic studies in Yogis. *Electroencephalography and Clinical Neurophysiology* 13: 452–56. Reprinted in C. T. Tart, ed., *Altered states of consciousness*.

———. 1961. Studies on Shri Ramananda Yogi during his stay in an airtight box. *Indian Journal of Medical Research* 49: 82–89.

Astin, V. H. 1968. Standards of measurement. *Scientific American:* 50–63.

Austin, M. D. 1971. Dream recall and the bias of intellectual ability. *Nature* 231: 59.

Baghi, B., and Wenger, M. 1957. Electrophysiological correlates on some yogic exercises. *Electroencephalography and Clinical Neurophysiology* suppl. 7: 132–49.

Bergson, H. 1976. *Duration and simultaneity*. New York: Bobbs-Merrill.

Beveridge, W. I. 1950. *The art of scientific investigation*. New York: Random House.

Bogen, J. E. 1969. The other side of the brain, I, II, III. *Bulletin of the Los Angeles Neurological Societies* 34: 3.

Brecher, E. M. 1972. *Licit and illicit drugs*. Boston: Little, Brown.

Breuer, J., and Freud, S. 1937. *Studies in hysteria*. Boston: Beacon Press. (Original work published 1895.)

Bruner, J. 1962. *On knowing: Essays for the left hand*. Cambridge, Mass.: Harvard University Press.

Budzynski, T. H.; Stoyva, J.; and Adler, C. 1970. Feedback-induced muscle relaxation: Application to tension headaches. *Journal of Behavioral Therapy and Experimental Psychiatry* 1: 205–211. Reprinted in T. Barber et al., eds., 1971, *Biofeedback and self-control*. Chicago: Aldine-Atherton.

Cadwallander, T. C. 1958. Cessation of visual experience under prolonged uniform visual stimulation. *American Psychologist* 13: 410 (abstract).

Carmon, A., and Nachshon, I. 1971. Effect of unilateral brain damage on perception of temporal order. *Cortex* 7: 410–18.

Carroll, J. B., ed. 1951. *Language, thought and reality: Selected writings of Benjamin Lee Whorf*. Cambridge, Mass.: M.I.T. Press.

Cohen, W. 1957. Spatial and textural characteristics of the Ganzfield. *American Journal of Psychology* 70: 403–410.

Dalal, A., and Barber, T. 1969. Yoga, yoga feats, and hypnosis in the light of empirical research. *American Journal of Clinical Hypnosis* 11: 155–66.

Davidson, R. W. 1966. *Documents on contemporary dervish communities*. London: Octagon Press.

Davison, R. 1984. Hemispheric asymmetry and emotion. In K. Sherer and P. Ekman, eds., *Approaches to emotion*. Hillsdale, N.J.: Lawrence Erlbaum.

Dement, W. C. 1974. *Some must watch while some must sleep*. San Francisco: W. H. Freeman.

Deregowski, J. B. 1973. Illusion and culture. In R. L. Gregory and G. H. Gombrich, eds., *Illusion in nature and art*. New York: Scribner's.

Domhoff, G. W. 1969/70. But why did they sit on the King's right in the first place? *Psychoanalytic Review* 56: 586–96.

Durrell, L. 1960. *Clea*. New York: E. P. Dutton.

Eliot, T. S. 1943. "Burnt Norton." In *Four Quartets*. New York: Harcourt Brace.

Filbey, R. A., and Gazzaniga, M. S. 1969. Splitting the normal brain with reaction time. *Psychonomic Science* 17: 335–36.

Frank, J. 1975. *Persuasion and healing*. 2d ed. New York: Schocken Books.

Freuchen, P. 1959. *The book of the Eskimos*. New York: Fawcett World Library.

Freud, S. 1954. *The interpretation of dreams*. New York: Avon Books. Trans. James J. Strachey. (Original work published 1895.)

Galin, D.; Ornstein. R. E.; and Adams, J. 1977. Midbrain stimulation of the amygdala. *Journal of States of Consciousness* 2: 34–41.

———; Ornstein, R. E.; Herron, J.; and Johnstone, J. 1982. Sex and handnesses differences in EEG measures of hemispheric specialization. *Brain and Language* 16(1): 19–55.

Gazzaniga, M. S. 1967. The split brain in man. *Scientific American* 24–29.

Geschwind, N. 1972. Language and the brain. *Scientific American* 226(4): 76–83.

Gibson, J. J. 1979. *The ecological approach to visual perception*. Boston: Houghton Mifflin.

———. 1960. *The perception of the visual world*. Boston: Houghton Mifflin.

———. 1966. *The senses considered as perceptual systems*. Boston: Houghton Mifflin.

———. 1970. On theories for visual space perception: A reply to Johansson. *Scandinavian Journal of Psychology* 11: 73–79.

Gunn, J. A. 1929. *The problem of time*. London: Allen & Unwin.

Hall, E. 1975. A conversation with Idries Shah. *Psychology Today* 9(2): 53–59.

Harton, J. J. 1939. An investigation of the influence of success and failure on the estimation of time. *Journal of General Psychology* 21: 51–62.

Hastorf, A., and Cantril, H. 1954. They saw a game: A case study. *Journal of Abnormal and Social Psychology* 49: 129–34. Reprinted herein.

Hebb, D. O. 1949. *The organization of behavior*. New York: Wiley.

Hilgard, E. R. 1973. A neo-dissociation interpretation of pain reduction during hypnosis. *Psychological Review* 80(5): 396–411.

Hobson, J. A., and McCarley, R. W. 1977. The brain as a dream state generator: An activation-synthesis hypothesis of the dream process. *The American Journal of Psychiatry* 134(12): 1335–48.

Hochberg, J. E. 1978. *Perception*. 2d ed. Englewood Cliffs, N.J.: Prentice-Hall.

Hoffman, A. Psychotomimetic agents. In A. Burger, ed., *Drugs affecting the central nervous system*, vol. 2. New York: Marcel Dekker.

Hubel, D. H., and Wiesel, T. N. 1979. Brain mechanisms of vision. *Scientific American* 241: 150–62.

———. 1962. Receptive fields, binocular interactions and functional architecture in the cat's visual cortex. *Journal of Physiology* 160: 106–154.

Humphrey, M. E., and Zangwill, O. L. 1951. Cessation of dreaming after brain injury. *Journal of Neurology, Neurosurgery, and Psychiatry* 14: 322–25.

Huxley, A. 1954. *The Doors of Perception*. New York: Harper & Row.

Ittleson, W. H. 1952. The constancies in perceptual theory. In F. R. Kilpatrick, ed., *Human behavior from the transactional point of view*. Hanover, N.H.: Institute for Associated Research.

———, and Kilpatrick, F. P. 1951. Experiments in perception. *Scientific American:* 50–55.

James, W. 1970. *The principles of psychology*, vol. 1. New York: Dover. (Original work published 1890.)

———. 1970. *The principles of psychology*, vol. 2. New York: Dover. (Original work published 1890.)

———. 1980. *The varieties of religious experience*. New York: Longmans Green. (Original work published 1917.)

Kapleau, P., ed. 1965. *The three pillars of Zen: Teaching, practice and enlightenment*. Boston: Beacon Press.

Kasamatsu, A., and Hirai, T. 1966. An electroencephalographic study of Zen meditation (Zazen). *Folia Psychiatria et Neurologia Japonica* 20: 315–36.

Kimura, S.; Ashiba, M.; and Matsushima, I. 1939. Influences of the air lacking in light ions and the effect of its artificial ionization upon human beings in occupied rooms. *Japanese Journal of Medical Science* 7: 1–12.

Kinsbourne, M. 1971. Generalized and lateralized effects of concurrent verbalization on a unimanual skill. *Quarterly Journal of Experimental Psychology* 23: 341–45.

———. 1971. Unpublished manuscript, Duke University.

Koestler, A. 1960. *The lotus and the robot*. New York: Harper & Row.

Kohler, I. 1962. Experiments with goggles. *Scientific American* 62–72.

Kotaka, S., and Krueger, A. P. 1967. Studies on air ionized-induced growth increase in higher plants. *Advancing Frontiers of Plant Sciences* 20: 115–208.

Kreuger, A. P. 1976. Biological impact of small air ions. *Science* 193: 1209–13.

———. 1969. Preliminary consideration of the biological significance of air ions. *Scientia* 104. Reprinted in R. E. Ornstein, ed., *The nature of human consciousness*. San Francisco: W. H. Freeman; New York: Viking Press.

———. 1969. The biological significance of air ions. In *Bioclimatology, biometeorology, and aeriontherapy*. Milan, Italy: Carlo Erba Foundation.

————, and Levine, H. B. 1967. The effect of unipolar positively ionized air on the course of coccidiodomicosis in mice. *International Journal of Biometeorology* 11: 279–88.

LaBerge, S. P.; Nagel, L. E.; Dement, W. C.; and Zarcone, V. P. 1981. Lucid dreaming verified by volitional communication during REM sleep. *Perceptual and Motor Skills* 52: 727–32.

Lee, D. 1950. Codification of reality: Linear and nonlinear. *Psychosomatic Medicine* 12(2). Reprinted in R. E. Ornstein, ed., *The nature of human consciousness*. San Francisco: W. H. Freeman, New York: Viking Press.

Lefort, R. 1968. *The teachers of Gurdjieff*. New York: Samuel Weiser.

Lehmann, D.; Beeler, G. W.; and Fender, D. H. 1967. EEG responses during the observations of stabilized and normal retinal images. *Electroencephalography and Clinical Neurophysiology* 22: 136–42.

Lettvin, J. Y.; Maturana, H. R.; McCulloch, W. S.; and Pitts, W. H. 1959. What the frog's eye tells the frog's brain. *Proceedings of the Institute of Radio Engineers* 47: 140–51.

Levy, J.; Trevarthen, C. B.; and Sperry, R. W. 1972. Perception of bilateral chimeric figures following hemispheric deconnection. *Brain* 95: 61–78.

Levy-Agresti, J., and Sperry, R. W. 1968. Differential perceptual capacities in major and minor hemispheres. *Proceedings of the National Academy of Sciences* 61: 1151.

Luce, G. 1970. Biological rhythms. In *Psychiatry and Medicine*. Bethesda, Md.: National Institute of Mental Health.

————. 1972. *Body time*. New York: Pantheon.

————, and Segal, J. 1966. *Sleep*. New York: Lancet.

Ludel, J. 1978. *Introduction to sensory processes*. San Francisco: W. H. Freeman.

Luria, A. L. 1966. *Higher cortical function in man*. New York: Basic Books.

Lynch, J. 1977. *The broken heart: The medical consequences of loneliness*. New York: Basic Books.

Miller, N. E. 1975. Biofeedback: Evaluation of a new technique. In Di Cara et al., eds., *Biofeedback and self-control, 1974*. Chicago: Aldine-Atherton.

————. 1969. Learning of visceral and glandular responses. *Science* 163: 434–35.

Milner, B. 1965. Brain mechanisms suggested by studies of temporal lobes. In F. L. Darley and C. H. Millikan, eds., *Brain mechanisms underlying speech and language*. New York: Grune & Stratton.

————. 1971. Interhemispheric differences in the localization of psychological processes in man. *British Medical Journal* 27(3): 272–77.

Naranjo, C., and Ornstein, R. 1977. *On the psychology of meditation*. Baltimore: Penguin Books.

Nebes, R. Hemispheric specialization in commisurotomized man. *Psychological Bulletin* 81(1): 1–14.

Neisser, U. 1968. The process of vision. *Scientific American* 204–214.

Nicols, H. 1891. The psychology of time. *American Journal of Psychology* 3: 453–529.

Nowlis, D. P., and Kamiya, J. 1970. The control of electroencephalographic alpha rhythms through auditory feedback and the associated mental activity. *Psychophysiology* 6(4): 476–84. Reprinted in R. E. Ornstein, ed., 1973, *The nature of human consciousness*. San Francisco: W. H. Freeman; New York: Viking Press.

Ogden, E., and Shock, N. 1939. Voluntary hypercirculation. *American Journal of the Medical Sciences* 198: 329–42.

Orne, M. T., and Scheihe, K. E. 1964. The effects of sensory deprivation: A critical review. Unpublished manuscript, University of Pennsylvania.

Ornstein, R. 1969. *On the experience of time*. London: Penguin Books.

————, ed. 1973. *The Nature of human consciousness*. San Francisco: W. H. Freeman; New York: Viking Press.

————; Herron, J.; Johnstone, J.; and Swencionis, C. 1979. Differential right hemisphere involvement in two reading tasks. *Psychophysiology* 16(4): 398–401.

————, and Swencionis, C. (in press). Analytic and synthetic problem-solving strategies in hemispheric asymmetry. *Neuropsychologia*.

————; Thompson, R.; and Macaulay, D. 1984. *The amazing brain*. Boston: Houghton Mifflin.

Poulain, A. 1950. *The graces of interior prayer: A treatise on mystical theology*. St. Louis, Mo.: Herder. Quoted in A. Deikman, *Deautomatization and the mystic experience*.

Pritchard, R. M. 1961. Stabilized images on the retina. *Scientific American*: 72–78.

Rahula, W. 1959. *What the Buddha taught*. New York: Grove Press.

Rice, C. 1964. *The Persian Sufis*. London: Allen & Unwin.

Ring, K. 1980. *Life at Death: A scientific investigation of the near-death experience*. New York: Coward-McCann.

Robinson, N., and Dirnfeld, F. S. 1963. The ionization state of the atmosphere as a function of the meteorological elements and the various sources of ions. *International Journal of Biometeorology* 6: 101–110.

Schwartz, G. E., and Shapiro, D. 1973. Biofeedback and essential hypertension: Current findings and theoretical concerns. *Seminars in Psychiatry* 5(4): 493–503.

Semmes, J. 1968. Hemispheric specialization: A possible clue to mechanism. *Neuropsychologia* 6: 11–16.

Shah, I. 1972. *Caravan of dreams*. Baltimore: Penguin Books.

———. 1985. *The exploits of the incomparable Mulla Nasrudin and the subtleties of the inimitable Mulla Nasrudin*. London: Octagon Press.

———. 1974. *Magic Monastery*. New York: E. P. Dutton.

———. 1968. *Oriental magic*. London: Octagon.

———. 1982. *Seeker after truth*. New York: Harper & Row.

———. 1971. *The Sufis*. New York: Doubleday.

———. 1970. *Tales of the dervishes*. New York: E. P. Dutton.

———. 1967. *The way of the Sufi*. New York: E. P. Dutton.

Shanon, B. 1979. Yesterday, today and tomorrow. *Acta Psychologica* 43: 469–76.

Sperry, R. W. 1956. The eye and the brain. *Scientific American:* 48–52.

———. 1964. The great cerebral commissure. *Scientific American:* 44–52.

———. 1951. Neurology and the mind-brain problem. *American Scientist* 40: 291–312.

———. 1964. Problems outstanding in the evolution of brain function. James Arthur Lecture, American Museum of Natural History, New York.

Spiegelberg, F. 1962. *Spiritual Practices in India*. New York: Citadel Press.

Stevens, S. S. The psycho-physics of sensory functions. In W. A. Rosenblith, ed., *Sensory Communication*. Cambridge, Mass.: MIT Press.

Stewart, K. 1972. Dream theory in Malaya. In C. T. Tart, ed., *Altered states of consciousness*. New York: Doubleday.

Stratton, G. M. 1896. Some preliminary experiments in vision without inversion of the retinal image. *Psychological Review* 3: 611–17.

Suefield, P. 1969. Theoretical formulations. In J. Fubek, ed., *Sensory deprivation: Fifteen years of research.* New York: Appleton-Century-Crofts.

Sulloway, F. 1979. *Freud, biologist of the mind: Beyond the psychoanalytic method.* New York: Basic Books.

Tanner, J. M. 1962. *Growth at adolescence.* 2d ed. Oxford: Blackwell Scientific Publications.

Tarchanoff, J. R. 1972. Voluntary acceleration of the heartbeat in man. Trans. David Blizard. In Shapiro, et al., eds., *Biofeedback and self-regulation,* 1972. Chicago: Aldine-Atherton.

Tart, C. 1971. *On being stoned: A psychological study of marijuana intoxication.* Palo Alto, Calif.: Science and Behavior Books.

Tepas, D. T. 1962. The electrophysiological correlates of vision in a uniform field. *Visual Problems of the Armed Forces,* ed. M. A. Whitcom. Washington, D.C.: National Academy of Science, National Research Council.

Thurlnas, C. 1980. *Current Sufi Activity: Work, Literature, Groups and Techniques.* London: Designist Communications.

Turnbull, C. 1961. Some observations regarding the experiences and behavior of the Bambuti pygmies. *American Journal of Psychology* 74: 304–308.

Valins, S. 1966. Cognitive effects of false heart-rate feedback. *Journal of Personality and Social Psychology* 4: 400–408.

Von Bount, E. E.; Shepherd, M. D.; Wall, J. R.; Ganong, W. F.; and Clegg, M. G. 1964. Penetration of light into the brain of mammals. *Annals of the New York Academy of Sciences* 117: 217–224.

Wallace, R. K., and Benson, H. 1972. The physiology of meditation. *Scientific American:* 84–90. Reprinted in R. E. Ornstein, ed., *The nature of human consciousness.* San Francisco: W. H. Freeman; New York: Viking Press.

Watts, A. 1957. *The way of Zen.* New York: New American Library: 123.

Index